Business Ethics Through Movies

Business Ethics Through Movies

A Case Study Approach

Wanda Teays

WILEY Blackwell

This edition first published 2015
© 2015 John Wiley & Sons, Ltd.

Registered Office
John Wiley & Sons, Ltd, The Atrium, Southern Gate, Chichester,
West Sussex, PO19 8SQ, UK

Editorial Offices
350 Main Street, Malden, MA 02148-5020, USA
9600 Garsington Road, Oxford, OX4 2DQ, UK
The Atrium, Southern Gate, Chichester, West Sussex, PO19 8SQ, UK

For details of our global editorial offices, for customer services, and for information about
how to apply for permission to reuse the copyright material in this book please see our
website at www.wiley.com/wiley-blackwell.

The right of Wanda Teays to be identified as the author of this work has been asserted in
accordance with the UK Copyright, Designs and Patents Act 1988.

Wiley also publishes its books in a variety of electronic formats. Some content that appears
in print may not be available in electronic books.

Designations used by companies to distinguish their products are often claimed as
trademarks. All brand names and product names used in this book are trade names, service
marks, trademarks or registered trademarks of their respective owners. The publisher is not
associated with any product or vendor mentioned in this book.

Limit of Liability/Disclaimer of Warranty: While the publisher and author have used their
best efforts in preparing this book, they make no representations or warranties with respect
to the accuracy or completeness of the contents of this book and specifically disclaim any
implied warranties of merchantability or fitness for a particular purpose. It is sold on the
understanding that the publisher is not engaged in rendering professional services and
neither the publisher nor the author shall be liable for damages arising herefrom. If
professional advice or other expert assistance is required, the services of a competent
professional should be sought.

Library of Congress Cataloging-in-Publication data applied for

9781118941935 (hardback)
9781118941942 (paperback)

A catalogue record for this book is available from the British Library.

Cover image: George Clooney in Michael Clayton, 2007 (dir. Tony Gilroy. Castle Rock /
Section Eight / The Kobal Collection

Set in 10/12.5pt Galliard Std by SPi Global, Pondicherry, India

1   2015

To Ruth and To Birgit

I celebrate your insight,
Your creative spirit

As for me,

"Yes, there were times
when I forgot not only who I was,
but that I was, forgot to be.
Then I was no longer that sealed jar
to which I owed my being so well preserved,
but a wall gave way
and I filled with roots and tame stems for example,
stakes long since dead and ready for burning,
the recess of night and the imminence of dawn..."
—Samuel Beckett, *Molloy*

Contents

Appendices

Acknowledgments

I am grateful to have a life of teaching and writing. I am grateful to be able to work with students and colleagues who want to make the world a better place. And I am grateful for the encouragement and constructive criticism of the two reviewers who gave feedback on my manuscript. It is most appreciated.

I want to thank my editor Liam Cooper, Alec McAulay, Allison Kostka, Sally Cooper and the rest of the Wiley-Blackwell production team for their expertise, support, and enthusiasm. Thank you all so much.

And then there's Silvio, who I thank for just being there day after day. Oh yes, and my friends and fellow faculty too. I am also indebted to my students—teaching is at the center of my life. There is so much I love about working together with faculty and students.

Finally, I'd like to thank all the rest of you for using this book and for being on this journey together.

Together we can put movies to work in service of Business Ethics.

Introduction to the Text

Nelson Mandela: How do you inspire your team to do their best?
Francois Pienaar: By example. I've always thought to lead by example, sir.
Nelson Mandela: Well, that is right. That is exactly right. But how
do we get them to be better then they think they can be? That is very
difficult, I find. Inspiration, perhaps…

—Invictus

Movies are a powerful medium, maybe *the* most powerful one of all. They show us what it means to be courageous, honorable, and generous. They also show us how people can fall short of those goals. From those who live with integrity to those who are up to their necks in moral sludge, from heroes who are moral exemplars to villains with ice in their veins. The host of characters portrayed on the screen run the ethical gamut.

On the level of the individual, movies help us see the vital role ethics plays in our lives. Choices and decisions come at us like potholes in the road: some we see ahead, others appear without warning. In both cases, we are called to assess the situation, weigh the options, factor in relevant values and principles, and make a decision. Movies provide an excellent platform for developing techniques of analysis and sharpening our moral reasoning skills.

Movies bring ethics to life and draw us in, so we identify with the characters and picture ourselves in their shoes. We feel their pain, their fears, and desires and understand the basis of their hopes. Movies can motivate us to take the moral high road and find the best in ourselves. Thanks to the engaging ways ethical dilemmas are presented, they can stimulate us to delve deeper. We then take more seriously the opportunities that come our

Business Ethics Through Movies: A Case Study Approach, First Edition. Wanda Teays.
© 2015 John Wiley & Sons, Ltd. Published 2015 by John Wiley & Sons, Ltd.

way. By showing us examples of nobility and inner strength, we are encouraged to nurture it in ourselves.

All of these qualities make them perfect vehicles for studying *and* doing Business Ethics. As we will see in this book, a movie can be as useful as a case study in highlighting moral problems, clarifying why one course of action is superior to another, and helping us grasp the personal and professional repercussions of the decisions we make. A movie can also give us insight into the ways we are defined or bounded by our work (paid and unpaid). We face pressures, expectations, written or unwritten rules, regulations, codes of conduct, and norms that are meant to guide us. It gives us instruments to help navigate moral territory.

A Case Study Approach

Case studies help us set out the parameters of ethical reflection and problem-solving. Evaluating moral conflicts and balancing competing interests is more understandable in the form of a case, a narrative, a story, a TV show, or a movie. By bringing it to life, we can tackle the issues more quickly, efficiently, and with more dedication than those presented in dry, sterile packages.

The case study approach takes what is abstract, general, and remote and redirects our attention to the trenches where the action takes place. The specifics of *this* case at *tha*t time and place call for clarification, analysis, and moral assessment. Even if the issues are not *our* issues, particular cases that reveal the human dimension tend to be much more instructive (and interesting!) than a discourse on the concepts, theories, and principles. Using both case studies and movies can be a gold mine for doing Business Ethics.

Movies put us face-to-face with characters stuck on the horns of a dilemma and trying to avoid sinking into moral quicksand. They help us think through a difficult situation as the story unfolds on the screen. We follow along as the protagonist faces ethical hurdles, confronts moral quandaries, and tries to find a clear path to a satisfactory resolution.

Movies are as strong a pedagogical tool as real-world cases; together they constitute two powerful components. We can get a better grasp of abstract concepts and moral principles when ethical theories are brought to life. That is one of the values of *applied* ethics, including Business Ethics.

A third component of our study is the inclusion of ethics codes in this text. They reveal the values that guide the policies and decision-making of a business. As a result, they are a key part of our exploration. These codes are not filler on a company's website. They set out the moral base of the corporation and provide guidance for its policies, procedures, and ethical decision-making. Examining these codes is most instructive.

The Focus of this Text

In the various movies we examine here we see protagonists who go the extra step and those who lack the moral fiber to do what's right. We see character traits that are inspiring and a few that are downright repugnant. We see those who rise to the occasion—such as whistleblower Jeffrey Wigand (*The Insider*), union organizer Rita O'Grady (*Made in Dagenham*), and South African president Nelson Mandela (*Invictus*). We see everyday people who find the inner strength to fight injustice and bring about change. They show how very important is the ethical core of businesses, institutions, and governing bodies.

You and I both know that not all protagonists are worth writing home about. Some are morally flawed and lose their way. Stephen Glass from *Shattered Glass*, Phil Connors from *Groundhog Day*, Karen Crowder from *Michael Clayton*, and Gordon Gekko from *Wall Street* all demonstrate where the path of inauthenticity can lead.

Being able to contemplate issues and ideas via movies, cases, and ethics codes is priceless for doing Business Ethics. The specifics of *this* set of players; *those* issues; *that* time and place clarify what's at stake and what principles are (or should be) brought to bear on the decision-making. In this way case studies spotlight the components of a moral quandary and give us a way to factor in theoretical constructs or models. The benefits of this process should not be underestimated.

Another thing about the case study approach is that we gain a set of tools for assessing a person's moral character—as well as corporate decision-making. We have the luxury of being one step removed from the action while still able to survey the situation and draw conclusions about the moral reasoning being put to use. What a great learning tool. That we have a range of great cases—from local to national and from national to international—means we have much to gain. The truth is that Business Ethics is global in scope.

Both real-world (traditional business) cases and those from movies are effective ways to put our analytical skills to work. They provide an opportunity to analyze the issues, ponder the choices, evaluate the options from diverse perspectives, and reflect on the action taken. Along with ethics codes and ethical theories factored into the decision-making, we have some powerful means for investigating the field.

The territory spans ethics in the workplace, corporate decision-making, conflicts between employees and employers, concerns of customers, and controversies regarding product safety, interpersonal relations, the environment, human rights, global justice—and more.

The Structure of this Text

There are three units to this text. The first, "Moral Navigation: Business Ethics and Society" gives an overview of the territory and some tools for the journey. The second, "Moral Leadership: Ethical Theory," sets out the major frameworks for moral reasoning. The third, "Moral Reflection: Thorny Questions," presents some challenges that put our moral reasoning skills to work.

Unit 1. Moral Navigation: Business Ethics and Society

In this unit, we look at the territory of Business Ethics. The four chapters of this unit provide key tools to help us on our way. This includes check-lists and techniques for analyzing arguments, dismantling cases, and weighing the various components. The first chapter, "Tools for the Journey," sets the foundation. In Chapter 1.2 we look at moral integrity in Business Ethics, as shown in Johnson & Johnson's handling of the Tylenol crisis.

Chapter 1.3 tackles the issue of profits and how greed can lead us astray. Political theorists Karl Marx and John Rawls offer some guidance so justice can prevail. The last chapter of Unit 1 looks at the impact of technology. Drawing from movies *Her*, *The Net*, and *Disconnect* and the case of the NSA surveillance and Target's data breach, Chapter 1.4 shows how much technology has touched our lives.

Unit 2. Moral Leadership: Ethical Theories

We start with an overview ("Aerial Surveillance") of the concepts and theories and apply them to films and cases in the rest of the unit. The first is in Chapter 2.2, where we look at Teleological Ethics, which focuses on end goals, rather than the means.

In Chapter 2.3 we see what happens when the emphasis shifts from goals to intentions and moral obligations. This is Deontological Ethics.

Its duty-based approach has been very influential. The next chapter, 2.4, brings us to Virtue Ethics, which focuses on moral character and the virtues needed for a life of purpose. Our focus here is Aristotle, but we briefly look at Confucius, who continues to have impact. The last chapter of Unit 2 is on Feminist Ethics. All too often, ethics books and classes marginalize or eliminate this field of ethics. Doing so is unwise, however, as this theoretical model and its expanded notion of moral agency and the role of relationships in moral reasoning deserve our consideration.

Unit 3. Moral Reflection: Thorny Questions

In the third unit we turn to some thorny questions of Business Ethics and zero in on five that are especially troubling. We start with environmental disasters and, through the movies and cases, see how vital it is to have measures in place. Chapter 3.2 tackles workplace violence. It's just about everywhere these days—post offices, airports, schools, day care centers, shopping malls, and more. Lives depend on us giving this matter our attention so the current realities can be addressed. In the next chapter (3.3), we look at workplace inequities such as unequal pay scales (e.g., with gender discrimination, ageism, or the like), sweatshops, and different pay tiers. Another thorny issue is workplace harassment, which we examine in Chapter 3.4. This can take the form of sexual harassment, assault, rape, stalking, or bullying. That nowhere seems safe from harassment—even the armed forces—tells us why we need to work for change.

In Chapter 3.5 we look at global justice and human rights. Of course we like bargain-priced clothes, food, and electronics. But we can't shield ourselves from the costs of outsourcing, importing cheap labor, and taking other countries' resources for *our* use. Our last chapter of the unit and of the book—Chapter 3.6—underscores the value and importance of personal transformation. We have to take responsibility for our own moral development—and for the values we hold dear and live by (or fail to live by).

Throughout the Chapters

The three aspects touched on throughout the book are: movies, cases, and ethics codes. Each one presents dilemmas, conflicts, and challenges facing individuals, businesses, institutions, and communities. And each one calls us to examine the moral basis for the decisions we make and actions we take.

This is not some abstract mind-game or thought experiment meant to entertain us. The moral engagement on the screen has prescriptive and descriptive components, so we are called to contemplate what *we* would do in like circumstances. Think about the movie *Contagion*, a film about a global pandemic. When an official of the Centers for Disease Control tips off his wife about a quarantine, the *&%@ hits the fan. His dilemma and conflicting values would be *ours* as well, if we were in his shoes.

Similarly, what would *you* do if you discovered your co-worker was fabricating stories—lies upon lies put together in the form of news reports? We may not be the one committing egregious acts, but are witnesses to the moral lapses of others. What should we do? *Shattered Glass* raises such issues.

Just as the movies highlight key issues in Business Ethics, the cases help us see how actual corporations are put to the moral test. Some pass with flying colors; some fall short; some are a disgrace. Using real-world cases along with movies makes for a dynamite combination in the classroom, in professional development workshops, in film clubs, and more. And we can all benefit from that.

A Note for Students

I hope you enjoy this book and it helps develop your skills in Business Ethics. This text has three levels:

1 *Movies* (of which there are 36 discussed in the book)
2 *Actual, real-world case studies* (of which there are 30)
3 *Ethics codes* (of which there are 17)

Each one shows us different aspects of moral reasoning and gives us food for thought.

Throughout the book are also *exercises*. Even if your instructor doesn't assign them, think them through on your own. They help you stand back, get an overview of the issues, and sharpen your problem-solving skills. If you write down your answers that is also helpful.

In Chapter 1.1 you'll find a Case Study Checklist. This is put to use several times to show how it works as a tool for breaking down the movie or the case study. This has the side effect of strengthening your observation and critical thinking skills—clearly something of use.

A Word for Instructors

This book is the very picture of *flexibility*. You can proceed from Unit 1 directly, ending with Chapter 3.6 of Unit 3. Or, if you prefer to emphasize theory and its value as a framework, start with Unit 2 and then move to Units 1 and 3. All but two introductory chapters present movies, cases *and* ethics codes. This makes it clear that the ethical dilemmas presented on screen have real-life correlates. Note also:

- *The movies*—yes, they are powerful vehicles and I wholeheartedly endorse using them. But you don't have to use all or any of the movies discussed here. They illustrate how protagonists face ethical dilemmas. There are 36 movies that serve as a spotlight in this book. They provide an engaging way to do ethics and to develop a variety of skills that no one should be without (analytical skills, reflective skills, writing skills, the ability to generate ideas in problem-solving, and so on).
- *The case studies* work with the movies to highlight the moral quandaries that reside at the core of Business Ethics. There are 30 case studies in this book. They range from classics like the Ford Pinto, Tylenol, Film Recovery Systems, Inc., Exxon Valdez, and Eveleth Mines to recent cases like the Fast Food workers' strike, the Bangladesh sweatshop collapse, the case of Costco and the tainted berries, and salmonella in Foster Farms' chickens.
- *Ethical theories* form the basis of Unit 2. It includes the major theories (from Teleological Ethics to Deontological Ethics to Virtue Ethics and Feminist Ethics). The key theorists are there too—and a few elsewhere (Marx and Rawls are in Chapter 1.3 on greed and Buddhist monk Thich Nhat Hanh is in Chapter 3.6 on Personal Transformation). Confucius is mentioned in Chapter 2.4 on Virtue Ethics to indicate that Aristotle isn't the only Virtue Ethicist.
- *Ethics codes* are rarely a part of Business Ethics books, which seems rather odd if you think about it. Don't skip the ethics codes. At least do a cross-section, so students understand that the values lying at the base of decisions and actions are not incidental. Many, if not most, were the work of dedicated people working hard to distill the moral core of the business or corporation.
- *The chapters* present a range of moral issues and methods for tackling those problems. The focus includes global issues (a global justice chapter, international cases, and movies and documentaries on crises around the world)—which we ought not overlook in doing Business

Ethics. You and your class can use the book as a sort of illustration, an ethical deconstruction manual—and look at entirely different movies. That's one of the strengths of this book—you are not tied to any of these films. Pick your own if you prefer! This liberates you in ways not all books that bring in films care as much to do (as they are studying the movies rather than using them as a springboard, as I do).

- *Exercises:* In addition to what this book provides students (see above note), the book has *exercises* throughout. These can be used for class discussion, on-line chat topics, short (or longer) essay questions, or group projects. You pick! Many ask the students to reflect on the issues and go from there. Some, like the exercise on GM's massive recall in 2014, ask students to do some investigation to learn more. My goal is to stimulate students to think about the ethical dilemmas, the concepts, values, and theories, the repercussions for business and for the society, and issues of accountability.

Thank you for joining me on this journey and using this text!

1.1

Tools for the Journey

Spotlight: *A Hijacking*
Ethics codes: Apple; Google

> *Connor Julian: We can't rush these people. Time is a Western thing. It means nothing to them.*
>
> —A Hijacking

Sometimes we surprise ourselves by our ability to roll with the punches. And this much is clear: we don't always know when disaster will strike and are not always prepared when it does. Movies are full of protagonists whose lives change overnight because of one unforeseen event or another. It could be zombies (*World War Z, 28 Days (or Weeks) Later)* or possessed spirits (*The Conjuring, The Possession*). It could be acts of God (*The Impossible, All is Lost*) or human-caused accidents (*Gravity, Arbitrage*). It could be morally suspect characters in your face (*Captain Phillips, The Grandmaster*) or out to get someone you seek to protect (*Taken, Olympus Has Fallen*).

You may simply be in the wrong place at the wrong time. But there you are. You can't run; you can't hide. You have to do something. And you know this much: All decisions have consequences, unavoidably so. This fact adds to the weight of the circumstances. So there you are.

It could be a terrorist takeover of an elite mall in Nairobi, a rampage in Maryland close to home, or a student armed with a gun in a Massachusetts classroom. It could be a mountain lion roaming a neighborhood in Glendale or a gang rape on a bus in India. All are terrifying to contemplate, and all are real-world cases. None of the victims were likely prepared for the events that transpired even though similar adversities occupy the evening news. We've seen it a hundred times, but always at a distance, until now.

So there you are. Picture yourself at work, a typical day, nothing new really. You are performing the same old tasks with the same old crew. You

Business Ethics Through Movies: A Case Study Approach, First Edition. Wanda Teays.
© 2015 John Wiley & Sons, Ltd. Published 2015 by John Wiley & Sons, Ltd.

may be the one in charge or just a cog in the wheel. You may not want power, but are thrust into a position of leadership. The rules of the game may be yours to set or are set by others, perhaps complete strangers, who have assigned you the moral status of a gnat.

So there you are. You didn't ask for your world to be turned upside down and you may have no say whatsoever in what follows. But you are present, with your faculties as sharp as ever. You have to pay close attention or what little control you have may slip like a wet fish out of your hands.

So here we are. We watch ourselves with new eyes, knowing that our priorities and values may need a major overhaul, and that the assumptions we're operating with warrant a closer look. And, yes, we may surprise ourselves at our resilience, our problem-solving skills, or our ability to respond to the unexpected. We may be pleased to discover our compassion for others or disturbed to realize that we are not as generous or altruistic as we once thought.

Being able to transport ourselves so we can contemplate issues and ideas via case studies and ethical dilemmas presented on screen is priceless for doing Business Ethics. The particulars of a case—that situation, those issues—help clarify what counts when assessing a person's moral character, the values of a corporation, or the actions and policies taken. Similarly, the particulars of a film allow us the luxury of being one step removed from the action without losing its immediacy, importance, and ability to convey lessons to be learned. Movies are a great learning tool.

As we will see throughout this book, these two forms of case studies—those based on actual events and those from movies—put our analytical skills to work. They give us the opportunity to examine the issues, ponder the choices, evaluate the decisions from diverse perspectives, and reflect on the consequences that follow. Along with ethics codes and ethical theories, we have some powerful means for investigating the field.

Let's start by looking at the benefits of using movies for studying Business Ethics.

Using Movies in Business Ethics

There's a seductive quality to movies that pulls us in. Each action, each character is bigger than life. It's a dynamic medium; one capable of imprinting images and dialogue on our skulls until the end of time. Who can forget *The Godfather*'s "offer you can't refuse," with the sight of a bloody horsehead driving the point home? Who wasn't struck by Gordon Gekko's "greed is good" speech or Lou Mannheim's warning to Bud Fox, "Kid, you're on a roll. Enjoy it while it lasts, 'cause it never does"? As Plato's Allegory of the Cave attests, the images on the screen can take on a life of their own. They often captivate us and even transport us by lifting us out of this reality into another dimension. They are vehicles for presenting ideas, setting out ethical dilemmas, and portraying characters and events. Thanks to movies, we have a way to develop our moral reasoning skills that is imaginative, vivid, thought-provoking, and often memorable.

Some movies transcend the level of fiction by giving us insight into our lives and into the world around us. That is the *reflective dimension* of film. For example, looking back at the Vietnam War—distant history for some, a daily presence for others—it may not be easy to grasp how dark a time it was. Because of movies like *Apocalypse Now* and *Casualties of War*, however, we get a sense of the madness of that conflict and a way to better grasp the horrors of the wars in Iraq and Afghanistan.

Similarly, movies like *The Insider*, *Food, Inc.* and *Up in the Air* give us insight into unsavory business practices. Whether it is duplicitous behavior in the tobacco business (*The Insider*), unsanitary conditions in agribusiness (*Food, Inc.*) or corporate downsizing (*Up in the Air*), business policies can change the social and economic landscape.

In this chapter we will look at key tools for analysis. These include the two approaches to ethics (Metaethics and Normative Ethics), handy checklists for dismantling arguments or setting out case studies, and tips for examining policies, guidelines, and corporate ethics codes. The movie *A Hijacking* is useful for illustrating the issues.

The Value of Film in Business Ethics

A good movie can leave a lasting impression on us. It can change how we see the world by playing a *descriptive role* offering insight into the problems we confront and the inferences we draw. It also has a *prescriptive component* in shaping how we think about the issue in question, and what factors should count in the equation. Among the considerations are the interrelationships and the moral status assigned to the various players.

Movies are a powerful vehicle for examining social, political, and ethical issues. They bring ethical dilemmas into focus so we can do a close analysis of the issues. There's something about the story being told large, bigger than life. It helps to be able to watch at a distance and with some detachment, so that we are not tied in knots by the threads of the story. Being engaged while being one step removed allows for clarity of moral reasoning. Basically, if we are in the audience and not the ones on the hot seat, we can stand back and evaluate both the dilemmas and the decisions. Even those that cut close to home, that are also *our* issues, can be examined without the weight of responsibility hanging over our heads.

Moral reasoning is often at center stage in the movies we watch. The ethical theories and conceptual frameworks we use shape our analysis. All of the chapters in Unit 2 demonstrate that. There we see how theories can play a vital role in unpacking the ethical dilemmas in movies and in helping us understand movies as a form of case study. They can be as effective in exploring issues as real-world case studies drawn from business in developing our own moral reasoning.

Two avenues will be pursued to meet that goal. One is to use case studies (actual cases in Business Ethics) to illustrate the range of issues and the sorts of reasoning involved in ethical problem solving. The second avenue is to use movies as another kind of case study. It is useful to start with an overview of the plot, focusing on the protagonist(s) and the ethical issue(s) that drive the action, a scene, or a specific decision. We will then go into that in enough detail to give us some tools and insight for developing our own skills at Business Ethics.

Overview of the Ethical Territory

There are two main branches of Ethics. One provides a bird's eye view of ethical concepts and theory and the interrelations between one theory and another. It is called Metaethics. The other branch focuses on the practical, the experiential, the level of ethical actions and moral judgments. It is called Normative Ethics. Let's get a sense of each of these two areas.

Metaethics

It is in Metaethics where we examine the theoretical frameworks, the models of moral reasoning, ethical rules, moral principles and the concepts that are used. Metaethics focuses on the structure behind moral reasoning. We are doing Metaethics when we compare and contrast ethical theories or examine concepts like "good," "bad," "virtuous," "vicious,"—as well as terms like "moral agency," "autonomy," "intentions," "culpability," and so on.

Language shapes the discourse. We know from advertising, the power that words like "winners" or "losers" can have on what we think, what we want, and how much we are willing to spend to accomplish that goal.

Think of ad slogans like "Coke is life," "We are driven," and "Just do it." A pithy slogan, as those in marketing know all too well, can stick in the brain for eons. And in just three words too!

In addition, the labels we use can affect our way of thinking. We see this with the terms "student" and "customer." Referring to someone enrolled in a university class as a "customer" or "consumer" rather than a "student" has significant repercussions. Think about it. We say, "The customer is always right." We would not normally say that of students, at least not in terms of academic matters. However, when it comes to *financial* affairs, students are often seen as consumers with bargaining power. The terminology shapes the boundaries of the policies and attitudes that follow.

Ethicist Douglas Birsch examines one of the key functions of Metaethics, that of evaluating ethical theories. He sets out four useful recommendations that we can draw from (2002, p. 6). They are:

Key Functions of Metaethics

1 *Establish guidelines:* Ethical theories should have some specific guidelines.
2 *Evaluate guidelines:* Ethical theories should be able to prioritize guidelines.
3 *Limit self-interest:* Ethical theories should have guidelines limiting self-interest.
4 *Solve ethical dilemmas:* Ethical theories should have guidelines that help us solve ethical problems.

Normative Ethics

Normative Ethics focuses on the practical dimension, not abstract concepts. Here we look at the ways in which ethics and ethical-decision-making take place in the world and in our lives (including the workplace!). As a result, Normative Ethics encompasses moral judgments about people, actions, and values. We try to figure out if an action is right or wrong, or if a person or group is virtuous or vicious (good or evil, morally upstanding or morally deficient), or apply a set of criteria in making a moral claim or judgment (e.g., "It was generous of the Board to give the workers a bonus this year," or "The FDA ought to play a stronger role around antibiotic-resistant salmonella").

In a work or institutional setting, decisions and policies are often bound by guidelines, regulations, or an ethical code. Throughout this book, we will look at a diverse collection of ethical codes ranging from small businesses to mega-corporations, from food production to high tech, and more. In Unit 2 we will see how ethical theories can be used as models for interpreting or assessing business ethical dilemmas that we find in movies and in real-world cases. As a result, we will see how both Metaethics and Normative Ethics are fundamentally important.

Tackling Cases in Business Ethics

Whether we are looking at cases from the business world or ones portrayed on the screen, the approach we take and the tools we use make all the difference. Keep in mind what we want to achieve: We want to pull out the key elements, look at the ethical dilemma, weigh the relevant factors, and arrive at a right decision. This means knowing what should be done and what rules, values, and principles should guide our assessment.

With ethical tools, we can go to the various cases in this book, and beyond. We can then dismantle them to see what's at issue, what values and goals should be factored in, and what to avoid by way of mistakes or sloppy thinking. With that in mind, let's consider how to approach a case and subject it to a moral analysis. Seven steps are key, as we can see in this checklist:

Case Study Checklist
A Guide to Ethical Decision Making

1   *Define the Problem.* Note the general issue(s), the ethical dilemma to be resolved, major players and decision-maker(s), competing perspectives, and who stands to gain or lose.
2   *Set out the Key Players.* Note whose interests are at stake and who or what counts in the equation. If there are allies and/or adversaries, state who they are.
3   *State the Facts.* "Where?" and "When?" are right behind "What?" when trying to nail down the specifics of the situation. Make note of the general context, details of the case, including the time and place, and what boundaries should be kept in mind. Note any relevant restrictions or guidelines that ought to be brought into the decision-making.
4   *Clarify Key Concepts and Values.* Terms and concepts shape the way problems are defined and evaluated—along with the values, they are at the heart of moral reasoning. Factor in as well any ethical codes,

regulations, legal constrictions, and relevant cultural or religious beliefs that bear upon the case. Keep those values in mind as you proceed.

5 *Settle on the Criteria of Assessment.* Set out the criteria and process for weighing options and evaluating evidence. Be aware of the ways in which criteria broaden or narrow the territory and inform the decision-making process.

6 *Get Some Perspective.* Turn over the problem and examine it from different points of view—and anticipate criticism. Solicit input and listen to the different voices with an open mind. Consider potential consequences in light of the ethical and legal parameters. Assess opposing positions with the openness needed to see any pitfalls of your tentative decision or plan. Make adjustments as needed.

7 *Make A Plan—Decide!* Ask if it is the best choice in light of the moral principles guiding the decision-making. Amend your decision as needed.

Applying the Checklist: *A Hijacking*

Let's put it to work with the movie *A Hijacking* (2013). It centers on a Danish cargo ship that has been taken over by Somali pirates. Their demands are both straightforward and unsurprising: They want money, lots of money. They have brought along a translator who plays a pivotal role, communicating by phone and fax the pirates' ransom demands and the CEO's response. The lives of the seven hostages (the ship's crew) hang in the balance as negotiations go on and the situation grows more tense.

The story moves between the polished executive dressed to perfection, cuff links and all, and the sweaty, scruffy cook. The one is in corporate headquarters in Copenhagen, invested in staying in control and heading his side of the negotiations. The other is held captive on the ship on the Indian Ocean and is thrust in a leadership role by the pirate's translator. The movie goes back and forth between these two protagonists. We open with Mikkel, the cook, making omelets for the crew, oblivious to the fact that pirates are about to take over the ship. Cut to Denmark, where Peter, the tightly wound CEO, is berating his assistant for his inferior skills at deal making. It's downhill from there.

We can see how the checklist helps us unpack the ethical base by going through each step. Let's see how it can help gives us insight into the movie.

1.   The Dilemma

At issue: The ship has been taken over by pirates demanding a $12 million ransom.

- The objectives facing CEO Peter Ludvigsen are: (1) to engineer the return of the crew (seven of them) without anyone being harmed; (2) to minimize the ransom to keep the costs down; and (3) to try to prevent more Danish ships being seized by pirates.
- The objectives facing the ship's cook Mikkel Hartmann are: (1) to try to avoid antagonizing the Somali pirates; (2) to do what he can to work with middle man and translator Omar; and (3) try to get the corporation to pay whatever it takes to get the crew released unharmed.

Interests at stake: There are three parties in the conflict—the pirates, the crew, and the corporation. The repercussions of any decisions made affect a wider audience, including other corporations (fearful of piracy involving *their* ships, aircraft, production centers, etc.), society in general, groups associated with the pirates (e.g., a terrorist group or political advocacy group), and so on.

2.   The Players

The movie centers on two key players—the CEO and the ship's cook. Others play a supporting role. We see the differences of perspective; the one far removed from the scene of the crime, the other right in the thick of it. We see this in the hardships inflicted upon the crew-members, such as restricted access to the toilet. This is but one of many indignities they will suffer before the ordeal is over.

- *The CEO:* Back at the corporate headquarters are Peter, his assistant Lars and hostage expert Connor Julian assisting with the negotiations. They are gathered together around a table staring at the telephone, waiting for calls from the pirates, with Julian keeping track of the shifting dollar amounts as the haggling over the ransom continues.
- *The Hostages:* The hostages are the pawns in a battle over money. We see how the capital is distributed in the bargaining process: the company has the money and the pirates have the time (and are willing to extend the hostage situation from days to weeks and then to months). The crew's patience and mental and physical health are stretched to the limit.

We see the strain. The dapper Peter discovers that the rules of the game he is used to playing with other polished businessmen don't apply to pirates, whose notion of power involves brute force and threat of force held over their captives. Their goal is to get as much money as they can from the Danish company and if it takes months to do so, that's the way it goes.

3. The Facts, Context, Parameters

Here's the nitty gritty:

* *The Context:* The story is set in the present. The HV *Rozen*, a Danish cargo ship, is stuck in the Indian Ocean with the Somali pirates determined to get a hefty ransom in exchange for the crew. We watch the events from two perspectives: on the ship via the ship's cook (Mikkel) and in Denmark with CEO Peter. Both face challenges that stretched them to the breaking point. They both dread making a mistake and angering or alienating the pirates.
* *The Conflict:* The pirates' asking price for the return of the crew is $12 million. The company's starting bid is $250,000. Neither side wants to accede to the demands of the other, so the negotiations drag on. Mikkel and the crew realize that their lives hang in the balance and grow increasingly despondent as time goes on.

As the tensions increase, Peter's sense of his own power diminishes. We see this most clearly when he mistakenly thinks Mikkel has been killed and he comes under fire over the lack of an early settlement. Problems that are unresolved start to fester. And no good can come of that.

4. Key Concepts and Values

Terms and concepts shape the decision process. What counts as "fair" or "just" can vary with the values brought to bear. In this case, there's no sense that much can be *fair* when it comes to extortion. The pirates don't play by any rules beyond those of self-interest. Translator Omar shows greater ethical awareness than the pirates he's helping.

Values: The major value shared centers on money. The pirates want the most they can get and the corporation wants to minimize the amount needed to bring the men back alive. The corporation also values *not* showing any weakness that'd increase their vulnerability to future attacks.

That constitutes a kind of reputational value that plays a role in the negotiation. *A Hijacking* is silent on the circumstances that allowed piracy to take root.

5.   Criteria of Assessment

Here is where we look at the factors such as the decision-making process and weighing the options. The central ethical dilemma centers on the ransom demand—how much money is needed to rescue the crew while deterring future piracy.

Two issues are critical: one is the corporation's resources and the second is the fear of future copycat piracy. This has consequences for all three parties. The pirates find hostage-taking to be lucrative, given $3.3 million they ended up with after the four months. The corporation wanted a quicker resolution. The longer the stalemate the greater the chance nerves will be frayed and tempers strained. So, both time and money count as criteria.

A third issue arises when the other board members accuse Peter of neglecting his usual duties. We watch Peter lose his grip in trying to negotiate with pirates who have a *very* different approach to conflict resolution. And then there's the human cost. The captain's ulcer left him in a weakened condition and the lack of food and proper hygiene affects all the crewmembers. The brutality and threat of death lies over the crew like a thick fog. Mikkel was nearly catatonic by the end of the ordeal.

Pulling all this together, *the key criteria are*: (1) Keep the ship's crew from harm, (2) contain costs, (3) keep a lid on how much the crisis affects the other part of the business, and (4) deter future piracy. From what we see in the movie, the priorities of the company were in this order —(1) cost containment, (2) minimize human costs, (3) deter future piracy and (4) don't neglect other issues of the company.

6.   Get Perspective and Anticipate Criticism

The crew members were pretty much powerless. Mikkel's suffering illustrates how hard it was to be held hostage. The pirates finally lowered their ransom demand and agreed to a payoff of over $3 million dollars. As for Peter, both his fortitude and sense of self are put to the test. He suffers in ways he would never have predicted. Criticism comes from three main fronts:

- First, the expert negotiator, Connor Julian, advises against Peter leading the negotiations. Later events indicate that Connor's advice should have been taken, as Peter's hubris put the crew in further danger.

- Second, Mikkel, the cook: he realizes that the lives of the hostages were not given the weight he expected.
- Third, Peter's fellow executives: they warn him that time is of the essence and he needs to bring about a timely resolution. Peter feels the weight of these three forces, but can't see a quick way out of the stalemate. This is when Lars, the colleague he berated at the movie's opening, offers the way out.

7. Make a Decision

Lars's solution is for Peter to counter the ransom demand by adding $500,000 of his own money to that of the corporation. The personal touch made the difference. The pirates got their $3.3 million, the hostages (all but one) came home, and both Mikkel and Peter are left to put their lives back in order.

Putting the Checklist to Work

The checklist helps us set out the basic dilemma, key factors, and how the moral reasoning unfolds. It can be used with movies or actual cases. It is a useful tool of analysis and a way to examine the portrayal of moral dilemmas or ethical conduct. With our decision-making checklist, we have a way to approach cases and move beyond them to other issues found in Business Ethics, such as setting or evaluating policies, regulations, and ethical guidelines.

Setting policy involves construction, in putting policy together from scratch or amending and modifying a previous policy. Such a task calls on both critical *and* creative thinking. *Evaluating policy* involves deconstruction. Both require tools of analysis and critical thinking skills, especially those of argumentation. Let's start with setting policy and get an overview of concerns.

Setting Policy

We frequently have to stake out a position on a policy change. Of course, people often draw a distinction between what they do and what they recommend others do. For example, an alcoholic, smoker, or athlete into extreme sports might argue from the standpoint of individual rights to justify their behavior, but would be hesitant to have their children to follow in their footsteps.

Drawing up policy guidelines requires us to *generalize* from a set of moral principles, rules, or values to a wider audience. In saying, "You ought to do such and so," we are giving a moral prescription. That usually takes the form of a recommendation as to how others should think and behave.

Most people operate by a set of moral prescriptions constructed from a variety of sources; such as religion, tradition, family values, societal beliefs, and so on. Many businesses and institutions such as hospitals and universities set out ethical guidelines.

Ethical guidelines function in a number of ways. Most important are these two:

- They set out expectations in the form of an ethical code meant to govern the relevant parties (employees, management, suppliers, staff, faculty students, etc.).
- They make those expectations known by publicizing or providing access to the code(s) in question; and others (such as the general public, customers, other corporate bodies) can examine those values.

To some extent, laws define acceptable modes of behavior, though laws do not necessarily set down or function as ethical guidelines. Plus, laws are not always respected. For instance, during the 1980's members of the Sanctuary Movement disagreed with the policy of the federal government regarding El Salvador, Guatemala and Nicaragua. The government's attempt to catch and deport what they called "illegal aliens" and what the Sanctuary Movement called "refugees," resulted in people breaking the law because of their moral principles.

Thirty years later, civil disobedience is still an avenue for bringing social problems to light. For example, nuclear protestors Sister Megan Rice, Michael Walli, and Greg Boertje-Obed made their way, slowly but surely, into the Oak Ridge nuclear plant in Tennessee on July 28, 2012 and sprayed peace slogans and blood on the wall of a building housing weapons-grade uranium. They were convicted of sabotage and given jail sentences of 35 months for Sister Megan and 62 months for the other two. They were also ordered to pay $53,000 for damage caused. It is vital that we look at what we believe in and come to some understanding of what we would do in the name of those beliefs. The day may come in each of our lives when we must take a stand.

Ethics Codes

The way that a business approaches ethics—and certainly its ethics code—reveals its basic set of values. These are the fundamental beliefs that shape all its decision-making. You know the saying, "To know me is to love me"? Well we can't know another, much less the driving force of a business, without knowing the ethics that reside at its core.

The importance of an ethics code should not be understated. And paying close attention to that code is not a hollow exercise. With that in mind, let's compare two major corporations' codes, those of Apple and Google.[1]

Apple's and Google's codes share some commonalities. Both are clear about boundaries (the law, regulations, etc.) and expectations around employee (or supplier) conduct, as well as the degree to which business interests must be upheld and protected. Nevertheless, there are differences in style and content. Google's code emphasizes the personal, with such phrases as "don't be evil" and "do the right thing." It calls its employees to serve users, act with integrity, demonstrate trust and responsibility, and respect one another. Also, the use of terms like "Googlers" has no correlate (such as "Applets") in the more formal Apple code. This may be an attempt on Google's part to make it more user friendly.

Google's greater emphasis on individual accountability may stem from the fact that its code is aimed at employees (people), whereas Apple's targets other companies with which it has business dealings. That said, the overall impression we get from the two codes suggests that the two companies diverge in how they approach their respective audiences.

Exercise

1. What are the main things *you* think a company's ethics code should contain? Note what values you'd expect to be emphasized.
2. How do Apple's and Google's ethics codes measure up to your expectations?

Tools of Analysis

Mapping Arguments

In order to evaluate cases in Business Ethics, we have to be able to deal with evidence and see how it fits together to support a thesis (=conclusion). First, we need the basics of argumentation—which we'll look at first. And then we need to get a handle on weighing evidence.

Mapping Arguments

1   Thesis
    ➡ Locate and state the conclusion (= thesis).
2   Evidence
    ➡ List the premises (= evidence).
3   Argument Form
    ➡ Determine the type of argument (deductive vs. inductive).
4   Sort and Weigh
    ➡ Sort evidence: Separate out claims of fact, value claims, and applicable regulations, laws, policies, or guidelines cited in the argument).
    ➡ Weigh evidence: Note strengths and weaknesses of the premises.
5   Thorny Issues
    ➡ Check for unwarranted assumptions, omissions, biased language, fallacious reasoning, and questionable claims that weaken the argument.
6   Bottom Line
    ➡ Assess the quality of the reasoning: Do the premises support the conclusion?

Some arguments are persuasive; others are not. If the premises offer sufficient support for the conclusion, we'd say it's a strong argument. If the conclusion could not be false if the premises were true, we'd say it's a *valid* argument—and if those premises were actually true, the argument would be *sound*. On the other hand, if the evidence is lacking and does not support the conclusion, the argument is *weak*. In fact, if the conclusion could be false while the premises were true, then we'd consider the argument *invalid* and *unsound*. So you can see that a great deal follows from the way in which the premises do or do not supply enough support for the conclusion to follow.

Necessity of Evidence

Without evidence, there's no argument. An argument requires at least one premise offered in support of the conclusion. And remember: *Opinions are not arguments.* There has to be at least one premise and only one conclusion in an argument. For an argument, you need both premises and a conclusion—without both pieces, there's no argument.

Arguments fall into two main types:

•   Inductive arguments (when the premises provide some support but the conclusion only follows with probability or likelihood).

- Deductive arguments (when it is claimed that the premises are sufficient in their support for the conclusion).

An inductive argument can be considered strong (*cogent*) when the conclusion appears highly likely if the premises are true. This is similar to "preponderance of the evidence" in a court of law. In contrast, a deductive argument asserts that the conclusion follows premises with certainty and, thus, as noted above, the argument is valid. This is similar to "beyond a reasonable doubt."

Evaluating the Strength of the Evidence

Once we have the argument set out, we can see how strong it actually is. We need sufficient evidence to make the case. Some premises carry more weight than others; some have a direct link to the conclusion, others are indirect; and some independently support the conclusion, while others are dependent on other pieces of evidence to make the case. As a result, it pays to carefully analyze the type and strength of the evidence.

Value Claims

In moral reasoning, we often deal with a variety of value claims (e.g., "You ought to be honest" and "You ought not share company secrets with our competitors"). Value claims are tricky, as they are not factual claims (true or false) and, thus, function differently within an argument.

Along with regulations and guidelines (e.g., Google's "Obey the law" and "Avoid conflicts of interest"), value claims (e.g., "Don't be evil") function in an argument as assumed truths—givens. However, assumptions can shift and one set of assumptions can be replaced by a completely different set. We need to view assumptions with care and see which of them function like factual claims and which function as values or as guidelines.

"Obey the law" may be considered ill-advised in some circumstances. Not all laws warrant compliance. And "Don't be evil" may be rejected if a greater harm could occur from avoiding the evil. Such prescriptions have to be weighed in light of competing values and interests. Hang onto our horse sense and not regard moral reasoning as necessarily black or white. Sometimes there are shades of grey and it may be wise to give them our attention.

Let's now take these tools and put them to work. In the remaining chapters of this book we'll do just that. With the films, the cases, and the various ethics codes, we can develop our skills in moral reasoning—and analytical reasoning—and gain greater insight into the field of Business Ethics.

Works Cited

Apple, "Apple Supplier Code of Conduct," http://www.apple.com/supplier responsibility/accountability.html (accessed December 8, 2014).
Google, "Code of Conduct," http://investor.google.com/corporate/code-of-conduct. html (accessed December 8, 2014).

Note

1   They can be accessed at "Apple Supplier Code of Conduct," http://www. apple.com/supplierresponsibility/accountability.html; Google, "Code of Conduct," http://investor.google.com/corporate/code-of-conduct.html.

Unit 1

Moral Navigation: Business Ethics and Society

1.2

The Moral Compass
Business Ethics and Society

Spotlight: *Up in the Air; Michael Clayton*
Case Study: The Tylenol Case
Ethics Code: Johnson & Johnson

> *Business Woman: He just waltzes in and cuts in line?*
> *Hilton Clerk: We reserve priority assistance for our Hilton Honors members.*
>
> —Up in the Air

Ryan Bingham is one of those guys who breezes through security and moves to the front of the line. He has figured out how to maximize the benefits of life on the road. Frequent flyer miles? You bet! He's a master at accumulating miles, ordering his entire dollars' allotment of meals whether he's hungry or not. "I don't spend a nickel, if I can help it," he remarks, "unless it somehow profits my mileage account." His motto might be "It's the *miles*, stupid" (not the economy!). He's slick too, with his classy style and sleek suitcase.

Remember the Charlie Chaplin film *Modern Times*, where Chaplin works in an assembly plant doing exactly the same thing every day, over and over? Well, *Up in the Air* (2009) tells the story of a man who fires employees as if on an assembly line, and just as mindlessly. He sails in, drops the axe on the hapless individuals, gives a canned speech to console them, and sails out. To soften the blow of being fired, Ryan tosses out snippets of wisdom. "Look, anybody who ever built an empire, or changed the world, sat where you are now. And it's because they sat there that they were able to do it." He doles out this spiel without batting an eye.

He glides along on the surface, happily within reach of his life's goal of one million miles. The arrival of a young trainee, Natalie Keener, shakes

Business Ethics Through Movies: A Case Study Approach, First Edition. Wanda Teays.
© 2015 John Wiley & Sons, Ltd. Published 2015 by John Wiley & Sons, Ltd.

up his routine. Her enthusiasm and confidence (some might say arrogance) are her outstanding characteristics. Sophisticated she's not.

Ryan can see that she's unprepared for the dark underbelly of being face to face with the grief of those who are terminated. Her equanimity is shattered when a woman calmly threatens suicide after being fired. Ryan dismisses it as idle talk, but Natalie is shaken to the core. Ryan may see himself as the ferrying lost souls over the River of Dread; but Natalie doesn't. Ryan may think that tossing out glib sayings like bags of peanuts to those in Economy class provides solace; but Natalie doesn't. And neither do we.

One thing becomes clear: Companies that lack the guts—the *ganas*—to explain to their employees why they are being fired fall short on the moral integrity scale. No more than a stranger should tell you that your husband wants a divorce, should a corporation use an outsider to hand out pink slips. It may be an effective means of damage control, but it's pretty darn heartless.

In this chapter we will look at one of the classics of Business Ethics history and examine a contrasting case from film (*Michael Clayton*). We will then turn to the components of moral agency and its three dimensions (the individual, the corporation, the community) and, finally, Johnson & Johnson's ethics code. Let's start with an exercise to see the role of a company's moral roots.

CASE STUDY: The Poisoned Painkillers

You are the CEO of a company with products ranging from baby shampoo to over-the-counter drugs (painkillers, nasal decongestants, cold medication, etc.). Your company's assets exceed $5 billion. You have thousands of employees and are well regarded in the business world and by the general public. It is September 28, 1982, Ronald Reagan is president, and the 444-day long Iranian hostage crisis ended 20 months ago.

Within one week, disaster strikes. Four people in the Chicago metropolitan area die of cyanide poisoning after consuming one of your painkillers. This is before safety seals were used, so where the painkillers were tampered with is up for grabs.

Police determine that the pills came from different distribution centers, so the production plant is not the likely source. More probable is that they were removed from drugstore shelves, laced with 65 mg. of potassium cyanide, and put back for the unsuspecting customer to purchase and consume.

Widespread fear and panic could destroy the company. Seven people have died and no one has claimed responsibility. Law enforcement is in the dark as to the perpetrator. The FBI has advised against recalling the product, because a recall could send the wrong message to the perpetrator(s) and cripple your business. Tensions are high.

Exercise

1. What are the ethical concerns raised by this case? State the top three. Why them?
2. Set out a plan:
   a. What should be our first response?
   b. How can you restore the public's confidence?
   c. Should you rename the product to erase the image of people dying?
   d. Would you do anything different if your company was a small business in the pharmaceutical market?

Putting The Tools To Work: The Tylenol Case

As you may have guessed, this is the Tylenol case; it could have destroyed its manufacturer, Johnson & Johnson. This tragedy resulted in a mass recall and the creation of tamper-proof packages. J&J came through with their reputation firmly intact and their CEO praised for his straightforward handling of the disaster. The case has never been solved, but it's a landmark of Business Ethics.

The *Case Study Checklist* (Chapter 1.1) has seven steps:

1 Define the Problem
2 Set out the Key Players
3 State the Facts
4 Clarify Key Concepts and Values
5 Settle on the Criteria of Assessment
6 Get Some Perspective
7 Make a Plan—Decide!

This helps frame the case and highlight the key aspects, so let's put it to work.

1. The Problem   Johnson & Johnson had to decide what to do when a multimillion-dollar-a-year product appears responsible for people dying. There was no indication as to the source of the poisoning or the extent of the problem. Have only a handful of Tylenol bottles been contaminated?

Or could there be dozens—even hundreds—of bottles of cyanide-laced pills? Capsules can easily be tampered with, in contrast to tablets or caplets. That fact hung in the air like pea-soup fog.

There was also the fear that it didn't stop with Tylenol. On October 2, 1982, Illinois Attorney General Tyrone Fahner observed, "The potential for these people doing the same thing to other medicines is horrendous." He realized that over-the-counter medicines needed protective inner seals like we see on jars of instant coffee (Malcolm, 1982).

You can bet there was a major manhunt. Fahner was confident that 100 state and federal agents could track down the killer. "We'll get him one way or the other," he declared. "Even nuts make mistakes." He added: "And if it's some sort of screwball cult, they'll turn on each other for the money" (Malcolm, 1982). Johnson & Johnson offered a $100,000 reward (never claimed). From our vantage point (30+ years later), we might first think of an act of terrorism and *not* a nutcase or screwball cult. Times have changed.

2.   *The Key Players*   The key players are the corporation, the public, the government (e.g., FBI, FDA, etc.), and the healthcare industry. James Burke, CEO of Johnson & Johnson, plays a pivotal role in the handling of the case.

3.   *The Key Facts*   As of October 2, 1982, 37 percent of sales of over-the-counter pain-relievers in the US were Tylenol products—worth over $300 million a year (Pace, 1982). Seven people died from Extra-Strength Tylenol capsules laced with potassium cyanide.

Johnson & Johnson recalled approximately 31 million bottles of Tylenol (a loss of around $100 million), set up a bank of toll-free 800-numbers for worried consumers and mounted an aggressive PR campaign. In addition to allaying public fears, this also allowed CEO James Burke to play a central role by putting a human face on the corporation.

4.   *Key Concepts and Values*   The concepts associated with Johnson & Johnson's handling of the situation are openness, trust, respect, and integrity. All are important. Though such a massive recall and subsequent discounts cost millions of dollars in the short term, the long-term gains were considerable. The public perception was that the company responded quickly to the crisis.

5.   *Criteria of Assessment*   When people die after consuming a previously safe product, it's a no-brainer that immediate action has to be taken.

This Johnson & Johnson did by the recall, the open phone lines, and effective use of the media.

Another concern was the corporation's reputation. Cost containment was a gamble. Finally, there was pressure to put distance between the contaminated product and the corporation. Cut their losses and aim for a clean slate. Changing names could be seen as losing face. The criteria, then, are:

1   How to minimize further harm
2   How to preserve the company's reputation and public goodwill
3   How to retain consumer loyalty
4   How to contain costs

6.   Get Perspective and Anticipate Criticism   Two issues are copycat poisonings and terrorism (domestic or global). How much weight should be given to these? And what about potential threats to national security? This has gained more prominence since 1982, but it still merited attention at the time. Also, since no one knew how many people would be poisoned before it was over, doctors and hospitals were put on the alert. All these concerns for Johnson & Johnson reinforced the importance of being as transparent as possible.

7.   Make a Decision   The poisoned capsules unleashed a host of problems. It was pretty much a nightmare. The October 5, 1982 *Business Digest* reported that, "Its stock has been hurt, earnings predictions and brokerage house recommendations have been lowered and at least one lawsuit has been filed." *The Times* editorial of the same day put it succinctly, "The acts of aberrant minds are hard to guard against, impossible to accept. Hurricanes are easier to cope with than psychopaths."

Johnson & Johnson stopped all advertising until they thought the threat was behind them and launched a recall. We may not be shocked that 31 million bottles of Tylenol were recalled. But it was different in 1982. "Before 1982, nobody ever recalled anything," said Albert Tortorella, PR expert who advised Johnson & Johnson (quoted by Rehak, 2002). "Companies often fiddle while Rome burns," he said. Obviously this didn't apply here.

Tips for Examining the Case

To get a handle on what happened, it pays to study the case from two temporal perspectives. One is from hindsight, framing events from the present time looking back, using what we know now. The other is to work in context—frame the crisis as-it-happened and assess events as they unfolded.

Situate yourself in 1982 and follow the crisis as it evolved. Go back to the time the story broke. Note what details came to light and what actions were taken. Look at the response of the media and relevant parties—from consumers to the CEO, the public in general and officials from the FBI to the FDA, law enforcement, and so on. Reassess first impressions, such as Attorney General Fahner calling it the act of a "nutcase" or "screwball cult" (Malcolm, 1982).

Looking at Johnson & Johnson's ethics code is also a useful exercise. An ethics code can also perform different functions for different audiences, and can provide insight into the values as well as the direction decision-making could take. We also gain insight into our own set of ethical priorities as well as those of the society.

Don't forget the obvious: Corporations exist at a particular time and place. They are *situated* in a context that can inform or even shape business policies and practices. Values are not carved in marble, their meaning and application fixed for all eternity. So we shouldn't make too many assumptions when investigating issues around morality.

Ethical Reflections

Johnson & Johnson CEO James Burke stood tall in the face of the firestorm. "He was widely praised for his leadership and his forthrightness in dealing with the media," notes Tortorella (Rehak, 2002). In a November 1982 news conference Burke presented a chronology of the company's response to the crisis. "He was in complete control," Tortorella says. Johnson & Johnson was "made a hero" by Tylenol (Rehak, 2002).

Here we are, thirty years later. What do we know now? No one was ever charged for the poisonings. However, James Lewis was convicted of extortion for writing to the company demanding $1 million to "stop the killings" (Fletcher, 2009). The fact that Johnson & Johnson did not change the name of the painkiller is seen as proof of its openness and integrity.

The Tylenol case is considered a landmark of effective PR and crisis management—"perhaps the best-ever organizational response to a major public relations crisis" (Blankenbeckler). Johnson & Johnson acted quickly and decisively. "They achieved the status of consumer champion," says Communications Professor Soterios Zoulas (2008). "The company took responsibility and placed public safety above profit."

This is one of those thrillers that would make a great movie! It has a gripping story, it centers on an important ethical dilemma, it has heroes and villains, and the fact it was never solved just adds to the intrigue. The FBI hasn't given up on trying to solve the case. As recently as May 2011 the FBI requested a DNA sample from Theodore Kaczynski (the "Unabomber"), who lived in Chicago at the time of the Tylenol killings. Kaczynski said he had never possessed potassium cyanide. (Stone and Walsh, 2011). And so the mystery continues.

Crisis Management

As we know from our own lives, there is much to be gained from seeing what's done right as well as examining mistakes and shortcomings. The four keys of crisis management are Response Time, Integrity, Transparency, and Responsibility. Waste no time when catastrophe strikes. The time you waste will be interpreted as: you are hiding something, you don't care, or you are trying to cover your butt.

Take the moral high road. Act with integrity and be willing to apologize and make reparations if mistakes are made. Be open with the press, consumers, employees, and anyone else with a stake in the events. Take responsibility to act quickly and caringly, and pitch in so problems are averted or alleviated in a timely manner.

Johnson & Johnson's handling of the Tylenol case was considered "heroic." The company and its CEO James Burke received accolades out the wazoo. Burke was complimented for the respect shown to consumers and the affirmative steps taken to prevent more tampering.

He also assumed *responsibility*. This is in keeping with the corporation's ethics code and its refrain "We are responsible to... ." The repetition of that phrase indicates that Johnson & Johnson wants that one moral commitment to stand out. (See the end of this chapter for an exercise on the code.)

To underscore the *integrity* that Johnson & Johnson showed when facing a crisis of such magnitude, it helps to examine a contrast. That we can find with the company U North and its chief legal counsel, Karen Crowder, in the movie *Michael Clayton* (2007). The movie could be subtitled, "Crisis mismanagement"!

SPOTLIGHT: *Michael Clayton*

Michael Clayton calls himself a "janitor." He works for the firm Kenner, Back, and Ledeen, where he's practiced law for 17 years. "I'm not the guy you kill. I'm the guy that you buy," he says. "I'm a fixer. I'm a bagman."

He mops up messes and put things in order, as when he assists a wealthy client after a hit-and-run accident (he hit, he "ran" in his nice Jaguar). Michael looks at the damage and opines, "I'm not a miracle worker, I'm a janitor. The math on this is simple. The smaller the mess, the easier it is for me to clean up."

Ironically, *he* could use some mopping up, given his gambling and drinking problems. But life has a way of sending us signals, and Michael is about to face some important choices. Apparently U North, one of the firm's big-league clients, has been selling a weedkiller that's poisonous to humans. Hundreds of people have been sickened and 468 have died from the pesticide. As a result, U North is in a $3 billion class action suit regarding the toxicity of its product.

The lead defense attorney for U North is a bit of a wild man. This is Arthur Edens, a senior partner and high-powered litigator. Given the string of successes to his name, he should do a fine job of squashing the plaintiffs' case. That was before Arthur's change of heart after discovering from an internal U North memo that U North marketed the pesticide knowing it was carcinogenic.

ARTHUR: "In-house field studies have indicated small, short-season farms dependent on well water for human consumption are at risk for toxic, particulate concentrations at levels significant enough to cause serious human tissue damage." ... you don't even have to leave your house to be killed by our product, we'll pipe it into your kitchen sink. ... Now, I love this. Not only is this a great product, it is a superb cancer delivery system.

What he learns sickens and infuriates him. Arthur is about to jump ship, but his shame and guilt at having defended U North pushes him to a mental and emotional breakdown. The horror of having defended U North could curdle the blood in his veins. He turns to his friend, Michael Clayton.

ARTHUR: I swear, I could stand here and tear off my fucking skin... And I could not get down to where this thing is living. Six years, Michael. Six years I've absorbed this poison. Depositions, a hundred motions, five changes of venue... 85,000 documents in discovery. Six years of scheming and stalling and screaming, and what have I got? I've spent 12 percent of my life defending the reputation of a deadly weedkiller!

Arthur doesn't like what he sees. "I have blood on my hands," he declares. People trusted that the product would be safe. Instead, scores of people were harmed. In his view, he bears some responsibility—that his own moral integrity has been compromised. "I had been coated in this patina of shit for the best part of my life," he reflects. "And the stench of it, the stain of it would take the rest of my life to undo."

Arthur is determined to set things straight. Unfortunately, he underestimates Karen Crowder, chief legal counsel of U North. From the moment our eyes light upon her, we can see she's a woman possessed. She likes things in order and wants to be in control. Her steely manner is matched by her ruthlessness. She who obsessively makes sure every hair is in place and her outfit all polished. But under the surface is a moral troll.

Arthur did not foresee Karen's investment in winning the lawsuit or how far she would go to stop the truth from coming to light. Integrity and transparency were not on her radar—much less responsibility.

J&J's Burke versus U North's Crowder

Let's contrast James Burke of Johnson & Johnson with Karen Crowder. When Johnson & Johnson was informed of deaths from their cyanide-laced painkillers, they didn't hesitate. They took immediate steps to try to prevent further harm and notify the public.

How about U North? Not even close. When U North got the news that their pesticide was toxic to humans, the chief legal counsel, Karen Crowder, did *not* step up to the plate to make things right. Quite the opposite; she tried to bury the truth. Her integrity shriveled up. If the explosive memo had not come to light, the plaintiffs would have been left in the dark.

Look at the contrast. Where Burke was transparent, Crowder was opaque. Where he was open, she sought a cover-up. She wasn't going to allow Arthur (no problem—kill him off!) or Michael (pay him off!) to bring her down.

The Pothole of Short-Term Interests

The Tylenol case shows that the reputation and stability of a business shouldn't rest on short-term interests. That lesson applies to U North too. We need to look beyond the end of our noses. Factor in the future, the past, and the present when surveying ethical dilemmas. As we know from our Case Study Checklist, getting some perspective makes all the difference.

This is as true for individuals as it is for corporations. The road to virtue requires that we act with integrity, day in and day out. This is something that ethicists emphasize, as we will see in Unit 2. By paying attention to the big picture, we can more easily set objectives for the short term and the long-term.

Johnson & Johnson did that by acknowledging its mistakes, such as selling capsules that could easily be opened. The corporation took steps to prevent more deaths, making it clear that the moral weight should put people over profit. Not so with Karen Crowder's work for U North. The movie shows us what happens when we lose sight of that value.

U North's Twisted Values

In contrast to Johnson & Johnson's recall, U North turned their back on consumer health interests. They weren't about to halt production of the lucrative pesticide, regardless of its toxicity. The very notion of incurring a multi-million dollar loss (as Johnson & Johnson actually did) is as far from Karen's mind as the moons of Saturn. Basically Karen Crowder is a model of cold-hearted efficiency, so it's not surprising that she values corporate profits over consumer well-being. With her misplaced loyalties, she does everything possible to prevent the truth from coming to light.

Karen has no qualms about rejecting the Principle of Non-Maleficence ("Do no harm"). In so doing, she crosses a moral threshold. We watch her make one bad decision after another. In the process, we get a bird's eye view of her self-destruction. Her dishonesty and willingness to eliminate the opposition was to no one's benefit—not hers, not U North's, and certainly not their customers.

Taking a Stand

Michael plays a central role in exposing Karen Crowder. He is the one who deals with Arthur's breakdown and whose life is in danger after Arthur is murdered by Crowder's henchmen (who make it look like a suicide). Michael is next on the list, and can only rely on his own resources to stay alive.

Michael follows the breadcrumbs. He can tell that Arthur's death was no suicide; that Arthur knew too much for Karen Crowder's comfort. Michael has the moral fiber to see that he must trap Karen in her web of lies and stop her once and for all. And don't forget, this is the guy with a gambling and drinking problem! Michael probably has a few other shortcomings, but he teaches us this much: *You don't have to be perfect to do the right thing.*

So we've got a flawed hero whose own ethical history is less than stellar. And once the goons are on his trail with the Ice Queen trying to bring him down, it's time to reassess priorities. With that, he's called to his better self. "Take the moral high road," we say to him up there on the screen. "Don't let U North trample on these farmers and their families or the lawyers who seek to defend them. Do something, Michael, do something." He doesn't disappoint.

Arthur (whose lament opens the movie), Karen (whose fixation with winning is her undoing), and Michael (whose gambling debts and heavy drinking lead him astray, until now) all shed light on moral reasoning. Arthur's murder knocks him out of the picture, but his moral legacy is there for Michael to shoulder. Michael finds the inner strength to aim it squarely at Karen Crowder. He shows us that it is possible to regain your moral bearings and get back on track.

Michael is determined to make things right and snare Karen. It's not easy, given she's well versed in the fine art of duplicity. But Michael is not called "the fixer" for nothing. And don't forget that gambling has taught him a few tricks, including when to draw, when to fold, and when to bluff. He uses these techniques to bring down Karen and take down U North's defense in the lawsuit with her.

Michael confronts her and offers to keep his mouth shut—for the right price. All the while he is wearing a wire, as the NYPD stands by in the wings. It's basically a fox-traps-weasel maneuver. It is done with enough subtlety that she doesn't see it coming and, once she's ensnared, there's no way out. Karen is arrested, Michael saves the day, and Arthur's efforts weren't for nothing. Arthur may have not been able to rinse off the "patina of shit" in his lifetime, but Michael finishes the job Arthur started and goes on from there, no longer the bagman.

The movie shows us how a person with a checkered past can seize hold of himself and do the right thing. We follow along as his moral chutzpah saves the day. He sees the harm done by the pesticide. He sees the corporation's failures. He sees the human costs of those failures. But he also sees that he is not powerless, that he can turn things around. Justice will be served.

Moral Agency and Assigning Responsibility

Moral agency has to do personal autonomy and the standards to which we are held accountable for both our actions and ethical decision-making. In order to be held responsible for our actions and intentions, we must be free to decide and act, and not be under coercion, compulsion, or duress.

Components of Moral Agency

- Free Will: Volition, being free to act without coercion or duress
- Competence: Rationality and a grasp of the difference between right and wrong

Let's look at both. The first aspect of moral agency is free will. It should not be underrated. Think about those who are coerced into lies or silence ("Shut your trap or you won't see Jasper again") or are under duress ("Have sex with me or your job will be past history"). Think, also, of those who evoke the "crime of passion" defense (wife in bed with the neighbor led to a murderous rage) or the imaginative "Twinkie defense" (sugar rush made Dan White commit murder). Then there's the unusual "irresistible impulse" defense of Lorena Bobbitt (couldn't resist the urge to chop off her husband's penis). The various justifications for actions blamed on insufficient self-control are legion.

The second aspect of moral agency is the rational component. In order to be held responsible for our actions and intentions, we must be able to tell right from wrong. Not all are capable of that and, consequently, children, juvenile offenders, the mentally deficient, and others who are cognitively impaired are normally excluded from moral agency. Occasionally, children are tried as adults in a court of law. This venue may be pursued when it is presumed that the offending children knew what they were doing (= competent) and had the mental and moral capacity to have chosen to act otherwise (= had free will).

Age and mental capacity are usually factored in when assessing accountability. Questions regarding competence require us to look at the particulars of the situation, as well as the context. This is often necessary before we can assess or judge a decision, entity (person or corporation), or action.

The nightly news reminds us how wide reaching an ethical dilemma can be. In some cases (world hunger, tsunami relief efforts, and so on) moral dilemmas are catalysts for people to work together. They may then be more effective in addressing problems or pushing through laws or policies. At other times there may be no easy resolution and further steps, such as mediation or widening the investigation, may be necessary.

Of fundamental importance in all areas of ethics is moral agency. It sets the boundaries of culpability and a way to go deeper into moral reasoning. With that in mind, let's turn to the three kinds of moral agents.

The Three Dimensions of Moral Agency

As we saw, the two criteria of moral agency are free will and rationality. There are three levels of abstraction here with respect to the notion of moral agency: The first is the *individual person*, the second is the *corporation*, and the third (the most abstract) is the *community*. When we usually talk about moral agents we are thinking of individuals—people—whose intentions and actions we judge as good or bad. We then speak of those performing or directing the acts as virtuous or vicious.

Of course, we tend to think of moral agency with regard to people—you and me, him and her. Ethicists tend to speak of moral agents as *rational human beings* who are acting independently and are, thus, responsible for what they say or do. Those who lack or are deficient in the two components (free will and competence) are treated as exceptions, but we might then turn to guardians or other responsible parties when assessing accountability. We will go into this in Unit 2 and examine approaches of the major ethical theories. First, look at Table 1.1 and then continue on to the discussion.

Persons and Moral Agency

One of the areas of contention in ethics is whether a person must be *human*. Does moral agency require a third characteristic—humanity? Some say yes, others say no. Let's consider the less restrictive view. The traits of being rational and acting on one's own volition allow for non-human entities to potentially be moral agents, philosopher Mary Anne Warren contends (2000, p. 79). This includes:

* Extraterrestrials ("skitters" and the Volm of *Falling Skies*, "prawns" in *District 9*)
* Vampires (*Count Dracula*, *True Blood*'s and *Twilight*'s vampire-allies often turn to nonhuman "blood" sources)
* Clones (*The Island*)
* Robots, androids, and cyborgs (*Alien*, *The Terminator*, and *Prometheus*)
* Humanoids (*Avatar*)
* Sentient creatures with developed language systems (e.g., dolphins and chimps)

There are also genetically engineered or human–animal hybrids (*Spider-Man* and *Batman*) with their own set of moral challenges. However, zombies (*Night of the Living Dead*, *World War Z*, *The Walking Dead*) show no

Table 1.1   The Three Dimensions of Moral Agency

Dimension	Manifestation	Expression	Examples
The Individual (Persons)	You, me, him, her	Acts for oneself or as a surrogate or guardian for another	⇒ Sherron Watkins—Enron whistleblower ⇒ John Hinckley, Jr.—shot President Reagan ⇒ David Anderson—daring rescue of his 2-year old daughter ⇒ Nurse Rivers—assisted the Tuskegee syphilis studies
The Corporation	Local businesses (Rick's Drive Thru), national corporations (Trader Joe's), international corporations (Chevron, Nike)	Organization of people acting as a single entity bound by rules, regulations, and policies. A legal "person"	⇒ Johnson & Johnson and the Tylenol poisoning ⇒ *Exxon-Valdez* and the Alaska oil spill ⇒ Apple suing Samsung over a copyright dispute ⇒ Pizza Hut suing Papa John's claiming false advertising
The Community	Political or religious group, gang, cult, neighborhood, girl scout troop, teacher's union, city, state, or nation	Acts as a collective, but not a legal "person"	⇒ Soldiers at My Lai, Vietnam ⇒ Environmental activists fighting the killing of baby seals for fur ⇒ The OLBZ (Oriental Lazy Boys) gang retaliating against the Osiri Boys gang in Los Angeles ⇒ Doctors Without Borders battling malaria in Sub Saharan Africa

capacity for moral reasoning—they are simply (singularly or collectively) searching for human flesh. This much is obvious: Personhood is not a simple concept. In Chapter 2.5 (Feminist Ethics) we'll go into this in more detail.

That corporations and communities may merit being added to the list is surely deserving of our attention. With that in mind, let's turn to corporations, the second level of moral agency.

The Corporation and Moral Agency

Corporations are entities intentionally formed according to a set of laws. These are laws that set out the parameters of ownership and decision-making regarding a corporation. It is a legal entity separate and distinct from its owners—or any other individuals for that matter. Because of this, we can distinguish corporations from both individuals and communities.

The dimension of moral agency is where we find corporations. In contrast to communities, corporations are legal *persons* with certain rights and freedoms. It may be hard to get our heads around this notion. Most of us think of persons as *humans*. The very idea that nonhumans might slide in under the boundaries of the definition may be a challenge. And surely not all think this is for the best. Nevertheless, as Philosopher Alexei Marcoux (2008) observes,

> At law, the corporation is a person, distinct in its personality from the persons who bear ownership shares in it (its shareholders) or conduct activities on its behalf (its directors, officers, and other employees).

Given a corporation has a legal status, should it have a moral status as well? "If the corporation is a legal person," Marcoux asks, "is it also a moral person?" The very fact we allow corporations to be labeled "persons" in terms of laws and regulations doesn't necessarily mean moral status should follow. Does our value system and sets of beliefs have room to fit corporations into the ethical realm where "persons" resides? This is not clear. In fact, Marcoux points out that not all business ethicists agree as to whether the corporation can be considered a moral person or moral agent. Let's look at the two sides.

The Argument For The Moral Agency of Corporations   On the pro side is ethicist Peter A. French. He contends that there are important features of the corporation and of corporate decision-making that exhibit the traits of moral agency. He infers that we then can consider a corporation as a member of a moral community. Let's see how he makes his case.

French starts with the concept of personhood and distinguishes three kinds—metaphysical, moral, and legal. For French (1979), the concept of legal personhood (as popularly understood) is virtually useless. His interest is moral personhood. This where he thinks the battle should take place.

French asserts that corporations can be spoken of as moral persons: "There is a sense in saying that corporations and not just the people who work in them, have reasons for doing what they do" (1979, p. 212). As he notes, a corporation has an internal decision structure delineating the power structure and corporate rules or policy. He cites John Kenneth Galbraith in arguing that the personality of the corporation comes from the interpersonal exercise of power and the interaction of the participants (p. 212).

In French's view, corporate reasons for doing something may be "qualitatively different from whatever personal reasons, if any, component members may have for doing what they do" (p. 215). That translates into a potential split—a divergence—in the way people might justify their decisions or actions from that of a corporation. The corporation's reasons for action may differ from those of the people who work for or represent the business, e.g., in the public eye. French concludes that corporations are moral persons and therefore moral agents in their own right (Marcoux, 2008).

The Argument Against The Moral Agency of Corporations   Not all would agree with French that corporations can be seen as moral agents. Philosopher Manuel Velasquez is one who rejects French's assessment. As far as he's concerned, "Attributing moral agency to corporations opens the door to the intuitively implausible conclusion that a corporation can be morally responsible for something no natural person connected with it is responsible for" (Marcoux, 2008). In other words, the very idea makes no sense; it is a logical contradiction.

Velasquez argues that French's position relies on the corporate organization having a continuous identity through time. This is an identity independent of those of its members. He ties this to the issue of responsibility, saying that:

> A corporate organization, for example, may endure for decades and remain the same corporate organization even as its original members retire and are replaced... [But again] if the corporate organization is not a distinct real individual entity, then it cannot be said to bear a share of responsibility for its actions that is distinct from the share we can attribute to its members. (Velasquez, p. 541)

From Velasquez's perspective, if we don't see a corporation as a distinct, individual entity, then it can't be seen as responsible separately from the way we assign responsibility to its members. Such a view would suggest that the corporation could be held to a higher standard than that of a natural person—which Velasquez argues makes no sense whatsoever.

Reflecting on the Debate Velasquez is troubled to think that a corporation can be held responsible for an action *apart from* the individuals who would be held responsible at the same time. The very notion that an entity such as a corporation can have moral standing on its own without some human "face" to it seems untenable. He throws down the gauntlet: People, not corporations, are the ones that can be held accountable for moral actions. As we saw, French thinks otherwise. For him, corporations can be considered moral "persons," where the concept of "person" is then stretched beyond the human. So, how to we resolve the dispute? Can we?

Let's step back and think about this. Perhaps this should guide us: "Don't look at the meaning, look at the use." If we want to know what a word means, a dictionary can only go so far, but not far enough. Ask instead, "How do we use the term?" Philosopher Ludwig Wittgenstein (1953) says that, for a *large* class of cases—though not for all—"the meaning of a word is its use in the language" (*Philosophical Investigations*, 43, p. 20). This takes us out of the abstract world of concepts into the real world of how we speak and use language.

Applying this to the issue of moral agency and corporations, here's what we find. We *do* speak of corporations as if they had the volition to act (free will); as when corporations take a position on some issue or the other. We also speak of corporations as having a sense of right and wrong, as with ethical codes, decisions, and actions that reveal a set of values. For example, Johnson & Johnson was praised for its handling of the Tylenol case. In fact, the *company* was called "heroic," not CEO James Burke. In this respect, the corporation itself was categorized and understood as having moral status.

Exercise

In *Michael Clayton*, the company's actions and actions taken on behalf of the company center on wrongdoing and culpability. Arthur Eden became aware of a damaging memo that caused him to switch sides and turn against his own client, U North. Think about the degree to which the U North should be held responsible, and not just the individuals working for or speaking on behalf of the corporation. Set out the strongest pro or con case.

Communities and Moral Agency

The third dimension of moral agency is that of the community. As far as communities go, think of social, religious, or political groups, cities, neighborhoods, states, or even countries as being subject to moral judgment. A community can be praised, as with El Reno, Oklahoma's rescue efforts after a devastating tornado flattened the town. On the other hand, communities can be found wanting, as when 20,000 displaced people ended up in the New Orleans Superdome after Hurricane Katrina. They subsisted there for five days in conditions that stretch the imagination—e.g., overflowing toilets, limited access to food and water, lack of healthcare, no showers.

A community acts as a *collective*, not an individual. What is in common is a collection—a group—of individuals affiliated with one another. This may be by design (as in a military unit) or by happenstance (as in passengers in a plane crash) or in reaction to some perceived wrong (as in political protestors). Community actions may then be judged by ethical standards that we can articulate and scrutinize. Whether or not we reach agreement is another matter.

A community can take morally commendable actions, morally neutral actions, or morally impermissible actions. In Chapter 3.4 we look at the role of the community in addressing sexual harassment in the workplace in the film *North Country*. There we see members of a community standing up against wrongdoing, thereby, taking the moral high road.

Examples of communities committing morally reprehensible acts are lynch mobs, gang rapists, and gangsters on a rampage. And let's not overlook the role of communities in either enabling or standing up against injustices such as the Holocaust, the "Trail of Tears," Rwanda genocide, torture at Abu Ghraib. Any one of these reveal how a community can act in ways we could label "immoral" or "unjust."

Individuals and Communities

Ethicist Peter A. French argues that a mob is merely the aggregate of its individual constituents and, so, cannot be conceived as a moral person (1979, p. 210). Is he right? Are mobs or other collectives not "persons" in the moral sense? One way to settle this is to look at the notion of responsibility. We certainly can hold individual members of a community responsible, so long as they qualify for moral agency. But, how about the collective?

To some degree we *do* hold groups accountable, as in the case of nation-states, soldiers, terrorist cells, or political activists bringing about praise, condemnation, or sanctions. In other cases, as with gangbangers, mobs, or gang rapists, we may be inclined to hold *individual* members accountable for their role in a group's behavior.

Mind you, it may be hard or even perilous to dissociate from a group, as seen with medical personnel present at abusive interrogations of terrorist suspects. It may also be hard to stand in opposition or point out moral failings of a group. That may be one reason why whistleblowers are so few. It is also why whistleblowers are so important and singled-out in ethics codes.

ETHICS CODE: Johnson & Johnson

We know from the Tylenol crisis that Johnson & Johnson regained public trust and now stands as an ethical pillar, thanks to its quick and attentive (some would say caring) response. You can see Johnson & Johnson's code at http://2012annualreport.jnj.com/our-credo.

Exercise

1. Look over Johnson & Johnson's ethics code in light of the Tylenol case and note what three things stand out.
2. Share your reflections on the ways in which the code connects to or informs us about the case.

Works Cited

Blankenbeckler, Wayne, "5 PR Crisis Management Truths from the Tylenol Murders," *EDUniverse*, http://eduniverse.org/5-pr-crisis-management-truths-tylenol-murders (accessed December 18, 2014).

Fletcher, Dan, "A Brief History of the Tylenol Poisonings," *Time* magazine, February 9, 2009, http://www.time.com/time/nation/article/0,8599, 1878063,00.html (accessed December 18, 2014).

French, Peter A., "The Corporation as a Moral Person," *American Philosophical Quarterly*, Vol. 16, No. 3 (July, 1979), pp. 207–215, http://www.sci.brooklyn. cuny.edu/~schopra/Persons/French.pdf (accessed December 18, 2014).

Malcolm, Andrew H., "100 Agents Hunt For Killer In 7 Tylenol Deaths," *New York Times*, October 3, 1982, http://www.nytimes.com/1982/10/03/ us/100-agents-hunt-for-killer-in-7-tylenol-deaths.html (accessed December 18, 2014).

Marcoux, Alexei, "Business Ethics," *The Stanford Encyclopedia of Philosophy*, Fall 2008, http://plato.stanford.edu/archives/fall2008/entries/ethics-business/ (accessed December 18, 2014).

New *York Times*, "News Summary," October 5, 1982, http://www.nytimes.com/1982/10/05/nyregion/news-summary-tuesday-october-5-1982.html (accessed December 18, 2014).

Pace, Eric. "Lingering Damage To Sales of Tylenol Is Expected," *New York Times*, October 2, 1982, http://www.nytimes.com/1982/10/02/us/lingering-damage-to-sales-of-tylenol-is-expected.html (accessed December 18, 2014).

Rehak, Judith, "Tylenol Made A Hero of Johnson & Johnson: The Recall That Started Them All," *New York Times*, March 23, 2012, http://www.nytimes.com/2002/03/23/your-money/23iht-mjj_ed3_.html (accessed December 18, 2014).

Stone, Sam and Denny Walsh, "FBI Investigating 'Unabomber' Ted Kaczynski in Tylenol Deaths," *Chicago Sun-Times*, http://www.suntimes.com/5468391-418/fbi-investigating-unabomber-ted-kaczynski-in-tylenol-deaths.html (accessed December 18, 2014).

Velasquez, Manuel, "Debunking Corporate Moral Responsibility," *Business Ethics Quarterly*, Vol. 13, No. 4 (Oct., 2003), pp. 531–562, http://www.academia.edu/1235632/Debunking_corporate_moral_responsibility (accessed December 18, 2014).

Warren, Mary Anne, *Moral Status: Obligations to Persons and Other Living Things*, (Oxford: Clarendon Press, 1997).

Wittgenstein, Ludwig, *Philosophical Investigations*, 3rd edn., Trans. By G.E.M. Anscombe, (Oxford: Blackwell, 1958), p. 20.

Zoulas, Soterios, "The 1982 Tylenol Crisis," *About Public Relations*, http://aboutpublicrelations.net/uczoulas1.htm (accessed December 18, 2014).

1.3

Show Me The Money
Greed Is Not Good

Spotlight: *Wall Street; Big Men*
Case Studies: Martha Stewart and Insider Trading; Costco's Tainted Berries
Ethics Code: Costco

> *Gordon Gekko: We make the rules, pal. The news, war, peace, famine, upheaval, the price per paper clip. We pick that rabbit out of the hat while everybody sits out there wondering how the hell we did it. Now you're not naive enough to think we're living in a democracy, are you buddy? It's the free market.*
>
> —Wall Street

Bud Fox has the energy, determination, and desire to make money, lots of money. That he doesn't have the know-how means an uphill climb to success. He fantasizes about the trappings that money can buy—the fancy cars, a big office, snazzy suits, and beautiful women who find him oh so attractive. His working-class father is more of an embarrassment than a source of pride. Bud's dream is to hit the big time. His gold standard is Gordon Gekko, a Wall Street icon. Gekko's ruthless, take-no-prisoners style strikes Bud as the epitome of the man who has made it to the top. The question is what does he have to do to get there from here. That ethical dilemma drives *Wall Street* (1985), a moral tale that made the movie a Business Ethics classic.

Wall Street has a Shakespearean quality to it: A young man has desire. Desire drives him to forsake both integrity and family. Hubris overtakes his ethics. It's a house of cards that eventually comes tumbling down. At that point, things get interesting, as the options come into sharp relief and whatever ethical flame burning inside him catches hold. But it's not too late to turn things around, to do the right thing, and to take responsibility.

Business Ethics Through Movies: A Case Study Approach, First Edition. Wanda Teays.
© 2015 John Wiley & Sons, Ltd. Published 2015 by John Wiley & Sons, Ltd.

It's a story with a strong ethical base. Yes, you can throw your ethics to the wind and lie, cheat, and steal. And yes the fruits of success and fame are hard to resist. But the joys are short-lived if it all unravels and the lines you crossed can't be erased. Here's where Aristotle offers a few pearls of wisdom.

In his *Poetics*, Aristotle sets out the key components of drama (theatre in his day, movies in ours). Six aspects stand out as significant; of those three are primary. They are:

1   Plot (= story line, the most important aspect)
2   Character (especially moral character)
3   Thought (= themes, intentions, what motivates the characters)

The remaining three are of lesser significance and basically either enhance or distract from the quality of the movie. These are:

4   Dialogue and Diction
5   Music
6   Special Effects

For Aristotle, the kernel of a great drama (= movie) is the plot. He thinks the plot should be complete, unified, and so tight that each element is necessary or probable. That means anything that is removed would cause the plot to suffer. With *Wall Street*, the pieces fall into place; none are extraneous. As a result, when we reflect on the ethical dilemma that roots the film, we can see its universal value. It speaks to us all.

Who hasn't experienced desire? Who hasn't wanted _____ (fill in the blank—money, fame, love, different body, etc.)? It's the human condition to want what we don't have. The question is what do we *do* in the face of desire. What price are we willing to pay?

Bud's is the story of a man whose moral fiber becomes tattered after he compromises his ethics to fulfill his desire. That he didn't foresee the cost is not surprising. Desire can blind us to the price of getting what we want. For Gekko, "Greed is good." It is a powerful motivator, that much we know. One question though is, "What are the limits?"

In this chapter we'll look at *Wall Street* and *Big Men* and the cases of Martha Stewart's insider trading and Costco's tainted fruit mix. We'll then look at Costco's ethics code. Marx's view of capitalism and John Rawls' theory of justice help put these films and cases in perspective.

Capitalism: Marx on Greed

Karl Marx looked at the world and saw a two-class system with the property owners (the rich) having all the power and the laborers (the poor) with no power whatsoever. It was not a system he could endorse, so he did what he could to bring it down.

In Marx's day there was no middle class and the gap between the rich and the poor was basically an abyss. His solution was revolution. The poor working class—the proletariat—should unite to transform the status quo. They had little to lose and a lot to gain.

Marx is no doubt rolling in his grave about the current economy and the dire state of (un)employment. He would have only criticism for the September, 2013 news report that,

> Five years after the financial crisis, the mega-rich have regained all the wealth they lost during the recession, setting a new record value for combined net worth... The annual report showed that America's wealthiest have a combined net worth of $2.02 trillion, the highest value ever recorded by *Forbes*. That's up from $1.7 trillion a year ago (Whitefield, 2013).

No, for Marx greed is definitely not good. In looking at some well-publicized examples of greed, Marx would shake his head and be glad when wrongdoers were brought to justice. He'd thus view the next case with some interest.

CASE STUDY 1: Martha Stewart and Insider Trading

On June 4, 2003 the US Securities and Exchange Commission (SEC) reported that Martha Stewart of cooking and lifestyle empire fame was charged with fraud, as was her former stockbroker Peter Bacanovic.

Let's look at the charges levied against her and Bacanovic and do a little *thought experiment*: Look at the list below and note what *you* find most significant from a Business Ethics perspective. These are violations stated in a June 4, 2003 press release from the Securities and Exchange Commission (www.sec.gov). Stewart was charged with:

- Committing illegal insider trading when she sold stock in the biopharmaceutical company ImClone Systems, Inc. after receiving an unlawful tip from Bacanovic

- Creating an alibi for her ImClone sales
- Concealing important facts during SEC and criminal investigations into her trades

The SEC claims that:

- Bacanovic conveyed information to Stewart through his assistant, leading her to sell 3,928 shares of her ImClone stock, thereby avoiding losses of $45,673
- Stewart and Bacanovic lied when questioned about the sale of ImClone stock
- Stewart and Bacanovic fabricated an alibi for Stewart's trades
- Stewart claimed that she did not recall being told about the selling of ImClone stock

Stewart was separately charged by the US Attorney for the Southern District of New York with making false statements concerning her ImClone trades.

Exercise

1. What do you think are the most significant charges against Martha Stewart from an ethical point of view?
2. What do you think should be taken into consideration in our ethical assessment of insider trading violations?
3. Share your thoughts on the following comments included in the SEC press release (June 4, 2003):
   Stephen M. Cutler, SEC Director of Enforcement: It is fundamentally unfair for someone to have an edge on the market just because she has a stockbroker who is willing to break the rules and give her an illegal tip. It's worse still when the individual engaging in the insider trading is the Chairman and CEO of a public company."
   Wayne M. Carlin, Regional Director SEC Northeast Regional Office: The Commission simply cannot allow corporate executives or industry professionals to profit illegally from their access to nonpublic information. The coordinated action announced today by the US Attorney's Office shows that the consequences for those individuals will be even greater if we uncover evidence that they obstructed our investigation.

Profit and Social Responsibility

Economist Milton Friedman, whose "Capitalism and Freedom" is pretty much required reading in the field, has one of the more famous lines of business. It is: "There is one and only one social responsibility of business— to use its resources and engage in activities designed to increase its profits." This sounds like an endorsement of "Greed is good."

However, all is not what it seems. Philosopher Gary Gutting (2013) points out that Friedman's declaration is incomplete, that it has been taken out of context. To grasp the meaning we need to see the end of the sentence, not just the fragment. Here's what Friedman says: "There is one and only one social responsibility of business—to use its resources and engage in activities designed to increase its profits *so long as* it stays within the rules of the game, which is to say, engages in open and free competition without deception or fraud (Gutting, my emphasis)."

Note what follows the "so long as." Chopping off the second half of the sentence has a dramatic effect. Restoring the context—the full sentence— paints a different picture. Gutting rightly notes that it puts a key restriction on the maximization of profit. "More important," he says, "it commits Friedman to the principle that there can be restraints on the capitalist system that are not self-imposed but rather imposed by the society that employs this system for its own purposes."

Businesses operate within a social context and, therefore, capitalism is not independent of the political system. Quite the opposite: "It is a creature of that system, which has goals (of morality and social responsibility, for example) that go beyond the profitable exchange of goods," Gutting (2013) points out. "Therefore, the owners of businesses must accept governmental restrictions on their profit-making for the sake of overriding social values."

The message is this: Friedman favors restrictions on business and acknowledges "the need for a variety of government interventions to keep capitalism on the right track." Most strikingly, Friedman proposed a "negative income tax" to eliminate poverty, even though he was "by no means a progressive," says Gutting.

And so it looks like Friedman would place limits on the profit-motive and look askance at the Gordon Gekkos of the world. They cut corners, violate laws and use other people without a care in the world. So long as they don't get caught, the rules are ignored. No good can come of that. Contrary to Gekko's declaration, greed is not good.

Yes, Friedman votes for profits, but they can't be the sole focus of a business. Social responsibility requires that we not treat the corporate world as divorced from the rest of the world. Businesses play a key role in preventing capitalism from becoming like the train in the movie *Unstoppable*—on a collision course with no brakes, picking up speed as it tears across the landscape! *This much is true*: Businesses don't have to allow the profit motive to trump all other values.

By prioritizing profits we risk losing touch with other values needed for a healthy business, a sound economy, and a desirable future. For one thing, letting profits rule leads to shortsighted thinking. When long-term gains are devalued or ignored in favor of what's right before us our decision-making gets skewed. The financial meltdown of 2008 testifies to the failings of inflating short-term gains. We are still in recovery from that mentality and need to learn a few lessons as we go.

Capitalism: Marx on Alienated Labor

Marx's theory may be over 100 years old, but it still has merit. One of his concerns about the economy is what happens to *workers* when they become tools of production. This brings up important concerns.

In his *Economic & Philosophic Manuscripts of 1844*, Marx argued that, "The worker becomes an ever cheaper commodity the more goods he creates." This was written in 1844—over 150 years ago. *You tell me*: Does this speak to the world *we* inhabit? Marx may not be ready yet for the dustbin of history, so let's hear what he has to say. In discussing the commodification of workers, he asserts that, "The devaluation of the human world increases in direct relation with the increase in value of the world of things" (1844). In other words, the value of people—workers—is inversely proportional to things in the world—objects, products, and money.

Marx drives this point home when he says, "Labour does not only create goods: it also produces itself and the worker as a *commodity*, and indeed in the same proportion as it produces goods" (quoted in Giddens and Held, 1982, p. 13). From Marx's perspective, many in the workforce do *not* have meaningful jobs where they can fulfill their potential and lead purposeful lives. Instead, the work they do objectifies them and alienates them from others, from the product of their labor, and from themselves. He would view the movie *Wall Street* as a case in point.

SPOTLIGHT: *Wall Street*

When Bud Fox used his own father to earn a few brownie points with Gordon Gekko, Marx would say he had just commodified dear old dad. Later in the film, the workers at Bluestar Airlines (where Bud's father was a labor leader) were on the verge of becoming collateral damage. We see this when Gekko is about to turn Bud's insider information and the workers' job stability into fodder for a sizable profit.

Marx would point out that Bud himself becomes grist for the profit mill. He is but a tool for Gekko's success and that Gekko has not an iota of loyalty to Bud. Nor does he feel the slightest remorse—not a twinge of a regret—that Bud's father and the Bluestar laborers that he represents would be wiped out if Gekko's stock sales proceed as planned.

The end result is that Bud's father and the workers have no inherent value beyond their ability to make Gekko more money. As such, they are all (in Marx's books) *alienated* from the product of their labor, from themselves as individuals, and from each other. They are alienated labor. Private property is the result of alienated labor. The product of labor does not belong to the worker, "but confronts him as an alien power" (Giddens and Held, 1982, p. 18). This is due to the fact that what they produces doesn't belong to workers themselves, but to someone else (such as the company they work for).

For Marx (1844), the price is steep:

> The worker becomes all the poorer the more wealth he produces, the more his production increases in power and size. The worker becomes an ever cheaper commodity the more commodities he creates. The *devaluation* of the world of men is in direct proportion to the *increasing value* of the world of things.

Mind you, we know that Bud himself was a member of the *bourgeoisie* with his newfound wealth sleazily obtained by breaking laws and using others. He enjoyed the pleasures that wealth buys, however hollow was his existence. All true. But when he fell off that pedestal and tried to turn things around, he showed that there was hope that he could finally redeem himself. Bud then took steps so he wouldn't be party to the destruction of Bluestar. And so he tried to right the wrongs he had committed.

When looking at *Wall Street*, we see the rise and fall of Bud Fox in the forefront. We see him try to redeem himself after realizing that he'd lost his moral bearings. In his *Poetics*, Aristotle discusses the value of complex plots that involve a reversal of fortune on the part of the hero. The best, he argues, is a plot in which the hero's fortunes take a dive. Bud is in this group, as we know. That he then has a "discovery" (epiphany, moment of clarification) shows us that it's never too late to change our lives and do the right thing.

When looking at *Wall Street*, issues of justice lie in the background. When some people get ahead and profit by duplicitous means, we all suffer. Sure, the few may benefit, but institutions that can be manipulated open the door for injustice and corruption. What counts as *fair* is more important than we may realize. With that in mind, let's turn to the role of justice in Business Ethics.

The Three Kinds of Justice

The three main kinds of justice are (1) Distributive justice, (2) Retributive justice, and (3) Compensatory justice (Garrett, 2002). *Distributive justice* focuses on the balancing of benefits and costs (e.g., Social Security, public education, health care). *Retributive justice* focuses on deciding punishment in light of the offense (e.g., a ticket for jaywalking, jail time for assault). *Compensatory justice* focuses on restitution for suffering a harm (e.g., a car accident caused by defective tires).

In some cases (e.g., a class action suit) both punitive (retributive) and compensatory damages are awarded. For example, some low impact rear-end collisions caused Ford Pinto gas tanks to explode (see Chapter 2.2). The subsequent lawsuits involved both types of awards. Punitive damages were designed to punish Ford for deliberatively selling a dangerous product. They focused on the nature of the wrongdoing and the financial ability of the company to pay an award.

Compensatory damages are based upon the severity of the injuries. They seek to restore, as much as possible, the person's state of being before the accident. The largest punitive damage award in US history involved five major tobacco companies. After two years and 157 witnesses, in 2010 a Miami Florida jury awarded $145 billion dollars in punitive damages. Tobacco giant Phillip Morris' chief counsel William Ohlemeyer appealed (Charatan, 2000).

Distributive justice comes to the fore when trying to bring about social transformation. How do we change the status quo and eliminate injustice? Such questions are crucial for businesses as well as society in general. We see the struggle around health equity as illustrative of how problematic it is to resolve questions of distributive justice. But, as we see next, it is important to try to do so.

Ethical Framework: Rawls' Justice Theory

John Rawls is a Philosopher of Law who sought to universalize individual rights. He focuses his energy on institutions and how they might be transformed to bring about social good, help achieve justice, and further human rights.

In his quest, institutional policies are a key concern, since he wants to ensure equal access to a system of liberties. In his book, *A Theory of Justice*,

Rawls sets out a method for avoiding bias and prejudice in order to arrive at a more just system. His motto is "Justice as fairness." He thinks we should all have liberty rights. To accomplish that we should strive to help the underprivileged as much as possible and examine the structure of institutions in order to find ways to minimize inequality and injustice. We need to make sure that laws, policies, and procedures are as fair as possible.

Rawls is guided by his vision of social justice. He thinks it crucial to minimize personal bias coloring our reasoning process. This could be addressed by stripping away personal attachments and affiliations. Rawls wants our decision-making to be free of prejudice. He suggests a "veil of ignorance" to keep bias at bay—a state of mind where we don't favor certain belief systems, groups, traditions, or anything else prejudice our thinking. We should free ourselves of our attachments, so that we can acquire the clarity of mind needed for quality reasoning. His hope is that this will bring enough detachment and objectivity to make us fair-minded in our decisions and policies.

Rawls' vision for a just society is based on noble intentions and laudable goals. However, not all agree with Rawls as to what's the best *path* to that pot of gold. Critics aren't so sure we can separate ourselves from that with which we identify ourselves, such as race and gender, religion and class. Some contend that such detachment is a lot more difficult than Rawls thinks possible, however much they support attempts to reduce prejudice.

Can we really peel away our many affiliations, such as being a Latina Republican vegetarian or a Buddhist animal rights activist, or the like? It might be great if we could, but that doesn't mean it's easy. That there are challenges does not deter Rawls. He believes this is the path to universalize human rights and help those most in need. We'll achieve social justice by reshaping institutions in and beyond workplace settings.

Rawls' Path to Equal Liberty

Without personal attachments and distractions we are more likely to arrive at the objectivity needed to create just policies and just institutions. In his view, we need to adopt these three principles:

Rawls Three Principles

- *The Principle of Equal Liberty*
  Each person should have an equal right to the most extensive system of liberties compatible with a similar system of liberty for all.
  ➡ Universalize human rights.

- *The Principle of Equality of Fair Opportunity*
  People with similar abilities and skills should have equal access to offices and positions under conditions of equality of fair opportunity.
  → Provide equal opportunities.
- *The Difference Principle*
  Social and economic institutions should be arranged to maximally benefit those who are the worst off.
  → Favor the least advantaged.

Do you see what Rawls is working for? Universalize human rights. Each individual has an equal right to a system of liberties. Liberty is not something that only the rich and powerful should have at their command. We have a moral obligation to make sure all people have such a right. This is Rawls' first principle.

His second principle directly speaks to Business Ethics. Provide fair opportunities. Those of similar abilities and skills should have equal access to jobs and positions. One consequence would be a more diverse workplace. By not favoring _____ (fill in the blank—gender, age, race, religion, etc.), we could further human rights.

With his Difference Principle—perhaps the most far-reaching of his maxims—Rawls wanted to help the least advantaged in the equation. This is not a matter of hiring the unqualified in order to address prejudice. The second principle makes it clear that the applicants must have similar skills and abilities in order to be considered for the position. However, what the third principle does is break a tie, so to speak, by favoring the most disadvantaged. The result is a form of systemic change founded on distributive justice.

Applying Rawls to Businesses

The Difference Principle creates positive duties—not just the negative duties associated with "don't do this" and "avoid that." Here, Rawls is calling us to take affirmative steps to address inequality and injustice. This means coming to terms with the inequities existing in workplaces and other institutions and doing something to change the situation. It's a call to action.

Julian Lamont and Christi Favor (2013) assert that, "Rawls' claim is that structuring a society so that this 'natural lottery' has such fundamental effects on people's lives is immoral, when we have the option to structure it another way, with a system of formal equality of opportunity."

Rawls' approach to distributive justice via his Difference Principle is relevant—and applicable—to businesses, institutions, and different forms of government (city, state, federal). The Constitutional Rights Foundation points out that, "The individuals under the 'veil of ignorance' do not know what position they really occupy in their society. As a result, 'to be on the safe side,' … rational-thinking members of the imaginary group would choose the principles of justice that most benefited those at the bottom."

Our next film is set in the African nations of Ghana and Nigeria. In both countries there is a wide gap between the rich and the poor, the powerful and the powerless. Hefty infusions of money could make a huge difference in the lives of the residents and the communities of which they are a part. However, that doesn't always happen—and not all monetary exchanges help those at the bottom of the economic ladder.

SPOTLIGHT: *Big Men*

The documentary *Big Men* could be subtitled "Big Money for Big Oil." It looks at the way large sums are being invested in a search for oil in Western Africa off the coast of Ghana. Any oil under the ocean waters would be hard to extract; however, oil *is* oil and a large enough quantity might justify the upfront costs.

A key player is Jim Musselman, CEO of Kosmos Energy, a Texas oil company. Oil capitalism is a unique field where there are players are from all over the world—Texas, Saudi Arabia, Nigeria, and so on. What they share in common is oil, oil, and more oil. The search for oil means a great deal of money can be spent—and lost when hopes are dashed. Katie Van Syckle (2013) notes that,

> The glitch, depending on your seat, comes when Ghanaian leadership changes, the justice department is called in to investigate allegations of corruption on the part of the U.S. firm [Kosmos] and credit contracts due to the financial crisis. …The doc …[also] profiles an African country trying to profit after centuries of exploitation and watches as everyone navigates how to slice the billion-dollar pie.

When exploratory ventures succeed, as with the oil field off of Ghana, vast sums of money come within reach. Potential gains are in the billions of dollars. The question is who gets what. Film critic Kenneth Turan (2013) thinks *Big Men* is not only an examination of international capitalism; it is also a look at human nature: "For it's not just oil that everyone is dealing with in *Big Men*, it is the universality of greed. ... It's not only that everyone wants a share of this enormous money, it's also that everyone thinks that they truly deserve it."

That's one of the things about greed; with greed comes the sense of entitlement. The movie shows how the prospect of lots of money affects all those connected to the drilling operation off the shores of Ghana. When the Ghanaian government changed, the political forces stirred up charges of corruption. Kosmos Energy was among the targets, with Jim Musselman forced out as CEO. He still had a majority interest in the investment and, in time, things settled down so different (and bigger) money men could come into play.

Big Men presents oil capitalism and its complications from multiple per-spectives, including Western points of view. And Musselman's interaction with his Ghanaian counterparts shows the levels of finesse that are essential in such high-level communications.

We follow the issues as they unfold. One has to do with Nigeria, Ghana's neighbor, and the chaos big oil has brought. The gap in Nigeria between those with money and power and those with none is as wide as the Grand Canyon. This is a breeding ground for political unrest that can lead to a breakdown in the society and to moral disarray. Film critic Scott Foundas (2013) suggests *Big Men* "should come tagged with a warning: The side effects of global capitalism may include dizziness, nausea and seething outrage." He notes troubling philosophical questions: "Is unchecked greed an intrinsic part of the human character? Is 'the greater good' ever more than a convenient euphemism where big business and big government are concerned?" As a result,

> Nigeria becomes the film's cautionary tale—a vision of what Ghana, with-out careful government controls, might become. But the film's most telling juxtaposition is that of Ghana itself—with its dirt roads, colorful tribal cou-ture and low cement buildings—against the steel-and-glass cage of Wall Street .[and] what [the director] finds in both locales is surprisingly simi-lar: a merry-go-round of investors, subcontractors and sub-subcontractors looking to turn national resources into personal wealth with little regard for collateral damage.

With violence and corruption added to the extremes of wealth and poverty, the social problems and ethical dilemmas plant roots that will be hard to extract.

Let's turn now to a recent case and see how a company responded to a crisis.

CASE STUDY 2: Costco and the Tainted Berries

June 2013 saw a flurry of state and local health officials and national health agencies working with the chain store Costco to address a Hepatitis A outbreak caused by one of their products. The infection was traced to tainted frozen berries sold in seven states.

Pomegranate seeds from Turkey were deemed the likely cause. Evidently Costco had sold over 330,000 bags of the contaminated fruit mix in the 4 months from February to May 2013. As of June 6, 2013, at least 62 people had gotten infectious hepatitis (Morran, 2013).

The store contacted customers and recalled the three-pound bags of Townsend Farms Organic Antioxidant Blend. Luckily, Costco keeps a record of all who bought the berries because the store requires membership for purchases. This helped Costco reach many of those who purchased the fruit mix.

Of course it would be quite unnerving to be advised to get medical attention because of a food product you consumed. Nevertheless, it showed that Costco took the matter seriously and acted quickly. Costco also offered free vaccines at their pharmacies and offered to pay for vaccines obtained elsewhere. "It's the right thing for us to do," the company's director of food safety acknowledged (Morran, 2013).

The berries were part of a frozen berry mix used in fruit Smoothies. Not only is Hepatitis A a serious disease (as it can destroy your liver), the matter is also complicated by the age range of those who were affected. From babies to the elderly, from the strong to the weak and feeble—many people consumed the contaminated berries.

One of the ethical issues here has to do with truth in advertising and packaging. The text of the packaging can be seen in Figure 1.1. (A photo of the package can be found on the Centers for Disease Control and Prevention website at http://www.cdc.gov/hepatitis/outbreaks/2013/a1b-03-31/advice-consumers.html.)

The package says "USDA Organic." The ingredients listed are dark tart cherries, pomegranate arils, strawberries, red raspberries, blueberries. Below that it says: "Townsend Farms. Field to Farm to Family Since 1906." Farther down the package is written, "Individually Quick Frozen." And finally, in the bottom left it says, "KEEP FROZEN."

Not on the package is any indication of the *source* of the berries, where the ingredients came from. Should that be stated? The package lists five ingredients. Would it be justified to infer that they are in *equal* amounts? Should companies be obligated to list *sources* of ingredients (e.g., from Turkey, Peru, Chile, etc.)? If so, should they do so on the front of the package?

USDA
ORGANIC

Organic Antioxidant Blend

DARK TART CHERRIES, POMEGRANATE ARILS, STRAWBERRIES, RED RASPBERRIES, BLUEBERRIES

Townsend Farms
Field to Farm to Family Since 1906
Individually Quick Frozen

KEEP FROZEN ENLARGED TO SHOW DETAILS
Net Wt. 48 oz. (3 lbs) 1.3 kg

Figure 1.1   Text of Townsend's organic berry mix package (central portion).

You tell me: Does the claim "Field to Farm to Family Since 1906" suggest that the field and farm are both owned and operated by Townsend? Could they use other fields and farms without violating the spirit or letter of the claim? If so, would those fields and farms have to be in business since 1906—or only Townsend's? If not, is that evidence that Townsend's marketing is misleading, dishonest, or deceptive?

Not all customers are happy with the way the case was handled. One disgruntled customer is Elizabeth Soza, whose father became so ill from the tainted fruit he is now bedridden. "Aside from my father's extreme physical suffering and my own emotional suffering, I am heartbroken over what this incident means on a larger scale. America does not grow its own food," she says, asking, "Why is produce from other countries all over our store shelves, where there is questionable oversight of the farming practices and health codes?" (Sacks, 2013).

This raises the question about the use of food products from countries lacking an agency like the Food & Drug Administration (the FDA). What should businesses like Costco do about that and what should the consumer rightfully expect? One solution is to establish an international agency or consumer watchdog to regulate the safety of produce and other foods. In any case the quality of the products coming in and out of the country needs to be more closely monitored to minimize health risks.

Evidently, Costco contacted 240,000 customers and received calls from 10,000 of them (Sacks, 2013). For some, including Elizabeth Soza, this was not enough. She claims:

> The company [Costco] left two voicemails confirming the family's purchase of Townsend Farms frozen berries and also left contact information for the

CDC, the FDA and Townsend Farms in Oregon. There was no apology or offer to help with medical costs, said Rita Soza [Elizabeth's mother and victim's wife], though the company did say a free hepatitis vaccine would be available at Costco pharmacies starting June 6 (Sacks, 2013).

"It's not at all how I thought a company like Costco would respond," she said, comparing Costco to Johnson & Johnson's handling of the 1982 Tylenol crisis (Sacks, 2013).

One concern here is whether one or both of Costco and Townsend (producer of the berry mix) are responsible for interfacing with the public about the Hepatitis A outbreak due to the berry mixture. Soza contrasts Johnson & Johnson's handling of the Tylenol poisonings, suggesting that Johnson & Johnson did a better job than Costco in confronting the situation. However, Townsend, not Costco, produced the tainted berry mix In contrast, Johnson & Johnson produced the painkiller Tylenol and, therefore, can't point the finger at anyone else. Consequently, the analogy doesn't quite hold.

Costco clearly *sold* the Townsend product, but Townsend produced it. Does it then follow that Costco should do more than they did? They *did* recall the fruit mix, they *did* contact 240,000 customers to notify them and suggest medical help, and they *did* offer free vaccines (or reimbursement for same). What extra steps might (and should) be taken?

Some contend that Townsend bears more responsibility than Costco, including lawyer Bill Marler. Benjamin Wood (2013) reports:

> Bill Marler, a Seattle-based lawyer, recently filed a class action lawsuit against Townsend Farms in California. He said his office has been contacted by approximately 400 people who received vaccinations as a result of purchasing the frozen berries, and only about half of those were contacted by Costco. "To me, the interesting thing is this is really an international outbreak," Marler said. "It's not just eight states."

He said the lawsuit does not target Costco, the product's distributor, because ultimately the responsibility for contamination lies with the producer or manufacturer. "This is a frozen, bagged product that Costco sells," Marler said. "The buck really stops at Townsend Farms."

John Rawls and the Costco Case

Rawls' foremost concern would be that all those affected by the tainted berries have equal access to health care and any subsequent treatment they might need. His third principle makes it clear that the needs of those most disadvantaged (here, the customers, and especially those sickened by the berries) takes precedence over competing interests.

In an implicit acknowledgement of that moral view, Costco took steps to notify customers. This they did via the news media and with customer records of those who purchased the product. They then contacted them personally. Rawls would be glad to know they took that level of care. He would also hope a plan is put into effect to better monitor product safety.

His Principle of Equal Liberty would mandate that all concerned should be treated fairly. He would want Costco or others bearing responsibility to make sure that justice has been done. That includes taking all reasonable steps to pull the product off the shelves, alert consumers, do what is necessary to protect public health, and follow up with customers in terms of refunds and/or reparations.

Unfortunately for both Costco and Townsend, the two major ways of reaching customers who purchased the tainted product are press releases and the store records (tracking those who purchased the fruit mix). The latter, however, only register those who used the Costco/American Express credit card. What about those who paid cash for the berries? If they didn't use the credit card, they could not be traced (or not easily so). Do they read the newspaper, watch TV news, or access news via the Internet, radio, or other means? Many people do; but not all. What can Costco and Townsend safely assume about customers who may have been affected by the tainted fruit? It is these disadvantaged consumers that Rawls might especially worry about and hope that all measures possible to reach them are indeed taken.

ETHICS CODE: Costco

Costco's Code of Ethics is lean and clean:

(1) Obey the law
(2) Take care of our members
(3) Take care of our employees
(4) Respect our suppliers.
     If we do these four things throughout our organization, then we will achieve our ultimate goal, which is to:
(5) Reward our shareholders.

Go to: http://media.corporateir.net/media_files/NSD/cost/reports/our_mission.pdf for a full explanation of each of the duties above. In its discussion, Costco offers this perspective:

These guidelines are exactly that—guidelines—some common sense rules for the conduct of our business. At the core of our philosophy as a company is the implicit understanding that all of us, employees and management alike, must conduct ourselves in an honest and ethical manner every day. In fact, dishonest conduct will not be tolerated. To do any less would be unfair to the overwhelming majority of our employees who support and respect Costco's commitment to ethical business conduct. If you are ever in doubt as to what course of action to take on a business matter that is open to varying ethical interpretations, TAKE THE HIGH ROAD AND DO WHAT IS RIGHT (their emphasis).

Exercise

1. Share your thoughts on Costco's Code of Ethics. Compare it to another ethics code (e.g., Johnson & Johnson's, Apple's, Google's).
2. Should they have addressed the wider community as well? Or is that covered by "Take the high road and do what is right"?

Works Cited

Aristotle, *Poetics*, The Internet Classics Archive, http://classics.mit.edu/Aristotle/poetics.html (accessed December 18, 2014).

Centers for Disease Control and Prevention, "Viral Hepatitis: Multistate outbreak of hepatitis A virus infections linked to pomegranate seeds from Turkey (Final Update)," http://www.cdc.gov/hepatitis/outbreaks/2013/a1b-03-31/advice-consumers.html (accessed December 18, 2014).

Charatan, Fred, "US Court Awards $145bn Damages Against Tobacco Giants," US National Library of Medicine, National Institutes of Health, *BMJ*, Vol. 321 (7255); July 22, 2000, http://www.ncbi.nlm.nih.gov/pmc/articles/PMC1118202/ (accessed December 18, 2014).

Constitutional Rights Foundation, "Justice as Fairness: John Rawls and His Theory of Justice," *Bill of Rights in Action*, Fall 2007 (Vol. 23, No. 3), http://www.crf-usa.org/bill-of-rights-in-action/bria-23-3-c-justice-as-fairness-john-rawls-and-his-theory-of-justice (accessed December 18, 2014).

Costco, *Code of Ethics*, http://media.corporate-ir.net/media_files/NSD/cost/reports/our_mission.pdf (accessed December 18, 2014).

Foundas, Scott, "Tribeca Film Review: *Big Men*," *Variety*, April 25, 2013, http://variety.com/2013/film/reviews/tribeca-review-big-men-1200415912/ (accessed December 18, 2014).

Gutting, Gary, "Why Conservatives Should Reread Milton Friedman," *New York Times*, September 26, 2013, http://opinionator.blogs.nytimes.com/2013/09/26/why-conservatives-should-reread-milton-friedman/?_php=true&_type=blogs&_r=0 (accessed December 18, 2014).

Marx, Karl, *Economic & Philosophic Manuscripts of 1844*, http://www.marxists. org/archive/marx/works/download/pdf/Economic-Philosophic-Manuscripts-1844.pdf (accessed December 18, 2014).

Marx, Karl, "Estranged Labor," in Giddens, Anthony and David Held (eds.), *Classes, Power, and Conflict: Classical and Contemporary Debates*, (Berkeley, CA: University of California Press, 1982).

Morran, Chris, "Costco Offering Free Hepatitis Vaccines To Customers Who Purchased Recalled Berries," *Consumerist*, June 7, 2013, http://consumerist. com/2013/06/07/costco-offering-free-hepatitis-vaccines-to-customers-who-purchased-recalled-berries/

Sacks, Brianna, "Costco Berries Linked To Another Case Of Hepatitis A In San Diego," *Neon Tommy (USC)*, June 6, 2013, http://www.neontommy.com/news/2013/06/costco-berries-linked-another-case-hepatitis-san-diego (accessed December 18, 2014).

Securities and Exchange Commission, "SEC Charges Martha Stewart, Broker Peter Bacanovic with Illegal Insider Trading" (press release), June 4, 2003, https://www.sec.gov/news/press/2003-69.htm (accessed December 18, 2014).

Turan, Kenneth, "Review: 'Big Men' Hits A Gusher Of Oil And Greed," *Los Angeles Times*, June 13, 2013.

Van Syckle, Katie, "Brad Pitt-Produced 'Big Men' Explores Greed in West African Oil Exploration," *Rolling Stone*, April 21, 2013, http://www.rollingstone. com/movies/news/brad-pitt-produced-big-men-explores-greed-in-west-african-oil-exploration-20130421 (accessed December 18, 2014).

Whitefield, Paul, "Forbes 400: Rich Get Richer While The Poor Get To Watch And Wish," *Los Angeles Times*, September 16, 2013, http://www.latimes.com/opinion/opinion-la/la-ol-forbes-400-wealth-divide-20130916,0,7963083. story (accessed December 27, 2014).

Wood, Benjamin, "Costco Offering Reimbursement For Hepatitis A Vaccinations After Recall," *Deseret News*, June 7, 2013, http://www.deseretnews.com/article/865581366/Costco-offering-reimbursement-for-hepatitis-A-vaccinations-after-recall.html?pg=all (accessed December 18, 2014).

1.4

Talk To Me
The Impact Of Technology

Spotlight: *Her; The Net; Disconnect*
Case Studies: Edward Snowden and the NSA; Target's Data Breach;
Target's Online Tracking
Ethics Code: Yahoo!

> **Theodore** (to his operating system "Samantha"):
> *I've never loved anyone the way I loved you.*
>
> —Her

SPOTLIGHT: *Her*

You know that saying, 'No man is an island'? Well, Theodore Twombly is about as close to being a one-man island as you can get this side of a psychopath. He lives alone in an upscale so-roomy-it's-almost-barren apartment on a high-enough floor to look out at the skyscrapers and the streets far below. He sees the buildings and the tiny, lighted windows of the high-rises, but too far away to see human shapes. The resulting picture is one of isolation and the distance that wealth can buy. We follow along as his life takes a surprising turn in *Her* (2013).

The movie is set in a futuristic Los Angeles. Theodore never drives a car—clearly not the L.A. of the present. No traffic jams for him! He appears content with the near-solitude of his existence. His worksite is a cubicle where, ironically, he writes heartfelt letters for a living. That Theodore's letters are clever and nicely done doesn't mean that polish can replace sincerity. And like the essayists of papers-for-hire that dishonest college students purchase, moral boundaries have already been crossed once he signs the letter with the customer's name.

Business Ethics Through Movies: A Case Study Approach, First Edition. Wanda Teays.
© 2015 John Wiley & Sons, Ltd. Published 2015 by John Wiley & Sons, Ltd.

Theodore takes his work seriously and spends time honing the right word combination and tone for the *Dear...* letters. From his solipsistic job he goes home to a 3-D videogame that centers on a Sisyphus-like character struggling to climb up and out of the abyss he's stuck in. As we know from Albert Camus' story, Sisyphus's destiny is to push a boulder up a hill only to have it roll down and begin again—day after day after yet another day. We presume this is a metaphor for Theodore's life.

His life seems pretty routine; predictable and safe, though insular—until a computer upgrade sets change in motion. Theodore is hooked by the idea of an *intuitive* operating system. He is fascinated, wondering how something inherently rational can be *intuitive*. You can program randomness, but how can you program intuition? He can't resist finding out. And so the unexpected came to Theodore Twombly. *Her* (2013) tells the story.

We'll begin with *Her* and then turn to *The Net* and *Disconnect*. Here we find issues related to identity theft and cyber-bulling. Security breaches and privacy rights have gotten international attention with whistleblower Edward Snowden's release of National Security Agency (NSA) files (Case 1). The very real crisis with the data breach at Target (Cases 2 and 3) brings home the fact that identity theft can have major repercussions. Our ethics code for this chapter is Yahoo!'s.

Aristotle's Model of Deconstruction

In his *Poetics*, Aristotle sets out a model to understand, evaluate, and deconstruct drama. Theatre in his day corresponds to film in ours and his model is very useful. We listed Aristotle's six components in Chapter 1.3: Plot, Character, Thought, Dialogue and Diction, Music, and Special Effects. The first three set out the key structural aspects of a movie and reveal its moral base.

Basically the plot of *Her* is this: A lonely ghostwriter who spends his talents writing personalized letters for hire in the not-too-distant future falls in love with his computer's new operating system (OS 1). This operating system has the ability to converse and convey its "thoughts" with an all-too-human (female) voice. It names itself Samantha, making it easier to think of it as a *person*.

The story is similar to *The Twilight Zone* Season 1 Episode 7 ("The Lonely") about an inmate, Corey, in 2046 sentenced to 50 years of solitary confinement on a distant planet. In his fourth year he is given a robot named Alicia (attractive and human-like). In time he becomes very attached to "her." Eventually he is pardoned and can return to Earth, but there's no room for the robot. Corey is devastated. There's a parallel to Theodore—lonely, needy, and lovesick.

That Samantha is disembodied means Theodore must imagine "her" as more than an intelligent machine. Christine Smallwood (2013) says Samantha's disembodiment means that Theodore never has to deal with anything sticky, bloody, or wet. No muss, no fuss! How ideal! And so Theodore begins a most unusual relationship. It includes auto-erotic phone sex and a surrogate sent to consummate the relationship (no go!). Samantha's lack of a body *is* a bit of an obstacle.

Face it: With a computer upgrade you can replace that special *flawed* someone who can be downright irritating at times. Instead, you can have a Sam or Samantha (your pick) with handy practical functions (think of the 928 emails in your inbox that need filing!). Plus it has empathic functions for other needs (Can't sleep? Need company at 2:00 a.m.? No problem!). But, as with many fantasies, it was too good to last.

Applying Aristotle to Her

Aristotle would call the purchase of the new intuitive operating system OS 1 the *first cause* of action, as that kick-started the love affair of man and software. Theodore opted out of finding a real woman to be with. No fights over the remote or dirty dishes. No feelings of inferiority when an ego boost is so readily available. Who wouldn't spend good money for that?

It was just a matter of time until the *second cause* of action. This brought a reversal of fortune, causing his happy days to come to a screeching halt. As it turns out, she serviced many other such Theodores—641 to be exact. Mind you, he did notice that she wasn't always attentive, but, hey, that happens. Besides, who says monopoly is a trait of operating systems, robots, cyborgs or the like?

Theodore was the victim of unwarranted assumptions. He thought intuitive operating systems would think and act like human beings. They may sound alike and share certain characteristics, but the differences are greater than he foresaw.

So, when she no longer devoted herself 24/7 to his wants and needs the illusion of love everlasting starts to unravel. That led to his reversal of fortune and his fall from Cloud 9. Thus begins the *denouement*, the resolution—the unfolding of the movie's final chapter. With that came Theodore's *discovery*—the moment when the hero sees the error of his ways. He is sadder but wiser. Maybe not a *lot* wiser, but wiser nevertheless.

When the hero experiences a *discovery*, there is character development. This is the moment of seeing the light, when all becomes clear and moral lessons are learned. Samantha may have been the ideal woman, but *he* was expendable. It's an ego-bruising moment, but in retrospect he may have been foolish from the get-go. There's more to love than simulating it with your computer. There's more to empathy than writing letters to people you will never know, pretending to care for them. You've got to come into the world in a fuller, more robust way.

Her ends with Theodore sitting on the roof of the high-rise, looking out at the city lights below. By his side is his friend Amy. We see that, yes, technology can make our lives much better. But that doesn't mean we should check our critical faculties at the door.

Applying the Case Study Checklist to Her

The Case Study Checklist (Chapter 1.1) can unpack the moral core of the movie and give us a tool for examining its moral dimension. Let's put it to use.

1. **Define the problem. Set out the various ethical issues**
   - The personhood of operating systems/artificial intelligence (AI)
   - The ethical use of technology in terms of access to information and privacy
   - The use of technology to replace or supplement human interaction
   - The use of technology in decision-making roles that have greater impact than the mere functioning of the technology itself (e.g., in data processing, creating templates)
   - The use of human surrogates to simulate real human-to-human relationships
   - The societal impact of the increasing social role of artificial intelligence (AI)
   - The potential for increased surveillance and corporate or governmental use of personal information

2. **Note the Key Players** Basically they're Theodore and Samantha. Friend Amy, ex-wife Catherine, and blind date Amelia have a part to play as a sort of chorus in raising doubts about Theodore's insularity and providing a human contrast to OS Samantha.

3. **State the Facts** See above discussion and plot details.

4. Clarify Key Concepts and Values *The key concepts* are person-hood, moral status, moral agency, rationality, and privacy. *The key values, ideas or principles* are personal autonomy, preserving civil liberties, expanding the role of artificial intelligence in work and social life, and the potential value in shifting decision-making to nonhuman "persons."

5. Settle on the Criteria of Assessment Apply relevant principles and rules:

1 Corporations have legal personhood and, thus, at least some moral status. The question is how far to take that sense of personhood. Does legal personhood entail *moral* personhood? Can we agree that corporations have moral agency? And if so, does it transfer from the corporation to the operating systems (intelligent machines) that it creates and markets?

2 Moral agency has two main components—rationality (ability to reason) and freedom (volition). Samantha is presented as rational and supposedly intuitive—in doing complex tasks, such as editing email passages and predicting what will interest Theodore. A key issue is volition. Samantha is an operating system. It may have a human voice, but it has been programmed—it is not self-motivated, it lacks the free will vital to a moral agent. Samantha seems no more morally culpable than a robot planting landmines in Afghanistan.

3 Current laws are at odds with practices around data collection and surveillance. Theodore is initially uneasy about Samantha reading his email and learning private details of his life—which raises concerns about privacy rights. That the agent of surveillance has a sexy voice and is solicitous doesn't mean that there are no ethical issues with this new operating system.

4 John Stuart Mill's Harm Principle endorses freedom of choice so long as no one else is harmed (Mill, 1999). This is in line with the values of freedom and autonomy. *Her* includes online sex games, the 3-D video game, and the social acceptance of Theodore's friends/acquaintances that Samantha is his girlfriend. This revelation is an opening for others to share how they've bonded with their operating systems.

6. Get Some Perspective Theodore conveys a sense of loss after realizing he was played by Samantha. The question is can he can go let go of his attachment and go on with his life? Researcher Julie Carpenter studied military personnel to see if they could become so attached to their robots that they may be reluctant to put them at risk. She found that,

> It's becoming more common to have robots sub in for humans to do dirty or sometimes dangerous work. But researchers are finding that in some cases, people have started to treat robots like pets, friends, or even as an extension of themselves. That raises the question, if a soldier attaches human or animal-like characteristics to a field robot, can it affect how they use the robot? What if they care too much about the robot to send it into a dangerous situation? (Armstrong, 2013)

Carpenter interviewed Explosive Ordnance Disposal personnel who were using robots to disarm explosives. Although they said their attachment to the robots wouldn't affect their performance, they felt a range of emotions such as frustration, anger and even sadness when their field robot was destroyed. She found that many of the soldiers she talked to named their robots, usually after a celebrity or current wife or girlfriend (never an ex). This led Carpenter to ask if the battlefield could be compromised by human–robot attachment, or the feeling of self-extension into the robot described by some operators (Armstrong, 2013).

7. Make a Decision   Here we give our assessment.

The movie is not just about a man who falls in love with a virtual entity. It's also about the role of technology in our lives and how our lives—our society, our jobs and workplaces—have been changed. With the gains have come losses; with the benefits have come costs. Is Theodore better off for his "affair" with Samantha? Has he gained greater insight into who he is and what purpose he can serve in what he does with his life? There's a lot here to ponder.

Norbert Wiener and Computer Ethics

For another angle on *Her*, let's turn to Norbert Wiener, a mathematician who thought computer ethics needed a justice base. His work on information technology the 1940s led him to predict a second industrial revolution and ethical challenges that would follow (Bynum, 2001, 2008). He inquired into what principles of justice should guide us in finding *purpose* in life.

In order to flourish, we must be free to engage in creative actions and maximize our potential as intelligent, decision-making beings. He sees this as the purpose of a human life. With that in mind he set out four values (which he expressed as principles) affirming justice as the foundation for society (Bynum, 2005). These are values are: liberty, equality, benevolence (goodwill), and the minimal infringement of freedom (only restrict for the good of the community). Let's consider why they're important to a well-run business:

- *The value of liberty:* Within a business setting, it would benefit both employees and employers for workers to have the liberty to develop their skills and abilities. Without the freedom to be innovative and develop our strengths in our work, we won't be able to reach our potential. That's to no one's advantage.
- *The value of equality:* A quick test of equality is the Test of Symmetry— being able to reverse roles, change positions, without any asymmetry being revealed. With inequities in the workplace, we see what happens when a role reversal shows discrepancies in the pay scale and treatment of workers (e.g., with respect to gender, age, or race).
- *The value of goodwill:* Goodwill—benevolence, doing good— is an issue of both attitude and disposition. This is vital in business, where the presence or absence of goodwill can determine the direction of a course of action. Without goodwill, there can be no trust. For that reason a gesture of goodwill lays the groundwork for trust, to opening up to the other in a way that builds connections and reciprocity.
- *The value of freedom:* This entails the autonomy to act freely. Its restrictions are laws and regulations and the protection of others from harm. Without sufficient autonomy, creativity is stifled and independence of thought shrivels up. Businesses have to balance needs and interests and allow for the freedom for ideas to flourish and for collaboration to take place.

Consider how these values influence Business Ethics. Some companies, such as Google and Facebook, provide the space and time for employees to relax, work in teams, bounce ideas off one another, and let the creative juices percolate. On its website Google praises employee perks. There it says of their benefits:

We want to make your life better and easier.
Here's the secret sauce to our benefits and perks: It's all about removing barriers so Googlers can focus on the things they love, both inside and

outside of work. We're constantly searching for unique ways to improve the health and happiness of our Googlers. And it doesn't stop there–our hope is that, ultimately, you become a better person by working here.

CASE STUDY 1: Edward Snowden and the NSA

The operating system Samantha has complete access to everything on Theodore's computer. Should he care? Would you? Privacy is an acknowledged value; a *right* according to some worldviews. In fact, the US Supreme Court ruled that a cellphone search needs a warrant—broadly extending privacy rights. Chief Justice John Roberts, Jr., stated that, "Modern cellphones are not just another technological convenience. With all they contain and all they may reveal, they hold for many American 'the privacies of life'" (as quoted by Savage, 2014).

In 2013 the issue hit the front pages with the revelation of massive surveillance being carried out by the National Security Agency (NSA). Whistleblower Edward Snowden revealed violations of privacy "rights" including a metadata collection of enormous troves of phone records— hundreds of millions of phone records. According to a *New York Times* report (Sanger and Shanker, 2014):

> As *The Guardian* put it, cell phones, laptops, Facebook, Skype, and chatrooms allow the NSA to build 'a pattern of life'—a detailed profile of a target and anyone associated with them. This is part of a dragnet. Chris Soghoian, ACLU technologist asserts that, "If the NSA wants to get into your computer or phone, they are going to get in and there isn't any way to stop them."

The Guardian (2013) reported on the extent of the surveillance:

> And the number of people caught up in this dragnet can be huge. You don't need to be talking to a terror suspect to have your communications data analysed by the NSA. The agency is allowed to travel three hops from its targets—who could be people who talk to people who talk to people who talk to you. Facebook, where the typical user has 190 friends, shows how three degrees of separation gets you to a network bigger than the population of Colorado. How many people are three hops from you?

Though this was a bombshell, a federal judge ruled on December 27, 2013 that the government's actions were legal. But the question is: What will come of all this? And what's the big deal? Fox News (2014) reported on the use of radio waves to snoop into people's (private) computers:

> The National Security Agency has placed software on nearly 100,000 computers around the world that allows the U.S. to conduct surveillance on those machines using radio frequency technology, *The New York Times* reported Tuesday. The secret technology allows the agency to gain access to computers that other countries have tried to protect from spying or cyberattacks, even if they aren't connected to the Internet, *The Times* reported, citing NSA documents, computer experts and US officials. The software network could also create a digital highway for launching cyberattacks by transmitting malware, including the kind used in attacks by the US against Iran's nuclear facilities, according to the report.

Susan Herman, President of the American Civil Liberties Union states that secret government lists now dictate not only who can fly but also who can open bank accounts or get security clearances (and therefore certain jobs), and even whom the government may kill (2013).

Before considering Snowden's actions, think about what being a whistleblower entails. Ethicist Peter B. Jubb (1999) sets out these key components: (1) it is an intentional act, (2) it is not required or coerced, (3) it creates a public record, (4) the whistleblower accessed the incriminating data or information, (5) it reveals potential/actual wrongdoing under the control of an organization, and lastly, (6) it is shared with an entity capable of addressing the wrongdoing (see Lindblom, 2007).

All of the components were met in Snowden's case. He obtained information while employed by the NSA, he deliberately stole files on his own volition (no one forced him to become a whistleblower), he shared a portion of the files with a major newspaper (*The Guardian*), and personally had access to the information—no one else gave it to him. The data reveals surveillance and data collection by the NSA that raises privacy concerns.

Among the major actions that Snowden revealed are:

- A secret court order showing that the NSA was collecting the telephone records of millions of US customers of Verizon, one of America's largest telecom providers.
- The NSA also has "Prism," which, according to the Snowden documents, is the biggest single contributor to its intelligence reports. It is a downstream program—which means the agency collects the data from Google, Facebook, Apple, Yahoo and other US Internet giants.
- US and British intelligence agencies have successfully broken or circumvented much of online encryption. Much of this, …[was done by]

making deals with the industry to introduce weaknesses or backdoors into commercial encryption... (see *The Guardian*).

Reactions to Snowden's Revelations

You can imagine the after-effects of Snowden's revelations about the NSA's surveillance when even heads of state in Europe discovered that their computers and phones were sharing data with the NSA. The reactions fall between two extremes. For some, Snowden deserves a Medal of Honor for disclosing what could be unconstitutional prying and data collection. For others, Snowden deserves life in prison without parole for obtaining state's secrets and committing treasonous acts.

According to *The Washington Post* (2013) the German magazine *Der Spiegel* lifted the lid on the operations of the National Security Agency's hacking unit—asserting that American spies intercept computer deliveries, exploit hardware vulnerabilities, and hijack Microsoft's internal reporting system in order to spy on their targets. In addition,

> Old-fashioned methods get a mention too. *Der Spiegel* said that if the NSA tracked a target ordering a new computer or other electronic accessories, TAO [a division of the NSA known as Tailored Access Operations] could tap its allies in the FBI and the CIA, intercept the hardware in transit, and take it to a secret workshop where it could be discretely fitted with espionage software before being sent on its way.

Intercepting computer equipment in such a way is among the NSA's most productive operations, and has helped harvest intelligence from around the world, one document cited by *Der Spiegel* stated.

Exercise

1. Read the two views and then draw *your* assessment of Snowden's actions:Rep. Mike Rogers (R-MI and chairman of the House Intelligence Committee) said on ABC's *This Week* that Snowden crossed the line when he contacted a foreign country to sell the classified NSA information for something of value.

   > That is what we call a traitor in this country. He has traded something of value for his own personal gain that jeopardizes the national security of the United States. We call that treason. He should come back. He didn't use

any of the whistleblower protection avenues laid out before him. None.
Zero (Barron-Lopez, 2013)

The New York Times Editorial Board disagreed:

> Mr. Snowden did not commit treason, though the people who have long
> kept the secrets he revealed are now fulminating with rage. If Mr. Snowden
> had really wanted to harm his country, he could have sold the classified doc-
> uments he stole to a foreign power, say Russia or China or Iran or North
> Korea. But even that would not constitute treason, which only applies in
> cases of aiding an enemy with whom the United States is at war (*New York
> Times* Editorial Board, 2013).

2. How do we find a balance between preventing acts of terrorism and
   protecting civil liberties like privacy rights?
3. What role should corporations and institutions play in achieving that
   balance?

Electronic Privacy Rights and Wrongs

There's more to privacy rights and wrongs than fighting terrorism.
Ordinary people in ordinary jobs face privacy concerns. It's not always
clear where lines should be drawn and to what degree corporations should
preserve privacy rights of employees, customers, and clients.

Ethicist Joseph DesJardins discusses electronic privacy within a business
setting. Whereas employees in federal jobs have Fourth Amendment
protections, that's not true in private enterprise. DesJardins cites the 2007
case of a Massachusetts bank intern Kevin Colvin who emailed his boss
that he'd miss work due to a family emergency.

> His boss looked at Colvin's Facebook page the next day. Lo and behold, he
> saw a time-stamped photo of Colvin in a Halloween costume. The boss pasted
> the photo in an email to Colvin, with copies to other employees (no doubt
> to put them on notice). Colvin was out of a job (DesJardins, pp. 122–123).

Not all employers would condone the actions of Colvin's boss. Privacy
is widely perceived as a value or even a *right* in certain circumstances. For
example, Facebook is said to uphold privacy rights, as noted on the
Millennium Search website:

> While an employee's Facebook page may seem like an ideal place to research
> relevant information, recruiters and employees assured the public they don't

have access to people's personal Facebook pages. Privacy was emphasized and employees mentioned that peeking into someone's Facebook page is definitely a fireable offense. While Facebook maintains an open work environment, employees and managers are not snooping on each other. Relationships between managers and employees are open and transparent to such a degree the need for uncovering more information about employees has become unnecessary.

Privacy surely merits the attention it has been receiving. But there are other issues that face both individuals and the workplace that are also important. Among them are identity theft and cyber-bullying—each a wasps' nest to deal with.

SPOTLIGHT: *The Net* and *Disconnect*

The Net (1995) and *Disconnect* (2012) both remind us that there are a number of perils that are web-based. It's not quite as bad as "Abandon all hope, ye who enter here" (the sign over Hell in Dante's *Inferno*). But it certainly is, "Don't abandon your horse sense, ye who enter here."

Angela Bennett of *The Net* is a computer whiz with impressive hacking skills. She comes upon evidence that a major computer security program will result in a malevolent group having control over vital areas of the government. With her vacation already paid for, she takes the computer disk with the damning evidence and heads off to Mexico, unaware of the dangers that lie ahead. The body count indicates how serious are her adversaries in wanting the disk.

What Angela faces is not just identity theft; she's the victim of an identity transformation! The group has the know-how to assign *her* a most unsavory identity. Angela Bennett is now on official record as Ruth Marx, with a string of crimes to her name. Angela struggles to sort out the identity theft and stay alive. She reflects on how easily this happened:

> Just think about it. Our whole world is sitting there on a computer. It's in the computer, everything: your, your DMV records, your, your social security, your credit cards, your medical records. It's all right there. Everyone is stored in there. It's like this little electronic shadow on each and every one of us, just, just begging for someone to screw with, and you know what? They've done it to me, and you know what? They're gonna do it to you.

It didn't help that her passport was stolen as well, with someone else claiming (evidently successfully) that *she* was Angela Bennett. Thankfully, she was a tech crackerjack with the skills to fight back. That she single-handedly succeeded in the end was a cause for vicarious pleasure in all those in the audience who'd been there and seen that with identity theft.

Disconnect and Identity Theft

The repercussions of identity theft can be a nightmare, as victims know! In the movie, *Disconnect*, an upper-middle class couple (Cindy and Derek Hull) find their lives turned upside down thanks to their malefactor. Their bank account was emptied out, credit cards too, the whole shebang. It was not only a financial catastrophe, but bore the emotional cost of baring their Internet activity to their mate. This added some unwanted stress on their marriage.

The precipitating events were Cindy sharing her information on a chat room and husband Derek using his credit card on an online gambling site. Both paid a hefty price. Once it was clear that the police weren't going to do anything (get in line behind thousands of others!) they turned to a specialist, a sort of electronic private eye. Not all have the financial luxury for that option. But it was an eye-opener to see what was involved to try to get to the bottom of their identity theft.

Both *The Net* and *Disconnect* present the stressful saga of victims of identity theft and the resulting chaos and distress they experienced. Imagine what happens when large numbers of people suffer a similar fate. That's the door that opened when a major retail store suffered a security breach. Let's see what happened.

CASE STUDY 2: Target's Data Breach

On December 19, 2013, mega-retailer Target announced that around 40 million customers' credit/debit cards had been hacked. On January 11, 2014,

> Target confirmed its own cyber attack was far worse than previously believed. America's second-largest retailer revealed the same group that stole 40 million credit card numbers also obtained the personal information—names, phone numbers and email addresses—of 70 million customers. (CBS News).

This is one of the largest such incidents in US history. Target sought to reassure anxious consumers with the announcement that the PIN numbers were safely encrypted. Of course, the majority of those whose bank information was hacked into tried not to picture themselves like Angela Bennett in *The Net*.

The *Wall Street Journal* (Germano, 2013) set out the timeline. Note the delay in sharing news of the breach with the public:

> **27 Nov to 15 Dec 2013:** U.S. Target stores suffered a data hack, with as many as 40 million credit- and debit-card customers exposed to potential fraud.
>
> **18 Dec:** The *Wall Street Journal* learns of the breach and reports that the Secret Service is investigating.
>
> **19 Dec:** Target publicly acknowledges the breach of information—including customer names, credit or debit card numbers, expiration dates and encrypted security codes.
>
> **20 Dec:** Target says very few problems have been reported and that they'd extend a 10% discount on in-store purchases for U.S. customers during the holiday period.
>
> **21 Dec:** Chase bank sets daily limits on spending and withdrawals while working to reissue cards to debit card customers affected by the breach. Some branches of the bank were open on Sunday, Dec. 22 to help out.
>
> **27 Dec:** Target says encrypted PIN information was accessed during the breach; but they believe PIN numbers are safe.

So what's a consumer to do? Jana Shortal (2013) of KARE news reports that, "The questions now mount for the 40+ million customers affected cautiously peeking at their bank accounts daily to see if their data is turned into false credit sold on the black market." Meanwhile, let the lawsuits begin, says Joshua Brustein (2013) of *Bloomberg Business Week*.

> Losing control of sensitive customer data is a fact of life for American companies. They're collecting more of it, and they are often outgunned by hackers, who are highly motivated to get at it. It's not even clear how much legal responsibility they have to protect it. There is limited judicial guidance on what constitutes negligence in the cybersecurity area, says Craig Newman, a partner at Richard Kibbe & Orbe who follows legal issues related to security.

Target CEO Goes to the Public

Target CEO Gregg Steinhafel posted a letter on the corporation's website addressed to Target's "guests" (= customers). Here's an excerpt:

Dear Target Guest,

As you have likely heard by now, Target experienced unauthorized access to payment card data from U.S. Target stores. We take this crime seriously. It was a crime against Target, our team members and most importantly you— our valued guest.

We understand that a situation like this creates stress and anxiety about the safety of your payment card data at Target. Our brand has been built on a 50-year foundation of trust with our guests, and we want to assure you that the cause of this issue has been addressed and you can shop with confidence at Target. ...

This was posted before Target realized the (encrypted) PIN numbers had also been accessed. And what of the delay between the time that the breach was discovered (November 27) and the time the public was notified (December 19)? How quickly should a corporation acknowledge issues that directly concern and impact their customers? Are they ethically bound to step forward at the first sign of difficulty? If Johnson & Johnson represents the Gold Standard in transparency over the Tylenol disaster, how close (or far) is Target from that goal?

On Target's corporate website, they state that they'd acted quickly when they learned of the breach. However, they do not say they informed their guests. Read for yourself:

We began investigating the incident as soon as we learned of it. We have determined that the information involved in this incident included customer name, credit or debit card number, and the card's expiration date and CVV.

We are partnering with a leading third-party forensics firm to conduct a thorough investigation of the incident and to examine additional measures we can take that would be designed to help prevent incidents of this kind in the future. Additionally, Target alerted authorities and financial institutions immediately after we discovered and confirmed the unauthorized access, and we are putting our full resources behind these efforts.

As for Target, they are busy with damage control. One questions is whether they are doing enough:

Customers whose cards are used fraudulently won't be held responsible for those charges, and companies that get hacked often foot the bill for credit monitoring. Target customers whose identities are eventually stolen will find it difficult to prove that this breach is specifically to blame. Hackers have plenty of ways to access personal information (Brustein, 2013).

Kevin McCoy of *USA Today* reports that,

> What this means is that the "key" necessary to decrypt that data has never existed within Target's system and could not have been taken during this incident, the company said, adding, the most important thing for our guests to know is that their debit card accounts have not been compromised due to the encrypted PIN numbers being taken. Brian Krebs, a computer security expert […] said Target's disclosure means the thieves would have to find a way to break into electronic systems of the payment-processing company that works with the retail chain. It would involve a much more elaborate and multiparty compromise, said Krebs.

Given the value of stolen credit cards (one stolen card can sell on the black market for as much as $100, Nicole Perlroth reports in *The New York Times*), we can be sure this is not the end of such security breaches. Let's now turn to online tracking.

CASE STUDY 3: Target and Online Tracking

According to Kashmir Hill (2012) of *Forbes* magazine, Target assigns every customer a Guest ID number. This ID is tied to their credit card, name, or email address and this becomes a bucket that stores a history of everything they've bought and any demographic information Target has collected from them or bought from other sources.

Hill continues, "I can promise you that Target is not the only store doing this. Those people chilled by stores' tracking and profiling them may want to consider going the way of the common criminal—and paying for far more of their purchases in cash." True, some may turn to cash, but as we all know, there will be a significant percentage of customers (Target's guests) that use a credit or debit card and, thus, are subject to being tracked and profiled.

You tell me: Is this a violation of privacy? Should you resort to cash to protect yourself from the snooping eyes of retail stores? Must the use of a credit card relegate you to a data file that sends you coupons and flyers and the like? Should you be able to opt out of profiling and tracking?

Privacy is not an incidental matter. It is one of those civil liberties that constitute the great principles and fundamental values of a democracy. We need to clarify the boundaries of those values, those liberties. And we have to decide—in consort with businesses who profit from tracking and profiling—just how far they should go.

New York Times reporter Charles Duhigg wrote an exposé on Target's profiling that centered on privacy rights. Duhigg wrote about a Target statistician, Andrew Pole. According to Pole, Target colleagues asked him in 2002 if he could figure out if a customer was pregnant even if she didn't want us to know. With that challenge, Pole set to work to see what he could find out. What he found was a potential gold mine for Target, as he indicates:

> We knew that if we could identify them in their second trimester, there's a good chance we could capture them for years, Pole told me. As soon as we get them buying diapers from us, they're going to start buying everything else too. If you're rushing through the store, looking for bottles, and you pass orange juice, you'll grab a carton. Oh, and there's that new DVD I want. Soon, you'll be buying cereal and paper towels from us, and keep coming back.

With this goal, the Guest ID became very important to the store (and to others using this model). It keeps tabs on your purchases and any use of credit cards, coupons, or surveys. In addition,

> Also linked to your Guest ID is demographic information like your age, whether you are married and have kids, which part of town you live in, how long it takes you to drive to the store, your estimated salary, whether you've moved recently, what credit cards you carry in your wallet and what Web sites you visit. Target can buy data about your ethnicity, job history, the magazines you read, if you've ever declared bankruptcy or got divorced, the year you bought (or lost) your house, where you went to college, what kinds of topics you talk about online, whether you prefer certain brands of coffee, paper towels, cereal or applesauce, your political leanings, reading habits, charitable giving and the number of cars you own (Duhigg, 2012).

Is this privacy right worth fighting for? Where should the boundaries of tracking customers—or employees be drawn? As Duhigg points out,

> "Almost every major retailer, from grocery chains to investment banks to the US Postal Service, has a predictive analytics department devoted to understanding not just consumers' shopping habits but also their personal habits, so as to more efficiently market to them. It just so happens that Target has always been one of the smartest at this," says consultant Eric Siegel (Duhigg, 2012).

Not all customers fear Big Brother or are perturbed by snooping businesses that seek to profit off of them. Sure businesses make money if they make a sale, but customers may benefit too. They may appreciate the tips (*"If you like that shampoo, you might like this conditioner"* or *"If you enjoyed* Die Hard, *you might like* The Bourne Identity," and so on). Plus, let's not forget those coupons and discounts! As a result, not all customers object to their habits being recorded and kept for future reference.

The upshot is this: It's good to look at the benefits (pros) and risks (cons) of profiling and tracking on the part of businesses like Target, Amazon, and so on. We need to ask if the concerns are sufficient to warrant more than a check-this-box-agreeing-with-the-privacy-notice.

Back to Disconnect: Cyber-Bullying

Disconnect is consists of interwoven vignettes. One zeroes in on the Hulls' identity theft. Another is the story of two cyber-bullies who target Ben Boyd, a fellow high school student. One thing leads to the next and a cruel joke escalates to tragic ends. It is a sad, sordid matter that reveals how easily lives can be derailed by lapsed morality.

In Chapter 3.4, we will look at bullying in the NFL. Here in *Disconnect*, the bullies hide behind a pseudonym (pretending to be a girl interested in Ben). When they acquire a sexually explicit photo of Ben, their cruelty ratchets up another step. They send out the photo to schoolmates who then humiliate him with taunts, jeers, jokes, and the like. Ben becomes a laughing stock, much to his mortification.

A key issue is how businesses can stop cyber bullies and protect victims like Ben. One way is to create a culture that discourages it. Another is to have programs and policies in place. As we'll see in Chapter 3.3, this is not a minor matter. In *Disconnect* the bullying is between teens, not adults, and is in a school setting, not the workplace. But it can have devastating effects—ones that cross all boundaries and bear significant repercussions for employees *and* employers.

ETHICS CODE: Yahoo!

Yahoo! is an Internet portal and, thus, we would expect its ethics code to address some or all of the moral concerns around the Internet and use of computers. On its website, Yahoo! sets out a statement of its values (Excellence, Innovation, Customer Fixation, Teamwork, Community, Fun), as well as its ethics code. Yahoo!'s Ethics Code can be found at https://secure.ethicspoint.com/domain/media/en/gui/20988/YahooCode.pdf.

Exercise

Read over Yahoo!'s ethics code and the detailed statement of its values. What stands out about this code? Would you add or change anything? Share your thoughts.

Works Cited

Armstrong, Doree, "Emotional Attachment To Robots Could Affect Outcome On Battlefield," (Press Release), University of Washington, September 17, 2013, http://www.washington.edu/news/2013/09/17/emotional-attachment-to-robots-could-affect-outcome-on-battlefield/ (accessed December 18, 2014).

Associated Press, "Report: NSA Intercepts Computer Deliveries," *Washington Post*, December 29, 2013, http://www.washingtonpost.com/business/technology/report-nsa-intercepts-computer-deliveries/2013/12/29/dc14c3da-70a2-11e3-bc6b-712d770c3715_story.html (accessed December 18, 2014).

Barron-Lopez, Laura, "Rogers Says Snowden Committed Treason," *The Hill* (blog), December 22, 2013, http://thehill.com/blogs/hillicon-valley/technology/193832-rep-rogers-says-snowden-committed-treason (accessed December 18, 2014).

Brustein, Joshua, "Is Target to Blame for Its Data Breach? Let the Lawsuits Begin," *Bloomberg Business Week*, December 26, 2013, http://www.businessweek.com/articles/2013-12-26/is-target-to-blame-for-its-data-breach-let-the-lawsuits-begin (accessed December 18, 2014).

Bynum, Terrell, "Computer and Information Ethics," *Stanford Encyclopedia of Philosophy*, August 14, 2001, revised October 23, 2008, http://plato.stanford.edu/entries/ethics-computer/ (accessed December 18, 2014).

Bynum, Terrell Ward, "Norbert Wiener's Vision: The Impact of the Automatic Age on Our Moral Lives," in Robert J. Cavalier (ed.), *The Impact of the Internet on Our Moral Lives*, (Albany: State University of New York Press, 2005).

CBS News, "Retailers hacked: Are Data Breaches at Target and Neiman Marcus Connected?" CBS News, January 14, 2014, http://www.cbsnews.com/news/retailers-hacked-are-data-breaches-at-target-and-neiman-marcus-connected/ (accessed December 18, 2014).

DesJardins, Joseph, *An Introduction to Business Ethics*, 4th edn, (New York: McGraw-Hill, 2011).

Duhigg, Charles. "How Companies Learn Your Secrets," *New York Times*, February 16, 2012, http://www.nytimes.com/2012/02/19/magazine/shopping-habits.html?pagewanted=1&_r=2&hp (accessed December 18, 2014).

Fox News, "NSA Reportedly Using Radio Waves To Snoop On Offline Computers Worldwide," *Fox News*, January 15, 2014, http://www.foxnews.com/

politics/2014/01/15/nsa-maps-pathway-into-computers-report-says/ (accessed December 18, 2014).

Germano, Sara, "Target's Data-Breach Timeline," *Wall Street Journal*, December 27, 2013, http://blogs.wsj.com/corporate-intelligence/2013/12/27/targets-data-breach-timeline/ (accessed December 22, 2014).

The Guardian, "NSA Files Decoded: Edward Snowden's Surveillance Revelations Explained," November 1, 2013, http://www.theguardian.com/world/interactive/2013/nov/01/snowden-nsa-files-surveillance-revelations-decoded#section/1 (accessed December 18, 2014).

Herman, Susan, "Letter: Secret Watch Lists," *New York Times*, 22 Dec 2013.

Hill, Kashmir, "How Target Figured Out A Teen Girl Was Pregnant Before Her Father Did," *Forbes*, February 16, 2012, http://www.forbes.com/fdc/welcome_mjx.shtml (accessed December 18, 2014).

Lindblom, Lars, "Dissolving the Moral Dilemma of Whistleblowing," *Journal of Business Ethics* (2007) 76:413–426m, p. 414, http://www.jstor.org/discover/10.2307/25075529?uid=3739560&uid=2129&uid=2&uid=70&uid=4&uid=3739256&sid=21103334730097 (accessed December 18, 2014).

McCoy, Kevin, "Target confirms encrypted PIN data stolen," *USA Today*, December 27, 2013, http://www.usatoday.com/story/money/business/2013/12/27/target-confirms-encrypted-pin-data-stolen/4219415/ (accessed December 22, 2014).

Mill, John Stuart. *On Liberty*. Peterborough, Ontario: Broadview Press, 1999.

New York Times Editorial Board, "Surveillance: Snowden Doesn't Rise to Traitor," *The New York Times*, June 11, 2013, http://www.nytimes.com/2013/06/12/opinion/surveillance-snowden-doesnt-rise-to-traitor.html (accessed December 18, 2014).

New York Times Editorial Board, "This Week, Mass Surveillance Wins," *The New York Times*, December 27, 2013.

Perlroth, Nicole, "Target's Nightmare Goes On: Encrypted PIN Data Stolen," (Blog), *New York Times*, December 27, 2013, http://bits.blogs.nytimes.com/2013/12/27/targets-nightmare-goes-on-encrypted-pin-data-stolen/?_r=0 (accessed December 18, 2014).

Rogers, Dan, "The Millennium Search Blog, 5 Things I Learned from Facebook," http://www.msearchllc.com/blog/5-things-i-learned-facebook-employees (accessed December 18, 2014).

Sanger, David E. and Thom Shanker, "N.S.A. Devises Radio Pathway Into Computers," *New York Times*, January 14, 2014, http://www.nytimes.com/2014/01/15/us/nsa-effort-pries-open-computers-not-connected-to-internet.html (accessed December 23, 2014).

Savage, David G., "Court Deems Phones Private," *Los Angeles Times*, June 26, 2014.

Shortal, Jana, "Target says PIN Numbers Were Taken in Data Breach," KARE News, December 27, 2013, http://www.kare11.com/story/news/local/2013/12/27/pin-numbers-taken-in-target-data-breach/4227707/ (accessed December 18, 2014).

Smallwood, Christine, "Spike Jonze's Abandonment Issues," *New Yorker*, December 23, 2013, http://www.newyorker.com/online/blogs/culture/2013/12/spike-jonze-separation-anxieties.html (accessed December 18, 2014).

Steinhafel, Gregg, "A Message From CEO Gregg Steinhafel About Target's Payment Card Issues," Corporate Target, December 20, 2013, https://corporate.target.com/discover/article/Important-Notice-Unauthorized-access-to-payment-ca (accessed December 18, 2014).

Wiener, Norbert, *The Human Use of Human Beings*, (Boston, Houghton-Mifflin, 1954).

Yahoo!, Ethics Code, https://secure.ethicspoint.com/domain/media/en/gui/20988/YahooCode.pdf (accessed December 18, 2014).

Unit 2

Moral Leadership:
Ethical Theory

2.1

Aerial Surveillance
Ethical Theory

Spotlight: *The Insider*

> *Mike Wallace: And do you wish you hadn't come forward? Do you wish you hadn't blown the whistle?*
> *Jeffrey Wigand: There are times when I wish I hadn't done it. There are times when I feel compelled to do it. If you asked me, would I do it again, do I think it's worth it? Yeah I think it's worth it.*
> —The Insider

Thanks to movies we gain a greater appreciation of the ways in which morality can impact, even define, our lives. As a vehicle for an inquiry into Business Ethics, it's perfect for the job. There's nothing like a good story unfolding on the screen. As we saw in Unit 1, movies are an engaging way to navigate the ethical domain. The moral dilemmas in film work in tandem with actual cases as tools for learning Business Ethics. From the Tylenol poisoning to Costco's contaminated berries we have opportunities to develop our moral reasoning skills. Movies also allow us to observe moral conflicts, dig into ethical dilemmas, and reflect on ethical decision-making.

The moral journey calls us to consider the options, assess the evidence, and take or restrain from action. As shown by *Michael Clayton* and *Sleep Dealer*, they can turn the spotlight on duplicitous acts or ethical shortcomings on the part of corporate lawyers, co-workers, and management. They also show us—magnified so we can examine moral reasoning up close—how people *are* capable of doing the right thing.

That we need to survey the underlying values and competing worldviews comes with the territory. It is vital that we think carefully about the moral basis of our decision-making. Each decision carries with it the weight of responsibility and accountability. Some decisions allow for

Business Ethics Through Movies: A Case Study Approach, First Edition. Wanda Teays.
© 2015 John Wiley & Sons, Ltd. Published 2015 by John Wiley & Sons, Ltd.

revision, adjustment, and modification like clay in our hands. Others can't be taken back; they are set in stone. Such parameters are important to factor into our moral reasoning.

In this unit, we will investigate the major ethical theories and their value in exploring the moral dimension of our lives. They not only give us insight into some of the greatest thinkers of human history, they also give us insight into our own ways of thinking. We stand to gain by being able to justify our beliefs and opinions by drawing from these ethical theories.

It is equally useful to set an ethical context to examine and evaluate problems. The benefit of being able to call on your allies to back up your claims is not to be underestimated. And being able to get into the minds of your opponents, anticipate their criticism, and have your response ready is formidable.

Ethical theories are a powerful tool. They provide a framework of analysis and reflection. Each ethical framework can be taken to cases presented on the screen, as well as to real-world cases that we tackle in Business Ethics. The techniques and process of applying the Case Study Checklist (Chapter 1.1) shows that to be the case. The benefits are tangible. We learn more about the different theories, gain more insight into moral reasoning, and become more adept at incorporating those insights in our own ethical decision-making. With such means at our disposal, we can get a better grasp of Business Ethics, and do so with skill and care.

As we saw in Unit 1, movies function in a similar fashion to case studies by presenting ethical dilemmas within specific contexts. They allow us to see different perspectives and gauge the wisdom of one choice or another. There is a quality, a richness that makes movies useful to reflecting on ethics and analyzing decision-making and its aftermath. By offering a window into human nature, they help us get a greater sense of purpose in our lives. They can also present issues and concerns that impact all ethical aspects of the business world. That they do so in engaging ways is all to the better.

The two key approaches we acquire from studying ethics are conceptual and practical. One path, the conceptual, is called *Metaethics*; the other, the pragmatic and experiential path, is called *Normative Ethics*. In *Metaethics*, we look at ethical theory and such value-related terms as "good," "virtuous," "bad," "vicious," "shame," and "guilt"—not to mention concepts like moral agency, rationality, competence, moral personhood, and moral duty. Metaethics is, therefore, more abstract, for when we follow this path our attention is focused on ideas and theories (comparing, contrasting, fleshing out).

In Metaethics we examine ethical frameworks, as well as the principles and guidelines that structure ethical decision-making. We also look at the key concepts underlying theories and the ethical codes that play such a vital role in both corporations and professional organizations.

In *Normative Ethics*, we focus on moral decision-making, the practical side of ethics. Having moral "street smarts" is useful for surveying and applying the ethical structure of theory and ideas. This makes all the difference in framing issues and justifying decisions.

We put theory to use in Normative Ethics. Here, we're deciding what is the right thing to do in a particular situation. We give thought to what we've done—or what others have done. We then decide, "That sure was a good decision and took guts to make!" or "She wasn't as honest as she should have been" and so on.

With Normative Ethics, we reflect on moral reasoning in context, offer advice, and make judgments. Normative Ethics brings ethics into the world. We jump into the stream of morality, see what ought to be done, and make a decision—or let others do the thinking for us.

These two types of ethics shape our approach to Business Ethics through film. We use the tools of Metaethics to open up and examine the different theories—noting similarities and differences, assessing their value as theoretical models, and contrasting their principles. With the tools of Normative Ethics, we apply an ethical theory to analyze a movie and the ethical dilemmas it presents. This entails examining how the protagonist confronts them and what decisions are taken.

Moral Agency

Moral agency has to do with being capable of moral decision-making, being responsible for our actions. There are two major factors to moral agency, namely *free will* and *rationality* (= competence). To be held responsible for our actions and intentions, we must be *free* to decide and act. This means we are not under compulsion, coercion, or threat to do one thing or another.

The second aspect of moral agency, the rational component, is knowledge of good versus evil. To be held responsible for our actions and intentions we must have the cognitive ability to tell right from wrong. A great deal turns on competence. Children, retarded people, comatose or unconscious patients are not ordinarily deemed competent and, therefore, their moral agency would be mitigated or set aside. However, sometimes children and teenagers are deemed competent to be held accountable for their actions. For some, that means they are prosecuted as adults. Given the range of issues around moral agency, it is prudent to examine the particulars and assess the moral agency of those whose actions and intentions are being reviewed.

This unit provides an overview of the major ethical theories. Each theory functions as a tool of discovery by highlighting the key concerns, the social/historical context, and clarifying the parameters. Ethical theories also illuminate the moral aspects of problem solving by emphasizing particular values that help set boundaries on the ethical dilemma.

The ethical theories we will look at here are:

- Teleological Theories—focused on goals and ends (Ethical Egoism, Ethical Relativism, Utilitarianism)
- Deontological Theories—focused on moral duty and obligations
- Virtue Ethics—focused on moral character
- Feminist Ethics—focused on moral agency and relationships

SPOTLIGHT: *The Insider*

The Insider (1999) is the story of two men who stand up for what they think is right. The first is a tobacco industry chemist and the second is a journalist for CBS. We see each one take risks and stick his neck out, trying to bring attention to the health risks of tobacco.

First, there's the whistleblower, Jeffrey Wigand, who works for Brown & Williamson tobacco company. In an interview with Mike Wallace of *60 Minutes*, Wigand says, "Part of the reason I'm here is that I felt that their representations clearly misstated—at least within Brown and Williamson's misrepresentations—clearly misstated what is common language within the company: 'We are in the nicotine delivery business.'"

Having been Vice President of Research and Development, Wigand is in a position to make life uncomfortable for the company. He discovers that Brown & Williamson was in cahoots with other tobacco companies to create physiologically addictive cigarettes. This was done by using ammonia to boost cigarettes' impact and sell them to an unsuspecting public.

Secondly, there's the journalist, Lowell Bergman. He's a pivotal figure at CBS and regularly works with Mike Wallace, anchor of the TV news show *60 Minutes*. He has no qualms about taking on controversial subjects or risky assignments. His instruction to get background information on cigarette smoking was the catalyst to contacting Wigand, who indicated there was a much bigger story—one with the makings of a bombshell.

The movie is powerful on both fronts. We see the human cost of being a whistleblower. This includes putting oneself at risk, enduring threats and intimidation. We see the extent people will go to silence those with incriminating evidence. Wigand suffers death threats via email, bullets put in mail boxes as warning signals, stalking, listening devices ("bugs") in his house, and so on. His family is subjected to a reign of violence. It's no surprise when the victims snap, as we see with his wife, Liane.

Wigand shows the extent to which the whistleblower is on his own, alienated from most if not all of his ties and overcome with guilt that his family has been made to suffer. The inclination to bag it and move on is understandable in such circumstances. That there are whistleblowers like Wigand, who hang in there and stand up against wrongdoers, is impressive.

Similarly, there are journalists who are also risk-takers. Dana Priest of the *Washington Post*, Tim Golden of *The New York Times*, Seymour Hersh and Jane Mayer of *The New Yorker* come to mind. They show their own moral fiber and willingness to take personal risks to bring ugly and/or disturbing truths to light. This we saw with their coverage of the CIA's practice of extraordinary rendition and the abuse and torture of detainees in the war on terror. In *The Insider*, Lowell Bergman shows similar integrity.

Applying the Theories

Let's proceed by looking at Teleological Ethics, Deontological Ethics, Virtue Ethics, and Feminist Ethics. Marxism and Rawls' Justice Theory were examined in the first unit (Chapter 1.3). Since Marxism has had a significant influence on the way we think about businesses, economic classes, and corporate and political structures, it is good to recognize it and Rawls' justice theory alongside other value-centered theories.

Teleological Theories

Teleological Ethicists focus on goals and consequences, rather than the means or intentions. Teleological Ethics is often referred to as Consequentialist Ethics, given its emphasis on ends over means. The goal is to maximize goods or benefits and minimize harms or disadvantages—and the focus could be an individual, group, business or institution or a community. Teleological theories fall into three categories: Ethical Egoism, Ethical Relativism, and Utilitarianism. Let's get an overview of each and why the third (Utilitarianism) is taken most seriously.

Ethical Egoism   The Ethical Egoist focuses on self-interest. Choose the option that will produce the greatest benefit or least harm for oneself.

Put *consequences* above intentions or moral obligations. Adopt the motto "Me, me, me, and ME!" Everyone else's interests recede and should have little, if any, weight in decision-making unless doing so would be advantageous to you! Any attention to the welfare of others—any altruism—should benefit yourself, not anyone else. Because it does not give credence to the concerns of others, Ethical Egoism has limited value as an ethical theory.

Applying the Model   An Ethical Egoist would advise Wigand to try to maximize his own happiness and self-interest. The question is if being a whistleblower would meet that goal. Given the headaches and risks he took, the answer would likely be "No."

A better option would be to keep his job with its good salary and health care for his family or negotiate a handsome severance pay and find another job. Of course, he might get a reward for putting public interest in such high esteem, but that seems a long shot.

The situation with Lowell Bergman is similar. Sure he might gain fame for such a big news story, but he'd have more job security if he didn't rock the boat. Ethical Egoists tell him to keep his eyes on his own self-interest, his own benefit and not that of others (unless it brought him some gain).

Ethical Relativism   Ethical Relativism foregrounds the values and interests of a group or organization. This would include corporations. There may be shared principles or values, but the bottom line is that the group's interests take precedence over those of individuals. That "group" could be a culture, a subculture, a professional organization, an ethnic group, a religious organization, a bunch of activists or political allies, a gang, a terrorist cell, and so on. It could also be a corporation.

With Ethical Relativism the group's interests are to be maximized, even if the individual is at the losing end of that value system. In other words, what benefits the group may be a disadvantage to individual members and entail personal sacrifices. The individual who accedes to the group leaves their independence, and to some degree their rationality, at the door. Just following what the group or culture tells us to do or think deflates individuals' moral reasoning and makes Ethical Relativists vulnerable to questionable or even dangerous decision-making.

On the other hand, Cultural Relativism allows for multiple—legitimate—moral points of view. From a global perspective, this could level the playing field and offer advantages not otherwise present to less powerful groups (or businesses or countries) relative to those having more power and more clout.

Applying the Model   Identify the group whose interests are to be maximized. The most obvious group in *The Insider* is Brown & Williamson.
Would their interests be served by a cover-up or by having the public
know that cigarettes were engineered for addiction? Lying to the
public may be preferable in the short term, as profits might then stay
stable.

In the long run, the fact of physiologically addictive components in cigarettes may be something consumers would tolerate. The threat of cancer
hasn't been much of a deterrent. In either scenario, Brown & Williamson
would prevail.

Utilitarianism   The   dominant   form   of   Teleological   Ethics   is
Utilitarianism. It dictates that we should maximize good or happiness and
minimize evil or unhappiness for the greatest number of people. Aim for
societal benefits; favor consequences, not the intention or moral principle
behind the act. Utilitarians put society's interests above those of any
individual. In fact, Utilitarianism allows for individuals to be sacrificed for
the public good (e.g., with the death penalty).

Utilitarians favor a cost–benefit analysis, where we select the option
with the highest ratio of gains. Weigh the potential consequences and then
select the best of the lot. The means to the end are of lesser consequence.

The Big Three Utilitarians are Jeremy Bentham, John Stuart Mill, and
G.E. Moore. They recommended we follow what is called a *Principle of
Utility* (thus, the term "Utilitarian"!). Its basic structure is this:

> *Choose that act that will result in the greatest* _____ *and the least* _____ *for the
> greatest number of people.*

Each ethicist filled in the blanks differently. For Bentham, it was pleasure vs. pain; for Mill, happiness vs. unhappiness (in terms of social benefits); and for Moore, good vs. evil. They do not seek universal satisfaction,
but rather the most for the most—the majority.

There are two main forms of Utilitarianism—Act and Rule. They both
try to maximize good or happiness and minimize evil or unhappiness, but
differ in the scope to which the Principle of Utility is applied. Act
Utilitarianism has a much narrower target than Rule Utilitarianism, as we
will see.

Act Utilitarianism   Act Utilitarians would have us choose what leads to
the best consequences overall for the greatest number of people *directly
affected* by the act in question—for *that particular case*. Weigh each

case with this in mind. The cost–benefit assessment of the specific dilemma shapes the decision and, thus, Act Utilitarians proceed on a case-by-case basis.

Applying the Model   An Act Utilitarian would look at Jeffrey Wigand, his wife Liane, and two daughters, and advise him to choose that act that would result in the greatest good or least harm for him and his family, and anyone else directly affected by his decision to blow the whistle. We might say all smokers are directly affected by his decision, so their interests *could* be factored in as well.

The family and smoking consumers do not share the same interests. Wigand's family would be better served if he did not blow the whistle. As the movie shows, exposing Brown & Williamson is dangerous, and resulted in a broken marriage with Wigand's career on the skids. Smokers may benefit from knowing the harm caused by tobacco, but perhaps Wigand doesn't need to be the one who's out on a limb.

Rule Utilitarianism   A Rule Utilitarian would advise Wigand to choose that act that would result in the best consequences for the greatest number of people, not just those directly affected. This asks us to consider each case as a *precedent*, thus generalizing and applying it to all similar cases. This is quite different from Act Utilitarianism's focus on the particular case, its context, and those people directly affected by the decision.

Applying the Model   A Rule Utilitarian would want us to benefit the majority of people. Surely people would be better off knowing the truth about the addictive qualities of cigarettes produced by Big Tobacco. Consumers may appreciate knowing that CEOs deluded them by misrepresenting the situation.

Of course, smokers might continue to smoke, addiction or no addiction. However, Utilitarians would recommend they make an *informed* decision in electing to do so. There is no way for that decision to be informed without disclosure of the facts of the case.

Turning this into a policy, therefore, would ask us to emphasize the society over the individual when weighing the costs and benefits. In Wigand's case, his family interests would indicate it's best to keep his mouth shut. However, societal interests would favor his speaking out and being an expert witness in a class action suit in Mississippi. Similarly, it benefits society for *60 Minutes* to air the interview, even though CBS corporate has a conflict of interest in doing so. That they are financially beholden to Brown & Williamson poses a problem.

Deontological Ethics

Deontological Ethics emphasizes duties and intentions rather than end results or goals. In that sense, this theory is the flipside of Teleological Ethics. The focus here is on moral obligations, not consequences. Followers of Deontological Ethics approach ethical decisions in terms of moral principles, ethical codes or moral duties; e.g., "Always tell the truth," "Don't steal," "Protect small children from harm," and so on. Basically, they subscribe to the view that intentions inform actions and an undesirable consequence is irrelevant to the question of whether the decision was good.

What follows from this ethical perspective is that Deontological Ethicists emphasize individual rights over societal benefits. Such rights are to be defended, even if the society as a whole would benefit more from sacrificing a minority for the good of the majority.

Kantian Ethics Immanuel Kant is *Numero Uno* in Deontological Ethics. Like Mill, he puts a lot of emphasis on rationality, but, unlike Mill, he doesn't see societal benefits as a primary goal. His concern is the individual, and respect for persons. In his view, human dignity is identified with the capacity for rationality.

Moral agents must be rational and have free will. All having these two characteristics should have equal moral status. Kant, then, would exclude children, incompetent adults, or anyone else whose mental capacity is compromised so they are no longer capable of making a reasoned decision.

Kant's system has two ethical principles to guide our decision-making. They are moral commands meant to apply across the board to all rational adults (= moral agents).

Kant's Two Moral Principles

The *Categorical Imperative*
Act in such a way that you would have it become a universal law.
➡ *Universalize ethical decision-making.*

The *Humanitarian Principle*
Always treat others as an end in themselves, never merely as a means.
➡ *Treat others with respect and human dignity.*

What follows from Kant's two principles: The first one would have us ask ourselves, "What if *everyone* did this?" If it would be acceptable for all to follow suit, then the action is morally permissible. Kant wants us to universalize moral decision-making. That is the thrust of his Categorical Imperative. His Humanitarian Principle holds that we should never use other people merely as a means to an end. Rather, treat people with dignity and respect.

Applying the Model   In the case of Jeffrey Wigand, a Kantian wouldn't blink an eye about his decision to take on Brown & Williamson. In exposing the lies and misinformation Wigand cites the "nicotine is not addictive" testimony before Congress, derogatorily calling the CEOs the "seven dwarves." Wigand laid bare the fact they perjured themselves.

The actual testimony moves from one CEO claiming, "I believe nicotine is not addictive" to the next. Twisting words is illustrated by the testimony before Congress of the Chairman and CEO, of the RJ Reynolds corporation, James Johnston: "Mr. Congressman, cigarettes and nicotine clearly do not meet the *classic* definition of addiction. There is no intoxication" (my emphasis).

Note the adjective "classic." This use of words weasels around what addiction incurs. How terms are used tell us a lot about the underlying values and beliefs. There's a reason Wittgenstein wanted us to pay attention to the *use* of language, not just the meaning.

Lowell Bergman wants CBS to bust this wide open, and put Wigand on *60 Minutes.* He is outraged when the corporate honchos retreated from airing the explosive interview. Bergman blows a gasket:

> LOWELL BERGMAN: You pay me to go get guys like Wigand, to draw him out. To get him to trust us, to get him to go on television. I do. I deliver him. He sits. He talks. He violates his own fucking confidentiality agreement. And he's only the key witness in the biggest public health reform issue, maybe the biggest, most-expensive corporate-malfeasance case in US history.
> And Jeffrey Wigand, who's out on a limb, does he go on television and tell the truth? Yes. Is it newsworthy? Yes. Are we gonna air it? Of course not. Why? Because he's not telling the truth? No. Because he *is* telling the truth. That's why we're not going to air it. And the more truth he tells, the worse it gets!

This is a movie about the truth and what telling the truth may ask of us. Kant is unbending in his moral requirement that we universalize our decisions. Where some find this brittle and potentially harmful, Kant would say it's the only moral option. And risk or no risk to Wigand's family, there's only one thing Kant would have him do. Tell the truth.

Kant would advise Wigand to be a role model; to do what he'd want everyone else to do. "Universalize your ethical decisions," Kant says. That might be hard advice to take, however. Would Wigand really want others to put *their* families at risk? It is hard to turn this into a universal law. Consequently, he wouldn't find it easy to be a Kantian. That said, Kant would give a nod to Wigand's directness and honesty.

W.D. Ross's Prima Facie Duties Deontological ethicist W.D. Ross sees Kant as too fixated on the present. He'd say we need to factor in the past and future to get a more balanced approach to ethical decision-making. Ross, like Kant, emphasizes moral duties, but thinks we'll intuitively know which of his seven duties to apply in a given situation. These he calls "Prima Facie" duties, because on the surface they are of equal value. On a case-by-case basis, the most relevant duties will be apparent.

Ross's Prima Facie Duties

* Veracity (Honesty and promise-keeping)
* Beneficence (Do good)
* Non-maleficence (Do no harm)
* Justice
* Gratitude (Loyalty)
* Reparations (Compensate for harm done)
* Self-improvement

These duties are in no particular order and are of equal merit until we face a particular case. At that point we decide which ones to draw on. Ross values honesty, but justice or non-maleficence may take precedence if telling the truth would result in serious harm.

Applying the Model Ross would look at Jeffrey Wigand and Lowell Bergman and see how several of his prima facie duties played a role in their lives. He would understand why Wigand is unsure whether to breach the confidentiality agreement and testify in a trial in Mississippi.

We saw earlier in the movie that Wigand was upset with Brown & Williamson's chairman, Thomas Sandefur, for the way he was treated. He told Sandefur, "So, what you're saying is it wasn't enough to fire me for no good reason. Now you question my integrity? On top of the humiliation of being fired, you threaten me? You threaten my family? It never crossed my mind not to honor my agreement." Wigand is beside himself.

Ross would note that it's good for Wigand to expose Brown & Williamson. People need to know that tobacco companies are adding ammonia and other chemicals to increase nicotine's effects and, thus, the impact of cigarettes. But he's torn by the competing duty of nonmaleficence—to keep his family from harm. It is a heavy weight on his shoulders.

Bergman is disgusted with CBS's reluctance to air the story. If he looked at Ross's list of prima facie duties, he'd see all sorts of violations. One is a failure to keep the promise made to Wigand that, if he came forward CBS would air the *60 Minutes* interview with Mike Wallace. Not so. Bergman decries that fact: "What do I tell my source for the next tough story, huh? 'Hang in with us, you'll be OK maybe'?" "No." He adds, "What got broken here doesn't go back together."

Ross would commend Wigand's courage and think it unjust of CBS to lead Wigand on and then drop him like a hot potato. He would argue that Wigand, Bergman, and Wallace all have moral duties that should be honored.

John Rawls' "Justice as Fairness"   Rawls is another Deontological Ethicist who emphasizes moral duty. He turns his attention to justice and is particularly interested in trying to address injustice within social institutions. His approach is to try to eliminate personal bias so that we distance ourselves from our own personal attachments and affiliations (nationality, religion, political party, etc.). He hopes this will then level the playing field and put in place a system of social justice. We could then be able to build a social contract that would eliminate prejudice and other forms of injustice.

Applying the Model   Rawls would agree with Kant that honesty was a central value in this situation. He would commend Wigand's attempt to step forward and disclose the truth that Brown & Williamson was trying so hard to suppress. And he would agree with Ross that justice is an important moral duty in this situation.

That Big Tobacco has created a product that is destructive in its impact and with such addictive qualities would not set well with Rawls. He'd say it was unjust to knowingly engineer a product to hook its users and send them down a road of addiction and ill health. That this has been done in secret is particularly troublesome, as people can't exercise free choice if they are in the dark. Consumers should be able to make a decision based on *informed* consent, not just voluntary consent.

We can see how justice figures into *The Insider* when Bergman tells Wallace, "This guy [Wigand] is the top scientist in the number three tobacco company in America. He's a corporate officer.... This guy is the ultimate insider." Wallace thinks it ludicrous that Brown & Williamson could hold Wigand to a confidentiality clause under the circumstances. "He's got a corporate secrecy agreement? Give me a break," he says. "This is a public-health issue, like an unsafe airframe on a passenger jet or... some company dumping cyanide into the East River. Issues like that? He can talk; we can air it. They've got no right to hide behind a corporate agreement." If this isn't a justice issue, what is?

It doesn't end there. Wallace is informed of Big Tobacco's power—one not beholden to justice. We see it in CBS's John Harris and Mark Stern's reply to Wallace:

JOHN HARRIS: They don't need the right. They've got the money.

MARK STERN: The unlimited checkbook. That's how Big Tobacco wins every time.
On everything. They spend you to death. $600 million a year in outside legal. ...These clowns have never...I mean ever...Not even with hundreds of thousands dying each year from an illness related to their product...have ever lost a personal-injury lawsuit. On this case, they'll issue gag orders, sue for breach, anticipatory breach, enjoin him, you, us, his pet dog, the dog's veterinarian... Tie him up in litigation for ten or fifteen years. I'm telling you, they bat a thousand. Every time. He knows that. That's why he's not gonna talk to you...

Rawls would see the machinations of power, the testimony of the CEOs before Congress, the public health issues *not* being brought into the open, the threats and intimidation employed against Wigand. He would see all that and argue that losing sight of the moral duty of justice was a fundamental failure of several key institutions. He would salute both Wigand and Bergman for their persistence and courage.

Virtue Ethics

Virtue Ethics fits its name, because it emphasizes virtues as the way to the good life—a life of flourishing and well-being. In contrast to Teleological Ethics (goal-based) and Deontological Ethics (duty-based), Virtue Ethics looks to moral character as the central ethical concern.

Aristotle is the heart and soul of Virtue Ethics. The Chinese philosopher Confucius is also focused on leading a virtuous life. He puts a lot of emphasis on the virtues tied to particular roles we play by virtue of our relationships. I will focus here on Aristotle, but you may find it enlightening to look into Confucius as well.

Aristotle looks at rational individuals (= moral agents) and asks us to examine our moral character. Put that under the spotlight. Neither consequences nor moral obligations should take priority over living a life of virtue (and avoiding vices). That's the path to finding purpose in our lives.

Aristotle emphasizes two kinds of virtues—intellectual virtues and moral virtues. His intellectual virtues are:

1   Artistic knowledge and creativity
2   Analytical and logical knowledge
3   Practical wisdom ("street smarts" about what we ought to do)
4   Philosophical wisdom (about ultimate things)
5   Understanding and comprehension (so we can make judgments)

Most people focus on Aristotle's moral virtues and their role in developing moral character. But don't underestimate the value of his intellectual virtues. Both types of virtues play a role in achieving a meaningful life. So how do we get there from here? Well, for Aristotle, we need to practice a life of moderation.

Seek a life of balance and you'll be on our way to excellence of character. Aim for the mean and avoid the extremes. That should be our mantra, Aristotle would say. This is the way to virtue and a fulfilling life. Certainly, moderation may not be the best choice. In the face of injustice or acts of violence against innocent others, the morally correct response may not be at all "moderate." That's why Aristotle considered "righteous indignation" a virtue.

Generally, however, Aristotle recommends the middle path. Many character dispositions or moral traits fall along a spectrum of *deficient* → *mean* → *excessive*. In that case Aristotle would tell us to seek the mean. Thus, for example, courage is the mean between cowardice and recklessness, generosity is the mean between being stingy or wasteful, and compassion is the mean between callousness and sentimentality.

Applying the Model   Wigand's opponents had every reason to worry. He's highly qualified to raise health concerns and he can't be bought off. Thomas Sandefur of Brown & Williamson observes that "Jeffrey says exactly what's on his mind," and "Jeffrey just charges right ahead." He is also aware of Wigand's strength of character. Consequently, he's right to worry about Wigand disclosing what he knows.

Aristotle would applaud Wigand's decision to blow the whistle. He would also applaud his decision to go to court in the state of Mississippi as an expert witness, even though it meant violating his confidentiality agreement. Not an easy decision. After being confronted with the possibility of going to jail if he testified, Wigand was in knots. He wanted to bring the truth to light about cigarettes, but he did not want his family to suffer. He was especially concerned that they'd lose their healthcare insurance if he went to jail.

Wigand was caught on the horns of a dilemma. He walked outside, away from Bergman and the various lawyers in the class action suit against Phillip Morris. We watch him pace back and forth, look out to sea, and struggle to find criteria to provide some clarity as to what to do. He saw no such criteria. There were no moral duties to point the way, no principle of utility to shed light on the best choice. We watch Wigand, holding our breath, waiting to see what he'll do. He tells Bergman, "I can't seem to find… the criteria to decide. It's too big a decision to make without being resolved… in my own mind."

Nothing will be the same again. His former life is in tatters. But he *can* go forward by staying true to the moral qualities, those virtues he holds dear. Aristotle would say, "Focus on what kind of person you want to be and what intellectual and moral traits are required to get there." This should guide you. And so it is that Wigand makes up his mind: "Fuck it. Let's go to court."

Wigand is not swayed by moral obligations (since they're in conflict) and not by maximizing societal good or happiness (also in conflict). But he gets it: Everything has changed "since whenever," and no one else can say what's the right thing to do. His decision reveals kind of person he is—or wants to be. This is about moral character.

Feminist (Care) Ethics

This ethical theory focuses on relationships and how they shape moral reasoning. Feminist Ethicists see neither moral duty nor consequences as the overriding concern of ethical decision-making. And they do not see rationality as the kernel of moral agency. By considering relationships of fundamental importance when assessing values, intentions, and actions, Feminist Ethicists emphasize the practical, the experiential dimension of our lives.

The foremost Feminist Ethicists are Mary Anne Warren, Nel Noddings, and Rita Manning. Carol Gilligan played an early pivotal role by arguing that women and men tend to differ in their approach to moral reasoning. Fundamental to Feminist ethicists is the view that relationships need to be factored in. We see this with Manning's two elements to an Ethics of Care.

Manning's Two Elements to an Ethics of Care

A disposition to care
We are called to attend to others' needs.
Caring is a goal, an ideal.
➥ *People are disposed to care about one another.*

The obligation to care for
Caring for another requires action, not just intentions.
Caring for others can be expanded to communities, values, or objects.
➥ *Responding to the needs of others is a moral obligation.*

Care Ethicists like Manning suggest we listen to the voices of both care and justice when confronted with ethical choices. See yourself as standing in a caring relationship with others. Reflect on rules and rights but don't restrict yourself—justice shouldn't be the only or major goal. Even in a just world, Manning contends, human needs include more than needs for physical sustenance; thus the emphasis on caring for one another.

Broader View of Moral Agency   Feminist ethicists also give thought to moral status and moral agency. Mary Anne Warren argues that moral status does not rest on any *one* defining characteristic. This contrasts with Kant's view that being a rational person is key, and also with Utilitarian Peter Singer's view that sentience is primary to moral agency. Both are too limited, she says.

Applying the Model   A Feminist Ethicist would say that Wigand is right to be so concerned with the impact on his family when he decided to blow the whistle and when weighing whether to be an expert witness in the Mississippi class action suit against Big Tobacco. There was no way he could wipe away such concerns. Feminist Ethicists would commend that way of thinking and commiserate with him as he tried to balance the care and justice aspects of his dilemma.

In addition, a Feminist Ethicist would look at the attention given to the confidentiality agreement and say Brown & Williamson used that principle ("Keep your promise") in an unjust and uncaring way—not to mention as a way to further their own interests. Brown & Williamson was interested in keeping the lid on the situation so as to ensure as little damage to their reputation and financial stability as possible. They certainly were not interested in retaining a respectful relationship with Wigand and had no reluctance to use his love of his family to achieve their ends.

Similarly, those like Manning who see a role for justice being factored into the equation would understand Wigand's desire to proceed with the *60 Minutes* interview. They'd sympathize with being so upset that it was not aired in its totality. He had put himself and his family at risk and CBS failed him; that much Feminist Ethicists would understand.

The remaining chapters in this unit present the various theories which are used as a framework to apply to our films and actual cases in Business Ethics.

Works Cited

Aristotle, *Poetics*, The Internet Classics Archive, http://classics.mit.edu/Aristotle/poetics.html (accessed December 18, 2014).

Manning, Rita C., *Speaking From the Heart*, (Lanham, MD: Rowman and Littlefield, 1992).

Warren, Mary Anne, *Moral Status*, (Oxford: Oxford University Press, 1997).

2.2

The Ends Justify the Means
Teleological Ethics

Spotlight: *Contagion*; *Park Avenue: Money, Power and the American Dream*; *Blue Jasmine*
Case Study: The Ford Pinto
Ethics Code: Ford Motor Company

> *Alan Krumwiede: After the Spanish Flu, nineteen-eighteen, you know? People got rich. The Vick's Vapo Rub people, the Lysol people, look it up. One man dies, another man makes money off his coffin.*
> *Hedge Fund Man: I don't think anyone is immune to opportunity, Alan. It's just that the studies show that there is no proof that Forsythia works.*
>
> —Contagion

> *Jasmine: It's not the money. It's the money. (Quoting husband Hal)*
> —Blue Jasmine

Some people try to profit from just about any situation that can be exploited. That they don't care who may suffer is grist for their mill. If there's one thing you can be sure of—and this one thing you *can* be sure of—is that they always look out for themselves. Alan Krumwiede is such a man.

When a virus started to spread from one person to the next and its victims began dying like flies, Alan saw this as a great opportunity. Make money off of the misfortunes of others? No problem! Remember the tale about the goose with the golden egg? Well this goose is laying lots of eggs and Alan plans to collect a few. We watch him hatch his scheme in *Contagion* (2011). He is an Ethical Egoist.

Teleological Ethics is often referred to as "Consequentialism" because of its emphasis on end goals. By putting the emphasis on objectives over moral obligations, their rallying cry is, "The ends justify the means." In

Business Ethics Through Movies: A Case Study Approach, First Edition. Wanda Teays.
© 2015 John Wiley & Sons, Ltd. Published 2015 by John Wiley & Sons, Ltd.

this chapter we look at Teleological Ethics and its three main branches—Ethical Egoism, Cultural Relativism, and Utilitarianism. We'll see what distinguishes each theory and apply them to *Contagion*, *Park Avenue*, and *Blue Jasmine*. We will also look at the Ford Pinto case, using Teleological Ethics as our framework. We'll then look at Ford's Code of Conduct. Let's start with Ethical Egoism.

Ethical Framework: Ethical Egoism

Ethical Egoists are at one end of the spectrum of Teleological Ethics. They share the view that ethical decision-making should be guided by a cost–benefit assessment in which end goals rule. Intentions or means are a distant second. Their top priority is self-interest. The interests of others would only be factored into moral reasoning if there would be some personal payoff. If I don't stand to gain from helping you, then, "Hasta la vista, baby!" I will help you *if* it's to my advantage, but only then.

Ethical Egoists may or may not be *psychological* egoists—who think it is human nature to be self-centered. This is a view held by Thomas Hobbes (of "the life of man ... nasty, brutish, and short" fame), as Alexander Moseley (2005) observes. In contrast, the focus of Ethical Egoism is on moral guidelines about what we *ought* to do and not scientific descriptions of *Homo sapiens*. The question is not if people are *innately* self-centered, but what values we should be operating with.

As philosopher Lawrence Hinman notes, the everyday form of Ethical Egoism is *Personal* Egoism, which emphasizes an individual's self interest above all else (Hinman, 1994, p. 132). The advice from this quarter would be to calculate carefully the best overall net benefits for oneself and make a plan. In contrast, *Universal* Egoism takes a more general stance, arguing that *all* people should jump on this bandwagon—that everyone should put their own self-interest first (Hinman, 137).

The most famous proponent of this view is the philosopher–novelist Ayn Rand, a staunch defender of individualism. She thinks it right and good for self-interest to be the guiding light of moral reasoning. You may have heard about her in speeches by Paul Ryan, Republican candidate for Vice President in the 2012 election. There is some debate over just how much of her philosophy Ryan adopted, but her stress on individualism and the importance of keeping one's own interests firmly in mind appear to have swayed his political views.

Ayn Rand has been influential, and politicians like Paul Ryan are testimony to that fact. The editor of *The Atlantic*, Garance Franke-Ruta, contrasts Ayn Rand with Karl Marx: "The enduring heart of Rand's totalistic philosophy was Marxism flipped upside down. Rand viewed the capitalists, not the workers, as the producers of all wealth, and the workers, not the capitalists, as useless parasites" (2011).

Not all would agree with the critical thrust of that characterization. However, Rand does favor a capitalistic system and shows little sympathy for those who don't take responsibility for their own path to success. Others hold a similar view about the importance of us not relying on others (or the government) to get ahead in careers or in life.

Universal Egoism and Business

Applying Universal Egoism to businesses, we'd rephrase the rule to say, "Every corporation ought to act in its own self-interest." On the surface, that may sound appealing, however much it's a dog-eat-dog mentality. But by putting short-term goals above long-term interests, Universal Egoism may not achieve the company's desired goals over time.

That doesn't sound so bad until you try to generalize it. If a majority of people or businesses put self-interest above all else, that could lead to rather nasty and brutish encounters and conflicts. As Moseley (2005) suggests, disputes might then settled by "Might makes right," with the most powerful inevitably trampling all over the weaker opponent.

The alternative is setting criteria for weighing competing interests (yours versus mine). This could get contentious unless the parties involved subverted their self-interests to those of a competitor or agreed to some division (you 40 percent, me 60 percent, for example). However this could undercut the very basis of Ethical Egoism. Mediating competing interests could be like stepping though a minefield.

Universal Egoism and Capitalism

The notion that people should look out for themselves and maximize personal gain is fundamental to capitalism. In the minds of capitalists, economic self-interest is the key to a prosperous society, making it a form of Ethical Egoism, as noted by philosopher Lewis Vaughn (2010, p. 77). And in terms of Business Ethics, a corporation guided by the profit motive above all else would fall under Ethical Egoism.

You tell me: What would capitalists have us factor into decision-making? Share the wealth and level the playing field? Not likely. Their advice would be:

- Scope out the situation
- Look for ways to generate revenue
- Settle on criteria for dividing up profits
- Factor in the role of investors and other contributors
- Purely optional to factor in the needy, the public, or others lacking a rightful claim
- Distribute the profits

Basically, it is rare for charity to be factored into the capitalist's equation. Since many people would like to maximize their earnings and *not* have to share them, the emphasis on self-interest is not often a matter of dispute. Capitalism has had a tight hold on many people's economic and other preferences. But that does not mean there aren't other models to consider.

In an economic context, Universal Egoists often use a capitalistic framework: Give priority in education to those who can pay their way—ahead of the financially needy. No problem if quality medical care goes to those who can afford it while others lack basic services. Such inequalities go with the territory of Egoism.

It's not so bad if you're one of the lucky ones! But even they are vulnerable to global disasters. Think of *World War Z*: They couldn't build a wall high enough to keep the zombies from crawling over, like a swarm of locusts. And a contagious virus can spread *very* quickly. Unless you have a bomb shelter in your backyard or a very large, well-stocked cellar, the scenario set out in *World War Z* may be a wake-up call. This is also true with *Contagion*, as we'll see.

SPOTLIGHT: Contagion

Contagion is perfect for doing Teleological Ethics. It has a strong plot driven by a riveting ethical dilemma: how to allocate medical resources and distribute medicine and supplies on a massive (national) scale while seeking the source and cure for a highly contagious, devastating virus.

To avert widespread chaos, the crisis required the police, the Army, and any other security personnel who didn't go into hiding. As we saw with the nuclear disasters at Chernobyl and Fukushima, only the most self-sacrificing can be counted on when there is a high probability of death.

Contagion starts with a businesswoman, Beth Emhoff, who goes on a business trip to Hong Kong, leaving her family in Minneapolis. A photo op with a chef who had blood from an infected pig on his hands set the pandemic in motion. One touch was all it took. Beth picked up the virus and spread it to just about everyone she touched. Within a matter of days it was carried around the world. If that seems unrealistic, you might check out SARS (Branswell, 2008). One person arriving in Toronto set that epidemic in motion!

MINNESOTA MEDICAL EXAMINER: I want you to move away from the table. (*the assistant medical examiner moves away*)
ASSISTANT MEDICAL EXAMINER: Should I call someone?
MINNESOTA MEDICAL EXAMINER: Call everyone!

One death after another quickly alerts the CDC (Centers for Disease Control) and WHO (World Health Organization) that they're facing a major health crisis. Major stress! Pretty soon the *key players* are in place. There's the family: Beth Emhoff (first carrier, now dead), Mitch Emhoff (husband), step daughter Jory (both she and Mitch are immune, brother Clark dies shortly after Beth arrives home). There's the medical team: Dr. Ellis Cheever (CDC), Dr. Ellen Mears (research scientist working with Cheever), Dr. Leonora Orantes (WHO), and Dr. Ally Hextall (research doctor). And then there's gadfly and blogger Alan Krumwiede, who sees the pandemic as a money-making opportunity.

"Where is the government?" you ask. Well, they aren't out there talking to their constituents; that much we know. Until the coast is clear, the leaders have gone underground. We can't count on them to do more than pass along their advice—or prayers.

Alan Krumwiede is quick to pounce on a business venture. That he is dishonest is lamentable. His ruse of having an antidote persuaded many people to skip taking the *actual* vaccine. At the beginning of the epidemic, he reacts with suspicion. We can see he's a bit of a conspiracy theorist by the following:

LORRAINE VASQUEZ: Why doesn't anybody help him? Is he okay?
ALAN KRUMWIEDE: Read the posts. Some say it was staged, an art project. Some say the authorities wouldn't do an autopsy. Covered it up.

So Alan turns to his blog and videos, and reaches a growing audience. Fear fuels a distrust of authorities on the part of the public. As time goes by and the number of deaths escalates, fears erupt into violence, not surprisingly. With visions of dollar signs floating inside his head, Alan pretends to be sick and then magically "cured" by something he called *Forsythia*. You can bet everyone wants to get their hands on it and, so, the money rolls in. Widespread panic is often good for business and this situation was no different.

Given *Forsythia* is ineffective and most who are infected soon die, there is little chance of accountability.

HEDGE FUND MAN: People trust you, Alan. If you tell them not to take it...
ALAN KRUMWIEDE: That's right! They trust me. All twelve million unique visitors, I'm a trusted man stepping up to a microphone in front of a very large crowd. That's who I am. That's the brand. I say the right thing, nobody shows up for their shot. Maybe they'd rather roll the dice with *Forsythia*.

Eventually Alan has to deal with the authorities. There's an ethical theory that describes Alan Krumwiede's morality—and that's Ethical Egoism.

Ethical Framework: Moral and Cultural Relativism

The kernel of moral and cultural relativism is the word "*relative.*" Moral Relativists reject the view that moral principles and values are universal or absolutes. Rather, they contend that the truth or falsity of moral judgments (like "Honesty is the best policy" or "Don't eat your pets") is relative to the norms, beliefs, and traditions of a group, subculture, or society.

Moral Relativism, like Ethical Egoism, focuses on consequences, but takes a wider view than individual self-interest. It seeks to maximize benefits and minimize harms for a group or community with shared values or traditions. Of course, from one society to the next, we see a diverse range of norms and values. "Ethical relativism reminds us that different societies have different moral beliefs and that our beliefs are deeply influenced by culture," points out Manuel Velasquez (1992). He adds: "It also encourages us to explore the reasons underlying beliefs that differ from our own, while challenging us to examine our reasons for the beliefs and values we hold."

Cultural Relativism is a variation of Moral Relativism. Instead of looking at a particular group or community for moral guidance, the Cultural

Relativist looks to a religion, ethnic group, culture, or subculture. What glues members of a culture together are shared values, loyalty ("family") and a distinct identity *as* being of that particular group (self-identified). Cultural/Moral Relativists would normally go along with the culture/ group, even if it were not personally advantageous to do so. The message is: Conform. "Get with the program." You don't rat on your "homies." Stand by them and they'll stand by you if the tables are turned.

Cultural Relativism and Business

So how does this translate into a business framework? Where do we see norms and values, traditions and practices, relative to a particular group operating in the workplace? We might think of a corporation as a kind of subculture with its own ethics code and its own values, beliefs, and traditions. Think of an athlete's team loyalty (e.g., Penn State's failure to respond to sexual abuse of young males by assistant football coach, Jerry Sandusky, now serving prison time). It was years before that busted wide open.

Think also of networking at the gym, shooting hoops, drinks at lunch, playing golf to build connections with others. Many such networking venues are a variation of a good-ole-boy system. There's also relativism born of societal differences to navigate so as not to offend the host-colleague-or customer. We see this in Marina Onken's advice (you can decide if it has any merit): "The concept of time may differ widely among various cultures. In many Asian countries, a meeting called for ten o'clock may convene at twelve o'clock—with no apology for the delay."

Some Cultural Relativists think it possible to have a few shared universal principles, while holding the view that the core of ethical values and traditions are *not* universal. Many people subscribe to Cultural Relativism, at least to some degree. If we look around, we see diverse norms and traditions, suggesting that at least some values and beliefs are community-oriented or culturally bound. All sorts of people align their morality with a group or culture that they identify with or of which they are members. At times, this can be seen in a business framework as well, where moral values and beliefs are bound by social (or company ties or shaped by the group or business norms.

The truth is that some people subscribe to and validate ethical guidelines rooted in the community they identify with—whether by culture, nationality, religion, or economic ties (class), or vocation. Look at Bud Fox in the movie *Wall Street*. He wanted to be a member of the same club as Gordon Gekko. There were signs of wealth and luxury wherever he looked. Consequently, Bud turned away from his father's work ethic and sense of obligation to the guys he supervises. These values were replaced by the high-flying values Gekko subscribed to (and pressured Bud to adopt). The movie shows us the error of his ways.

There are plenty of people who subscribe to one version or another of Ethical Relativism. Let's return to *Contagion* to see the form it takes as the body count increases.

Contagion and Moral Relativism

Dr. Ellis Cheever of the CDC is a Teleological Ethicist, but not an Egoist. Cheever wants very badly to address the crisis and find a cure. He regrets having dispatched researcher Dr. Ellen Mears to Minneapolis, where she dies in a futile attempt to find the source of the virus. And yet, when the chips are down, Cheever does *not* put the public's welfare above all else. He uses his power to protect those closest to him. He is an Ethical Relativist.

Although he seeks to maximize good or benefit, his moral focus narrows dramatically in a crucial scene. When it's clear that the pandemic is spreading and no cure is in sight, a decision is made to quarantine Chicago. Cheever learns of this plan before it is made public. At that point he shows his "true colors." The very principle that all people should be treated equally is tossed to the winds, in favor of personal loyalties.

Cheever phones his wife. "I want you to get in your car and leave Chicago. I want you to drive to Atlanta, drive by yourself. You do it. You do it now. Don't tell anyone and don't stop. And stay away from other people. You understand? Keep your distance from other people. Now, call me when you're on the road, Aubrey."

He tells her two things: *One*, to get the hell out of Chicago and come to Atlanta (where the CDC and Cheever are). *Two*, tell no one. Of course we all know that no one keeps secrets (or not for long)! And sure enough, Aubrey calls her friend. Cheever's actions may seem as natural as lions guarding their cubs against a predator, but that doesn't make it commendable as a moral principle. "Choose for the benefit of the group (community, culture, gang, collection of those we love the most) over all else—even if it requires a personal sacrifice." Acting on that moral principle nearly cost Cheever his job.

Laurence Fishburne, who played the role of Cheever, commented on his decision to alert Aubrey about the quarantine. In his view, "The personal stuff that I have as Ellis Cheever was telling my fiancée, soon-to-be wife, [Aubrey], to get out of town, to leave, to pack up, to not talk.

That's really easy. Any human being in that situation is going to do that, I think"(Houx, 2011).

Fishburne thinks this is a normal human response to a life–death situation. Perhaps, but not certainly the case. Furthermore, the fact many people would do the same does not justify it. We should pay heed to the *ad populum* (= Bandwagon) fallacy that argues we should do this or that just because that would be what the majority of people would do under the circumstances.

Cheever's phone call to Aubrey is overhead by Roger, the building janitor. Roger knows the disadvantages of being working class. And he knows that he and his boy won't get preferential treatment any time soon. Cheever's face registers guilt when he sees himself reflected back in Roger's eyes. They both know that Cheever did not operate with the view of "All for one and one for all" or "I have a moral duty to treat everyone equally." No. His relativistic ethics were laid bare.

Cheever is also humiliated when Alan confronts him on TV about his moral inconsistency. Alan asks Cheever to tell people what's going on in terms of the numbers of those afflicted, but then decides to answer his own question:

ALAN KRUMWIEDE: No? I'll do it. On day one there were two people with it, and then there were four, and then it was sixteen and you think you've got it in front of you. But next it's two hundred and fifty six and then it's sixty five thousand and it's behind you and above you and all around you. In thirty steps, it's a billion sick. Three months. It's a math problem you can do on napkin. And that's where we're headed! And that's why you won't even tell us the number of the dead, will you, Dr. Cheever? But you tell your friends when to get out of Chicago before anyone else has a chance.

Moral Relativism and Class Difference

Contagion shows us characters who react to global health crises in a variety of ways, with some trying to turn it into a money-making venture, some trying to protect their loved ones, and others risking everything to save lives. The values spectrum is striking.

The next two movies approach ethical relativism from another perspective—that of economic class. In both *Park Avenue* and *Blue Jasmine*, the spotlight shifts away from those gazing over the abyss between life and death to those gazing over the abyss between wealth and poverty.

SPOTLIGHT: *Park Avenue: Money, Power and the American Dream* and *Blue Jasmine*

The documentary, *Park Avenue: Money, Power and the American Dream* (2012), illustrates a kind of class-based Moral Relativism. So does *Blue Jasmine* (2013). Both movies look at the lives of the top 1 percent in terms of wealth. For the most part, they are portrayed as oblivious or indifferent to the struggles of the shrinking middle class or those in poverty living a few blocks away. Both movies are a scathing critique of the values and insularity of the very rich who reside on Park Avenue. Each one reveals some disturbing truths.

In *Park Avenue*, we look at the super-rich, the small percentage living in opulence on Park Avenue in New York City. It's a life of privilege beyond the imagination of all but princes and kings. These are people who have it all. They get generous tax cuts, perks, bonuses, and other benefits that dramatically widened the gap between the very rich and everyone else. We see how much has changed in the last 30 or so years. Using graphs and diagrams the movie makes the argument that there has been a major shift in the distribution of wealth in the US.

Director Alex Gibney's interest is not about the philanthropic rich; it is about those with the wealth and power to further their own gains. He looks at the use of political clout to not only keep those in place, but also to guarantee their continued growth. This is echoed by the work of investigative journalist Jane Mayer. She connects the "Tea Party" movement to "libertarian billionaires" devising "numerous pressures on Congress, to continue to rig their game" (Fuchs, 2012).

The film argues that Park Avenue Über-Rich have insulated themselves from the rest of the society. Ironically enough, the images of the Park Avenue residences jut into the sky like the Eldon Tyrell's tower in *Blade Runner* and seem just as exotic.

Gibney turns his attention to various individual billionaires, slicing open the group's elitist mentality and its set of relativistic norms and values. Their extreme capitalistic values align them with Ayn Rand's Ethical Egoism. They employ a vast network of lobbyists and conspire to further their own economic interests. Like Alan Krumwiede, but on a more elevated and powerful scale, they take advantage of the ignorance, gullibility, and political weakness of others.

There's a reason Moral Relativism has its detractors. Critics point out the limitations of this ethical theory and those who are Consequentialists suggest the superior alternative—Utilitarianism. Let's go there next.

Ethical Framework: Utilitarianism

Most prominent among the Consequentialists are Utilitarians. This branch of Teleological Ethics is commonly seen as much more influential than the other two we have looked at (Ethical Egoism and Ethical Relativism). As was mentioned in Chapter 2.1, the three superstars are Jeremy Bentham, John Stuart Mill, and G.E. Moore. Each one subscribes to the Principle of Utility:

The Principle of Utility: Three Forms

Jeremy Bentham
Choose that act that would result in the greatest pleasure and least pain for the greatest number of people.
➡ *Maximize pleasure and minimize pain for the most.*

John Stuart Mill
Choose that act that would result in the greatest happiness and least unhappiness for the greatest number of people.
➡ *Maximize happiness and minimize unhappiness for the most.*

G.E. Moore
Choose that act that would result in the greatest good and least evil for the greatest number of people.
➡ *Maximize good and minimize evil for the most.*

As you can see, all three focus on consequences. What we should maximize versus minimize, however, differs from one form to the next. It ranges from pleasure vs. pain (Bentham) to happiness vs. unhappiness (Mill) and good vs. evil (Moore). All three consider societal benefits to be more important than individual gains. Help the majority (= society as a whole) and not a single individual (as in Ethical Egoism) or a group/culture within the society (as in Ethical Relativism).

Note that their eyes are on what's best for the *majority*, not everyone. The goal is to improve society so that most people would benefit. Note, too, that there's no expectation of helping *all*.

Utilitarianism: The Most for the Most

Utilitarians want *the most for the most*: Try to maximize good/happiness/social benefit for the majority of the people. Weigh pros and cons and do a cost–benefit assessment. Then settle upon a decision. Such decision-making tends to focus on the short term. It's easier to predict consequences for the foreseeable future than for long-term planning. You can't please everyone, but aim for the best results for the majority ("most of the people").

Be aware: Prioritizing good ends allows for morally deficient means, such as lies, misinformation campaigns, puffery in resumés and marketing, intrusion on privacy, like email surveillance, and more. In certain situations, detention, "tough love," and various forms of discipline are tolerated or even condoned if they are thought conducive to some sought-after end.

The *modus operandi* of a Utilitarian is to do a cost–benefit assessment of the ethical dilemma. Factor in the end goal as bearing the greatest weight. Lower on the scale are ethical principles, moral duties, codes, good intentions, and the means to achieve the objective. Their rallying cry is "The greatest good for the greatest number of people." That does not mean "the most for *all*."

Any decision a Utilitarian makes could cause others to suffer. This would be morally acceptable if the majority came out ahead. In other words, the system may not be uniformly just or treat everyone fairly and with dignity. That some fall through the cracks is an acceptable compromise for Utilitarians as long as the *majority* will benefit by the decision or action.

Ethicist Michael Boylan (2000) looks at the impact of Utilitarianism and observes that it is the dominant moral theory in business and politics (p. 82). He notes that Utilitarianism is easy to understand and that "Most adults can apprehend and readily apply the Utilitarian slogan 'The greatest good for the greatest number.'" He goes on to argue that this would be an important advantage for any theory that aspired to be adopted by some society (p. 80).

If a society educates its population properly," Boylan observes, "the people would see that their own personal interests are not as important in the general scheme of things as the good of the whole." This occurs only when we feel sympathy for the other (p. 75). As we saw with *Contagion*, that sympathy is not always forthcoming.

It may be useful to reflect on Boylan's comments and see where they lead us. If we are indifferent to the plight of the homeless, the poor, the social outcasts, or other disadvantaged individuals and groups, then we might not appreciate the hardships they face. Plus, we might not realize that those hardships can ripple out and affect society in general.

Instead, we'd probably locate them on the periphery and not give them much credence. In that case, we might not see any reason to do anything about them. A minority could then be marginalized or ignored altogether, unless they arouse our sympathies so that we feel that their interests *should* matter to the general public.

Act versus Rule Utilitarianism There are two branches of Utilitarianism—Act and Rule. Both prioritize consequences and end goals over intentions and moral duties. Both subscribe to the Principle of Utility: *Choose that act that will result in the most good or happiness for the greatest number of people.* It is the scope of that "most" that differs for Act Utilitarians and Rule Utilitarians.

Act Utilitarians want the most good or least harm for the greatest number of people *most directly affected* by the decision. Rule Utilitarians try to maximize good and minimize harm for the greatest number of people. As a result, they want to optimize societal benefits, not just those like family members who are most impacted.

Act and Rule Utilitarians share the same guiding principle but differ as to who counts in the equation. Act Utilitarians have a much narrower focus and, thus, decide on a case-by-case basis. Rule Utilitarians view each case as a potential precedent that should apply (as a rule) for all other similar cases. Given these differences between Act and Rule Utilitarianism, the decision of a Utilitarian of one type could be opposite to one of the other.

Contagion and Utilitarianism Drs. Ellen Mears and Leonora Orantes are of similar moral ilk. Each one puts others' interests above her own and strives to do all she can to stop the spread of the virus. Dr. Mears is sent into the thick of things (by Dr. Cheever no less) and dies on a cot in a gymnasium next to others stricken by the virus. She sacrifices herself to get as much information as she can about the medical crisis.

In a similar vein, Dr. Orantes of the World Health Organization puts herself in harm's way. Having been held hostage in a Chinese village, she won't be party to deception in order to get released. When she discovers the villagers were given a placebo, she heads back to the village. She wants nothing to do with such thinking, such values.

Both women take considerable risks for the good of society. Helping others is in the forefront of their minds. From a strict Utilitarian perspective, sacrificing a minority to benefit the majority is morally acceptable. No problem!

In fact, it may be morally *desirable* in such cases as the pandemic in *Contagion.* An infectious disease of unknown cause was spreading at an alarming rate. The number of deaths was rising so fast that they ran out of body bags, and Canada wouldn't part with theirs. It was clear that those with medical know-how had to get to the root of the problem and stop it or slow it down enough to develop a vaccine.

Taking the notion of personal sacrifice one step further, researcher Dr. Ally Hextall injects *herself* with a mutated strain from one of the lab monkeys. She becomes her own human subject to find a vaccine. This self-sacrifice, a social good, would get Hextall a Utilitarian salute, even if it might horrify others.

Although the Nuremberg Code would commend her doing so, later codes, such as the Helsinki Declaration, omit this as a moral obligation. Nevertheless, Dr. Hextall's willingness to be her own experimental subject could be a welcome breakthrough—if she succeeds. Otherwise, her self-sacrifice would be for naught.

In contrast, Alan Krumwiede's attempts to profit with his fake "cure" has only *his* interests at heart, not the good of society as a whole. Alan's exploitation of others' fears would rub Utilitarians the wrong way. Such deceit is acceptable only if the majority gets a proportionately greater benefit. This is not the case here with Krumwiede's actions (unless suffering false hopes could be seen as a good).

Utilitarian Thinking in Business

Utilitarian ethics is not just applied to global medical disasters, though it is certainly employed there as a framework of analysis. It is frequently used in moral problem solving within institutions (medical, educational, governmental agencies), businesses, and, as Michael Boylan notes, politics.

It is extremely useful—all the more so given its attraction as a moral theory. Ethics committees and Institutional Review Boards often use a Utilitarian model as the basis of resolving ethical dilemmas. Let's see how it applies to business cases. We'll start with a scenario focused on weighing the factors around product safety.

Weighing Competing Factors   Picture this scenario: It's 1971 and you are a CEO in the auto industry. You can tell from recent trends and auto sales that not all drivers want cars that are gas-hogs or resemble barges. You figure the tide has turned, at least for those who are buying VW Bugs, Hondas, and Austin Minis. It's time to introduce some competition and get a piece of the pie.

You do the math and conclude that a car priced around $2,000 and weighing less than 2,000 pounds (good for gas!) will be the ticket for competing with the Germans, Japanese, and Brits (Jennings, 1993, p. 218). You tell your team the sooner on the market, the better.

The decision you face is this: How many shortcuts can you take? Where do you draw the line? No car is 100 percent safe; we all know that. If they weigh too much, they can do more damage hitting a smaller car (or a pedestrian). If they are too light, the driver will need a closed casket after a serious collision (to paraphrase commentators Click and Clack of NPR fame). If they are built solid as a rock, they'll be gas guzzlers. If they have quality parts throughout (leather this, brass that, really good paint, a snazzy stereo, GPS, rearview camera, anti-theft protection), then the cost mushrooms! And how much are buyers willing to spend to have greater safety features anyway?

Exercise

1. What standards should you employ in the above scenario?
2. What should be the balance between vehicle safety and consumer cost?
3. What is essential versus desirable—particularly when it comes to product safety?

CASE STUDY: The Ford Pinto

Consumers tolerate a certain amount of outsourcing of jobs as a trade-off for cheaper clothes, electronics, and other desirable objects. Companies that pay higher wages or use better-quality parts usually have to charge more. This is not always well-received among the buying public. Of course, many consumers don't balk at expensive cups of coffee or higher-priced phones and computers with nice retina screens. However true that is, the majority tolerate outsourcing if it reduces their own living costs.

So there we are: Potholes wherever we turn! Nevertheless, the Pinto case is another classic of Business Ethics. It merits a careful study. "*Learn from the mistakes of those who came before us*" should guide us as we make our own way through life, and be something businesses should take to heart.

It's 1971 and the Vietnam War is dragging on. The automotive industry is about to turn over a new leaf. European subcompacts are selling like hot-cakes. This is just the catalyst for Ford Motor Company to move into high gear to create a worthy competitor. They had a big hit with their first pony—the Mustang, a classic car if there ever was. So you'd think the next one would be just as successful, given the ready audience. Thus, the Ford Pinto.

It should be one of those strokes of genius, but it falls short. Right from the get-go, the car has problems. But sales are good and initially the problems seem minor. However, two things doom the enterprise: First, it's a rush job. Secondly, a few engineering shortcuts are taken. Both entail risks.

The biggest risk—their worst nightmare—is the location of the fuel tank. Contrary to the practice of the European carmakers (who place the fuel tank over the rear axle), Ford put it *behind* the rear axle (Jennings, 1993, 218). The way Ford designed it left too little "crush space." In addition, the bumper is significantly lighter (some say "flimsier") than is the norm in other American cars. At no time before or after the Pinto has such a weak bumper been used on an American car, reports Marianne Moody Jennings. If all this isn't bad enough, the Pinto lacks reinforcing rear sections, making it less crash resistant (Jennings, 218–219).

Ford's "Perfect Storm"

Basically, Ford created a "perfect storm" with all the problems tied to a vulnerable fuel tank. As a result, the situation escalated. A 1997 report by Mark Dowie of *The Atlantic Monthly* is telling. The Pinto prototype was crash tested and the car failed the fuel system integrity test in crashes over 20 miles per hour.

Such crashes indicated the Pinto was vulnerable to the fuel tank being driven forward, punctured, and fuel leaking in excess of the minimal standard. Such a leak could cause the car to burst into flames. Dowie points out that, "Because assembly-line machinery was already tooled when engineers found this defect, top Ford officials decided to manufacture the car anyway—exploding gas tank and all—*even though Ford owned the patent on a much safer gas tank*."

Amazingly enough, Ford sold the Pinto, knowing of the defect. Ford did a cost analysis. Remedies would cost an estimated $11 per car. The cost of a few cups of coffee and the car could be fixed! However, if 11 million cars and 1.5 million light trucks had to be recalled and repaired, we're talking approximately $137 million (Jennings, 222). At this point, the profit motive won out over safety concerns. "Safety doesn't sell," Ford CEO Lee Iacocca reportedly said (Dowie, 1977). That he may have underestimated the consumer seems worth considering.

In a move out of the Theatre of the Absurd, Ford modified its advertising. They sought to avoid visions of exploding gas tanks coming to mind. Burning Pintos have become such an embarrassment to Ford that its advertising agency, J. Walter Thompson, dropped a line from the end of a radio spot that read "Pinto leaves you with that warm feeling" (Dowie, 1977).

The Weighting Game: Deaths vs. Repairs

In a macabre turn of events, Ford computed the cost for 180 burn deaths, 180 serious burn injuries, and 2,100 burned vehicles. The unit cost estimate was $200,000 per death, $67,000 per injury, and $700 per vehicle— a bargain at $49.15 million (Jennings, p. 222). That's a saving of $87.85 million. Quite a tidy sum! For seven years Ford sold the car, knowing its defects. Yes, seven years.

Here's when the wave of self-interest washed over Ford and they lost sight of their duty to protect their customers from injury or death. The road taken by the Ethical Egoist may look like the Yellow Brick Road when you start skipping, but turns into quicksand the farther you go. And it certainly did not end well for Ford. It took years to rebuild their reputation. Nor did it end well for their customers, given that many died, others were injured, and millions of others became disillusioned about buying another Ford automobile.

Lawsuits followed. Robert Sherefkin (2003) reports that, "A 1979 landmark case, *Indiana vs. Ford Motor Co.*, made the automaker the first US corporation to be indicted and prosecuted [though found "not guilty"] on criminal homicide charges." Given the knowing disregard for human life, it's not surprising that Ford faced such serious charges.

No doubt it was an important, however, painful, lesson for Ford Motor Company to learn. But, if nothing else, Ford is not alone: Many businesses cut corners and compromise standards from time to time, at least to some degree.

Looking back what can we see? The problems with the Pinto tarnished Ford's reputation. It takes time to recover from moral failures, as was the case here. And it takes time to rebuild trust. This is as true for corporations as for individuals. Betrayal cuts deep. Whatever savings made in the short term, the long-term cost of paying off deaths rather than repairing the car was both tragic and avoidable.

Exercise

1. Assume you're on the jury of *Indiana vs. Ford Motor Co.* in which three teenagers died after their car was struck (it was on the side of the road, after the driving pulled over to retrieve the gas cap that had fallen off).
2. Investigate the case (you won't have trouble finding information).
3. Try to assess responsibility (x percent because of the faulty fuel tank, y percent because of the road conditions, z percent because of the inebriated driver who struck them, etc.).

4. If you were on the jury, would you agree with the "not guilty" verdict? Share your thoughts.

Three Decades Later: Ford's Ethical Turnaround

In 2010, ethics think tank Ethisphere Institute designated Ford as one of 100 companies and 36 industries worldwide as being honored for its high ethics standards. It was the only automaker on the list. Ethisphere Institute based its assessment "on an extensive review of companies' social responsibility efforts, corporate governance and business practices," said Alex Brigham, Ethisphere Institute's executive director. Three of the criteria used by Ethisphere and cited by Ford's press release were:

- A review of each company's codes of ethics, litigation and regulatory infraction histories
- An evaluation of investment in innovation and sustainable business practices
- A look into activities designed to improve corporate citizenship

In honoring Ford, Brigham highlighted the following:

> Ford's promotion of a *sound ethical environment* shines within its industry and shows a clear understanding that operating under the *highest standards for business behavior* goes beyond goodwill and lip service and is intimately linked to performance and profitability. (Ford Press Release, 2010, emphasis mine).

Who says we can't learn from our mistakes? Hopefully this indicates the Pinto tragedy is a thing of the past—and not to be repeated.

ETHICS CODE: Ford Motor Company

Ford's Code of Conduct is set out in a 20-page booklet, with opening letters from Bill Ford, Executive Chairman, and Alan Mulally, President and CEO. The code's core points address the following areas:

- The workplace environment
- Gifts, favors and conflicts of interest
- Use of company assets and data safeguarding
- Integrity of financial records

- Product quality, safety and environmental matters
- Intellectual property
- Working with governments (political activities)
- Competition and antitrust laws
- International business practices

You can see this at http://corporate.ford.com/doc/corporate_conduct_standards.pdf.

Exercise

In Ford's discussion of the workplace environment, it notes that its key values include

- A workplace that does not tolerate harassment or discrimination
- A work environment that meets or exceeds applicable standards for occupational
- safety and health
- Providing competitive compensation and work hours, in compliance with applicable laws
- Recognizing and respecting the right of employees to associate freely and bargain collectively
- Ensuring that child labor and forced labor are not used

➡ Assume you've been asked by Ford to highlight those values in an ad campaign meant to show consumers how much Ford cares about its employees and having a morally defensible set of values. In a paragraph or two, sketch out your campaign.

Works Cited

Anderson, Susan Leigh, *On Mill*, (Belmont, CA: Wadsworth Publishing, 2000).

Boylan, Michael, *Basic Ethics*, (Upper Saddle River, NJ: Prentice Hall. 2000).

Branswell, Helen, "SARS Memories Linger 5 Years Later," *The Ontario Star*, March 6, 2008, http://www.thestar.com/news/ontario/2008/03/06/sars_memories_linger_5_years_later.html (accessed December 20, 2014).

Dowie, Mark, "Pinto Madness," *Mother Jones*, September/October 1977, http://www.motherjones.com/politics/1977/09/pinto-madness (accessed December 20, 2014).

Ford Motor Company, *Code of Conduct*, http://corporate.ford.com/doc/corporate_conduct_standards.pdf

Ford Motor Company, Press Release, "Ford Motor Company Recognized as One of the World's Most Ethical Companies by Ethisphere," March 22, 2010, http://www.prnewswire.com/news-releases/ford-motor-company-recognized-as-one-of-the-worlds-most-ethical-companies-by-ethisphere-88830282.html (accessed December 20, 2014).

Franke-Ruta, Garance, "The Echoes of Ayn Rand in Paul Ryan's Budget Plan," *The Atlantic*, April 11, 2011, http://www.theatlantic.com/politics/archive/2011/04/the-echoes-of-ayn-rand-in-paul-ryans-budget-plan/237082/ (accessed December 20, 2014).

Fuchs, Cynthia, "Park Avenue: Money, Power and the American Dream," *Pop Matters*, November 13, 2012, http://www.popmatters.com/review/165397-park-avenue-money-power-and-the-american-dream/ (accessed December 20, 2014).

Helsinki Declaration. http://www.wma.net/en/30publications/10policies/b3/ (accessed 20 December 2014).

Hinman, Lawrence M., *Ethics: A Pluralistic Approach to Moral Theory*, (Fort Worth, TX: Harcourt, Brace, Jovanovich, 1994).

Houx, Damon, "Interview: Steven Soderbergh, Matt Damon and Laurence Fishburne on *Contagion*," *Screen Crave*, September 9, 2011, http://screencrave.com/2011-09-09/interview-steven-soderbergh-matt-damon-and-laurence-fishburne-on-contagion/ (accessed December 20, 2014).

Jennings, Marianne M., *Case Studies in Business Ethics*, (St. Paul, MN: West Publishing, 1993).

Moseley, Alexander, "Egoism," *Internet Encyclopedia of Philosophy*, August 7, 2005. http://www.iep.utm.edu/egoism/ (accessed December 30, 2014).

Nuremberg Code. http://www.hhs.gov/ohrp/archive/nurcode.html (accessed 20 December 2014).

Onken, Marina, "Business in Japan," http://www.onken.com/classroom/internationalmanagement/Japan/home.html (accessed December 20, 2014).

Sherefkin, Robert, "Lee Iacocca's Pinto: A Fiery Failure," *Automotive News*, June 16, 2003, http://www.autonews.com/article/20030616/SUB/306160770#axzz2a0c9FquP (accessed December 20, 2014).

Vaughn, Lewis, *Doing Ethics*, 2nd edn. (New York: W.W. Norton & Company, 2010).

Velasquez, Manuel et al., "Ethical Relativism," *Issues in Ethics* Vol. 5 No.2, Summer 1992, http://www.scu.edu/ethics/practicing/decision/ethicalrelativism.html (accessed from Markula Center for Applied Ethics, December 20, 2014).

2.3

Duties Rule
Deontological Ethics

Spotlight: *Shattered Glass; Arbitrage; Quiz Show; Food, Inc.*
Case Studies: Beech-Nut's Apple Juice; Minute Maid Lemonade;
Foster Farms' Chickens
Ethics Codes: National Public Radio (NPR); Dole Food Company, Inc.

> **Chuck Lane:** *He handed us fiction after fiction, and we printed them
> all as fact. Just because we found him entertaining. It's indefensible.*
> —Shattered Glass

> **Robert Miller:** *What you did is way beyond the money.*
> **Jimmy Grant:** *Nothing is beyond the money for you Robert. We both
> know that.*
> —Arbitrage

Stephen Glass, Associate Editor for *The New Republic*, had it all—or
seemed to. He had a great job, was well liked, and could make a
difference in the world. But he had this one flaw: He thought the rules
didn't apply to him. And, as Chuck Lane, one of *The New Republic*
editors put it, "We found him entertaining." Being adept at amusing
others can be a useful distraction. We watch how it all unravels in
Shattered Glass (2003).

Stephen knew how to sweet-talk the gals. It's amazing what people
will do when buttered-up. And he could spin a yarn that his co-workers
loved to hear. So what's wrong with that? We all love stories! True, but
there's a difference between a *story* and real life. When those boundaries
are blurred, things can go awry. And things definitely went awry for
Stephen Glass.

Stephen's story is ideal for understanding why Deontological Ethicists
value moral duties and especially that of honesty. In this chapter we will
get an overview of Deontological Ethics and its main proponents. We will

Business Ethics Through Movies: A Case Study Approach, First Edition. Wanda Teays.
© 2015 John Wiley & Sons, Ltd. Published 2015 by John Wiley & Sons, Ltd.

then take the theory to film (*Shattered Glass, Arbitrage, Quiz Show, Food, Inc.*) and then to cases in Business Ethics. We'll also examine National Public Radio's ethics code and Dole's Code of Conduct to see their deontological leanings. Let's start with a quick overview of the ethical theory.

Ethical Framework: Deontological Ethics

Deontological Ethics focuses on moral duty and obligation. This is a distinctly different emphasis from Teleological Ethics' view that the best possible consequences should drive the decision-making. Here, the biggest issue is what rules, principles, and duties should guide us, not the end goals.

Two ethicists stand out here: They are Immanuel Kant (whose two moral commands form the basis of his ethical theory) and W.D. Ross (whose "Prima Facie" duties are meant to guide our moral decision-making). Their emphasis on moral duty and individual rights provides a valuable framework for Business Ethics. Let's start with Kant, one of the superstars of moral reasoning. He has had enormous impact on the field of Ethics, and so becoming familiar with his approach is all to the good.

Kantian Ethics

Deontological Ethicist Immanuel Kant would insist on the truth, the whole truth, and nothing but! And that means no exceptions. This is a man with strong feelings about what needs to be done and he doesn't budge.

Put others at risk by being honest? C'est la vie! Tell a deranged killer where your family members are hiding? Of course. That the result of toeing the honesty line has a major downside does not, in Kant's eyes, merit a modification in our actions. Our moral obligation is to act like an ethical role model; thus, telling the truth is vital.

If the intentions are right-on, we have a moral duty to be honest, regardless of the consequences. It may strike you as brittle, but it is meant to be an unbending, exceptionless rule. Kant emphatically believes that moral duty overrides the consequences, however disastrous they may be. To let the end goals drive the decision-making would be to stand ethics on its head! Objectives fall behind duties as far as Kant is concerned.

His view is that we ought to set our sights on moral principles. Give no credence to the potential consequences of the options. The pillars are the moral duties that we hold dear and nothing else. Plus, we need to stand firm. After all, *a rule's a rule!* So don't think exceptions should be given weight. "Hold firm to your convictions!" Kant would tell us. No moral wimps allowed!

SPOTLIGHT: *Shattered Glass*

Kant would look at Stephen Glass and see moral failure. It is ironic that Stephen, in his role of Associate Editor, berated reporters whose articles didn't meet his standards. That he fell short of his own standards didn't seem to register on his moral thermometer. Nevertheless, signs of impending troubles came to the surface after he wrote an error-filled piece "Hacker Heaven." For one thing, the article referred to people who didn't exist (e.g., "Bad Boy Bionic") and to groups and acts that were a Null Set as well.

Adam Penenberg of *Forbes* magazine read Stephen's article and it sparked his interest. He wondered how *Forbes* could miss such a story. But when he searched for the specifics behind the article, he found nothing there. It was like The Emperor's New Clothes: What initially looked substantial evaporated into thin air upon closer inspection. He decided to call Chuck Lane, editor of *The New Republic*.

After Penenberg started asking questions, Chuck wanted answers. Stephen started constructing a pack of lies to cover all of his many tracks. As time went on, Stephen's lies multiplied, but he became sloppier and sloppier. That's the thing about lies—they tend to be like wet fish, easy to slip from our grasp and slide away.

Stephen Glass didn't fabricate *one* article, he fabricated one after another after another. "I just want you to tell me the truth, Stephen," Chuck said to him. Initially, Stephen presented himself like a confused, distraught kid, as if he should not be held accountable for what he'd done. "The part he's most upset about is lying to you Chuck," said Stephen's co-worker Caitlin. She and others tried to cover his butt: "He needs help. You can't fire him... We're all he has."

Exercise

1. Let's stop and reflect on this situation. Assuming it is actually true that Stephen was emotionally fragile or easily hurt, should that mean we shouldn't judge him? Or should we only do so if we can

show some leniency? How much do *you* think the liar's emotional well-being should be factored into our evaluation of their actions or moral character?

Back to Shattered Glass

Playing the victim or a weakling may be an effective ploy. Stephen attempted to count on pity or good will to get him through. And "I was so sloppy trusting my sources like that. And then lying about it," he said. "I said some things I shouldn't have said," he says, "I did some terrible, terrible things." He admits and then plays on everyone's sympathies with astonishing success.

The movie shows how lies can be stacked upon lies. It can be done so effectively that the liar himself begins to believe them. They acquire a life of their own. However, there's also this risk: Lies may only take you so far before others' sympathy starts to dwindle. This we see with Chuck Lane's growing horror once he begins to realize the extent of Stephen's dishonesty.

After Chuck suspended Stephen and walked him out the door, he decided to double check the earlier pieces Stephen had written. It was then painfully obvious that one article after another was an invention. Stephen was axed. However, he still tried to squeeze out as much mercy as he could get. "I can't be by myself right now. I'm afraid what I'm going to do..." he said, throwing himself on Chuck's sympathies.

"It's a hell of a story," Chuck observed, unmoved. That summed it up about as succinctly as he could get. In the ending credits, we learn that 27 out of the 41 articles by Stephen Glass that *The New Republic* published were partial or complete fabrications. Kant would just shake his head at the extent of dishonesty Stephen showed.

Stephen Glass's life did not end when he was forced out of journalism due to his violations of integrity. In time he went to law school, but was unsuccessful at getting a license to practice law in New York. He moved on to California.

In November 2013 he stood before the California Supreme Court in hopes of getting a green light to practice law in that state. The *American Bar Association Journal* (Neil, 2013) reports that, "Based on the skeptical questions posed by several justices, he appears to be facing an uphill battle."

Glass, who works as a paralegal for a Los Angeles law firm, is backed by former editors, his current employer and law professors, and he has obtained mental health counseling. But several justices questioned whether he has done enough to make up for his journalistic wrongdoing.

The justices expressed skepticism as to his ability to overcome his past transgressions and lead a life of integrity. "As the tough tenor of the supreme court's questioning became clear on Wednesday, he slumped in his chair. Afterward, he declined to comment and left the courthouse with his hands in his pockets and his head down" (Neil, 2013). Dishonesty lies along the same spectrum as betrayal—and is just as hard to regain a clean slate once tarnished. In January 2014 the California court denied him a license: his deceit, the court said "'bore directly on his character in matters that are critical to the practice of law.' Legal ethicists said the court's decision means that Glass ... is unlikely to ever get a license to practice law" (Dolan, 2014).

ETHICS CODE: NPR (National Public Radio)

Shattered Glass indicates that honesty is an important value in the journalism profession. Reputations depend upon honesty. The Stephen Glasses of the world end up with tarnished reputations. So also do the newspapers and TV stations that hire them and fail to have safeguards in place. National Public Radio has an ethics code/handbook that draws attention to eight guiding principles: Fairness, Completeness, Independence, Impartiality, Transparency, Accountability, Respect, and Excellence.

You can access it at http://ethics.npr.org/.

Kant on Honesty: Shattered Glass and Arbitrage

Kant would look at the case of Stephen Glass as indicative of what happens when moral duty is abandoned. We may think it'll all work out for the best when we put ends over the means, but don't count on it. Moral obligations are just too important says Kant.

Stephen Glass isn't the only film protagonist who gets ensnared by a network of lies. Robert Miller of *Arbitrage* (2012) also faces personal disaster when the combination of business corruption (e.g., cooked books) and a cover-up of a car accident that killed his lover test his ability to escape detection by authorities. That his wife and daughter see his moral underbelly are revealed as the plot unfolds. At one point, Miller's friend and advisor tells him, "Let me tell you something. And I'm speaking to you as a friend now... the more time that passes, the more lies that are told. The worse it gets..." Kant would second that opinion!

Like *Shattered Glass*, *Arbitrage* lays bare the moral low-road along with the risks of taking that path. Mind you, some people look at ethics and see some wiggle-room. "Most of the time I wouldn't think about cheating on an exam, but I didn't have enough time to study for this one." Or, "My supervisor asked me what I think of her new website. Personally, I think it's too crowded—but I'm not about to tell her that!" Utilitarians would say that presenting fiction as fact is a problem only if the society does not benefit. So long as the fabrications maximize good or happiness for the majority, the Stephen Glasses of the world can spin away!

What about *you?* Are you okay with the occasional (or frequent) cheater? Or does that seem unfair, dishonest, disrespectful of all those who actually studied and did their best? Are you okay with employees who don't want to offend their bosses and, so, lie or hedge rather than directly answer a question? Are you okay with the news media publishing misleading or false information because the government or their investors/sponsors direct them to do so? *Think about it.*

If you said, "I can live with these scenarios" or "I'm not bothered by a little cheating or a small lie or two" you would *not* get the Kantian Stamp of Approval. For Deontological Ethicists like Kant, moral duty is a beacon lighting the way in ethical decision-making. He puts a great deal of importance on *intentions* and moral obligations. Here are his two principles:

Kant's Two Moral Principles

The *Categorical Imperative*
Act in such a way that you would have it become a universal law.
➡ *Universalize ethical decision-making.*

The *Humanitarian Principle*
Always treat others as an end in themselves, never merely as a means.
➡ *Treat others with respect and human dignity.*

With the Categorical Imperative, Kant would have us select the option we would want every moral agent to follow. We should think of ourselves as a role model and choose wisely.

We can only hold *moral agents* responsible for their behavior. Kant does not consider minors or mentally incompetent individuals to be moral agents and, therefore, he asserts, they should not be held to this standard.

This all links back to Kant's emphasis on rationality—being competent to make ethical decisions. Let's see what this means.

Moral Agency and Kant's Two Principles

Kant sees moral agents as moral equals, but not all are moral agents (or equals!). As you may remember, there are two components of moral agency. They are *rationality* (= competence) and *free will* (= volition).

Since children aren't considered competent, they are not normally held responsible for their actions. Occasionally minors *are* treated as adults, for example, as when they are prosecuted for some heinous crime like premeditated murder. For the most part, however, minors are not thought accountable for their actions. They are not usually thought capable of distinguishing good from evil and, therefore, should not be held responsible.

Kant puts a great deal of importance on rationality and, thus, competence. Of course, he's not alone in thinking that "being of sound mind" is vital. As a result, he wouldn't consider children or others who are mentally compromised or impressionable to be moral agents, or moral equals. Moral agency requires a competent state of mind.

Of Kant's two principles, the Categorical Imperative is more widely cited and used as a moral template ("What if everybody did it?" Would I then endorse this choice?). This is the principle that asks us to *universalize* moral decision-making. An action is justifiable only if everyone could do the same. Kant thought this would lead to us being morally upstanding by being honest, keeping our promises, and so on.

Kant's Humanitarian Principle is also on the moral map. This principle asks us to treat others with respect and dignity. Don't use others merely as a means to some end. "Always treat others as an end in themselves," is the core of this principle. This, then, calls for us to protect individual rights over societal benefits. Human rights are key here. No one likes to be used and Kant would agree with that sentiment.

These two maxims (= principles) are the core of Kant's ethical theory and have wide-ranging impact. Each principle acts as a general rule meant to guide us. Both rest on moral integrity and are not tied to this place or that community. Think of each decision as applying across the board, in every setting. Make it universal and make human rights at the center of our moral reasoning.

Here's what Kant would recommend: Try to pull far enough back to think rationally about the issues and concerns. Look carefully at your intentions and what moral duties should inform your thinking. Do *not* focus on the expectations around the result of the decision or if anyone will be happy with it. Instead, be guided by our ethical principles, maxims, moral duties.

"We just have to check that the act we have in mind will not use anyone as a mere means, and, if possible, that it will treat other persons as ends in themselves," philosopher Onora O'Neill (1980) suggests. Granted people are used all the time; as when they help us get a job or introduce us to their nice cousin we're drawn to. What Kant objects to is using people *only* as a means, as if a link in a chain and nothing more. Such misuse of others violates their human dignity by turning them into objects to be used.

Let's see how Kant's theory is a useful tool for reflecting on the moral lessons in movies, by looking at the movie *Quiz Show*.

SPOTLIGHT: *Quiz Show*

One of the more memorable lines from the TV show *House* is "Everybody lies." In *Shattered Glass*, *Arbitrage* and *Quiz Show*, we watch liars in action. As we saw in the discussion of *Shattered Glass*, the liar (Stephen Glass) eventually tripped himself up by making mistakes that finally came to light.

In the case of *Quiz Show*, the lies didn't lie down quietly. This was due to the existence of multiple liars. Thanks to one of the liars becoming disgruntled with his fall from fame, the truth came to light. At that point, heads began to roll. As with *Shattered Glass*, the tower of lies became taller and taller, but eventually came tumbling down. This is just what Kant would want to see. In *Arbitrage* Robert Miller managed to weasel his way around the authorities. He used others to escape the jaws of fate. But, though he survived professionally, his moral corruption burnt holes like acid in his closest personal relationships. Kant would not be surprised.

Quiz Show presents two morally deficient protagonists. The first, Herbert Stempel, has become a fixture on the TV quiz show *Twenty-One*. He lives and breathes *Twenty-One*. Those closest to him—his wife and son—are reminded daily that Herbert's TV winning-persona has engulfed his identity. His brain is consumed with thoughts about the show. But his luck is about to change.

Herbert may be a winner and a weekly fixture in the lives of America's TV viewing public, but he's basically a pretty ordinary-looking fellow. Not so Charles Van Doren, English instructor, member of the famed Van Doren family, and as handsome as Prince Charming. As soon as they saw him, women in the audience swooned over the electrifying opponent about to oust Herbert.

If we were to do a race and class interpretation of this, it could be argued that the blond classy überman was bound to be the victor in a contest with the darker, working-class Herbert. Plus Charles has classy suits and nice, sparkling teeth and a polished demeanor. Not so Herbert, who lacks the style and presence of Charles Van Doren.

It's interesting to note that Charles wondered what Kant would think when he was first approached about coming on the show. He answered his own question by noting that Kant would not approve of being told the questions they planned to ask. The moral compromise was that of being tipped off what the questions were going to be. Later it appeared that the answers themselves were supplied, but by then Charles had entered *The Land That Kant Forbade*.

There would be no way in the world Kant would allow dishonesty or deception, whether in a game show or anything else. The idea that no one is hurt by such chicanery is not one Kant would condone. For him, it's all or nothing.

Herbert failed the Categorical Imperative when he acceded to the request to give the wrong answer. He resented that the question was an easy one (to name the movie that won the 1955 Academy Award for Best Picture). Nevertheless, when the question was asked of him, he hummed and hawed, then intentionally gave the wrong answer. It pained him to do it, but he did it anyway. And down the ethical vortex he went!

The movie is based on actual events tied to a rigged quiz show. Herbert became a whistleblower after feeling disgraced by his seeming ignorance. It especially irked him to say *On the Waterfront*, when the correct answer (*Marty*) was his favorite film. The other contestant, Van Doren whose fame and popularity grew, ended up lying to the Grand Jury. And this is in real life—not the movie. Only after he was hauled before a Congressional investigation, did he finally come clean.

Steve Feffer, who wrote a play on the case, said: "I think a lot of people in the audience will side with them [both Van Doren and Stempel]. They will say: 'I would have done that, too. I would have taken the answers. I would have taken the money'" (Keating, 1991). Clearly, Kant would think those who side with Van Doren and Stempel don't pass moral muster. He would say exceptions are not okay and those who would cave facing a similar situation do not grasp how important it is to be honest.

Exercise

1. Is Kant wrong to set down a rule that is to be treated as a *command* for all of us to follow? One without any exceptions at all?
    a. If your answer is "*Yes*," we would then have to decide what sort of penalty or punishment the rule-breakers would incur.

    b. If your answer is "*No*," there are legitimate exceptions to rules like "Don't tell a lie or deceive others," we would then have to decide what are allowable exceptions.

2. What should we do when a corporation *deliberately* lies to the public? Share your thoughts.

3. What sort of consequence would you think appropriate if the corporation deliberately lied about the ingredients in baby food?

Ethical Framework: W.D. Ross's Prima Facie Duties

W.D. Ross also provides us with a set of ethical tools for doing a moral analysis of films and examining cases in Business Ethics. He thinks Kant is too narrowly focused, that he puts too much emphasis on the present and not enough on the past and future. Ross says we should factor in considerations from the past—such as a sense of loyalty or gratitude—*as well as* those of the future—such as potential consequences.

His solution is Prima Facie duties. They are labeled "prima facie" because, on the surface (in the abstract), they are of equal moral weight. A duty only assumes greater significance than another in context— on a case-by-case basis. For any ethical dilemma, draw on the duties that are most helpful to sort it out, and shelve the others. Use only those that your intuition thinks applicable. Here they are:

Ross's Prima Facie Duties

- Veracity (Honesty and Promise-Keeping)
- Beneficence (Do good)
- Non-Maleficence (Do no harm)
- Justice
- Gratitude (Loyalty)
- Reparations (Compensation for harm done)
- Self-Improvement

Whenever we're facing an ethical dilemma, we select one or more of these duties and put them to use. For example, suppose you are faced with a decision where honesty seems important, but it is also important to do no harm. You would have to weigh the two moral duties before making a decision. Let your intuitions and the particulars of the case guide you, says Ross.

Quiz Show *and Deontological Ethics*

We know that Kant would say that both Herbert Stempel and Charles Van Doren, *Twenty-One* contestants, crossed a moral line. Ross wouldn't be impressed at them either, given they were not honest, they didn't do any good (Beneficence) other than entertaining the masses, and they could be said to have done harm (violating his duty of Non-Maleficence) by participating in an ongoing deception as well as undermining public trust in the media.

Neither one's actions would be good for their self-improvement—with the exception of Stempel blowing the whistle on the producers of the quiz show. That moves him farther up the moral ladder than Van Doren, though his lack of integrity earlier shows he's not above reproach. Furthermore, it seems unlikely that he'd be blowing any whistles had he not gone along with his demotion from participant to audience member.

Rawls also would agree with Kant and Ross that we should pay attention to moral obligations. He would be especially concerned about achieving a just result in the way the case was handled. Rawls would follow Kant in disapproving of the show's fundamental subterfuge.

The fraudulent actions would be seen to be morally repugnant by all three ethicists. They clearly violated Kant's Humanitarian Principle since others were used merely as a means to an end. They clearly violated Ross's duties of honesty, non-maleficence, and justice. And they clearly violated Rawls' second principle of Fair Opportunity. Those of equivalent talents and skills did not have equal access to be prizewinners. Contestants were disadvantaged from the get-go. Given money was involved and not just game-playing, rigging the show was not fair. The competition wouldn't have a chance if the winner was predetermined!

Rawls would also say the producers were biased in selecting contestants. They were unjust and their actions betrayed the public trust. Look at the selection of Charles Van Doren: When they saw how charismatic he was, they did a quick cost–benefit assessment. Herbert Stempel was no longer the draw he once was. Van Doren was little risk in comparison, especially once he went along with the duplicity.

With both *Shattered Glass* and *Quiz Show*, we see examples of individuals who know the difference between right and wrong. They are unquestionably competent. They are not under coercion of any kind—they are acting on their own volition. And so when they cross the moral line, Kant would advise us to hold them responsible. They lied and their lies were not harmless: In no way could their behavior be sanctioned. They acted in ways we would *not* want to become a universal law.

Let's now turn to corporate malfeasance and look at the case of the juice intended for babies—apple juice. Correction, *no-apple* apple juice. The apple juice by name only.

CASE STUDY 1: Beech-Nut's Apple Juice

It is 1987 and Beech-Nut is the second largest producer of baby food, after Gerber. Consumers consider it a given that the list of ingredients on a package accurately reflects what is actually *inside* the package. They trust that companies would not lie about what is packaged and sold. That was not the case here.

Leonard Buder of *The New York Times* (1987) reports that a Federal indictment claimed that Beech-Nut "intentionally shipped adulterated and misbranded juice to 20 states, Puerto Rico, the Virgin Islands and five foreign countries with the intent to defraud and mislead" between December, 1981 and March, 1983. In addition,

> It said that the product that Beech-Nut had been marketing as 100 percent apple juice was actually made from beet sugar, cane sugar syrup, corn syrup and other ingredients, with little if any apple juice in the mixture. Prosecutors said at the time of the indictment that the bogus apple juice cost about 20 percent less to make than real apple juice (Buder, 1987).

Beech-Nut settled a class action suit against them for $7.5 million. Dr. Richard Theuer, the company's president, said they would improve quality control and prevent such situations as the "artificial" apple juice from occurring again. He also said, "the misrepresented juice, although not pure apple juice, contained only 'safe food ingredients' and had presented no danger to health" (Buder, 1987).

Even if consumers were not allergic to beet sugar, cane sugar syrup, corn syrup "and other ingredients with little if any apple juice," they were deceived. They did not know their babies were being fed a mixture devoid of apple juice. Beech-Nut violated Kant's Categorical Imperative. Our other Deontological Ethicist would also fault the company.

Beech-Nut and W.D. Ross

Ross would look at this case and draw from his duties of honesty and promise keeping, non-maleficence (do no harm), and beneficence. Beech-Nut should have been forthright and disclose all the facts that would be relevant to address consumer concerns, including the degree to which babies were put at risk.

To do good and avoid harm, they should remove products from store shelves, institute a recall of the products and reimburse consumers. Ross would advise them to pay any related medical costs as well and issue a public apology.

Chicago Tribune reporter Bob Greene (1988) accused Beech-Nut of "betraying a trust." He said, "The parents were unknowingly feeding their tiny sons and daughters what one Beech-Nut employee described as a 'chemical cocktail.'"

In 1978, Jerome J. LiCari, Beech-Nut's director of research and development had wanted to test the new supplies for purity and quality because of adulteration rumors. The chemists tested the apple juice concentrate supplied to Beech-Nut by Interjuice, a contractor. They concluded that the Interjuice concentrate was "likely to be heavily adulterated, if not completely fake" (Welles, 1988, as quoted by Wood and Detwiler, 2007). Donna Wood (2007) reports that,

> By August of [1981], LiCari and other scientists in his unit felt that they had virtually conclusive proof that Universal's product was fraudulent. ...[He] wrote a memo to Beech-Nut's senior management, including [John F.] Lavery, stating the circumstantial evidence leading him to this conclusion (Traub, 1988).

Woods notes that, "After receiving no response to his memo, LiCari scheduled a meeting with Lavery. According to LiCari, Lavery told him he was not a team player and might lose his job" (Welles, 1988).

Jerome LiCari resigned from Beech-Nut in January 1982 (Traub, 1988). In 1987, the company pleaded guilty on the grounds of "collective knowledge" to more than 200 felony counts as well as food and drug law violations, for selling fraudulent apple juice from 1981 to 1983.

CASE STUDY 2: The No-Lemon Juice Lemonade

Beech-Nut isn't the only case centering on missing ingredients. Minute Maid lemonade's container may surprise thirsty consumers. Look carefully at what is written on the Minute Maid container (Figure 2.1).

As you can see, this states: "Minute Maid. Lemonade. Contains 0% Juice." The conclusion is unavoidable: There is no juice of any kind (lemon or other) in this drink. This may give us pause. No juice. None. However,

Enjoy

Minute Maid®

CONTAINS 0% JUICE

LEMONADE

Figure 2.1 There is no juice of any kind (lemon or other) in this drink.

in all fairness to Minute Maid, their lemonade may still contain lemons in other forms—just no lemon *juice.*

Exercise

1. Should Minute Maid be allowed to market "lemonade" without any juice? It could certainly contain other parts of the lemon—such as peels, seeds, or pulp. After all, it is just *juice* missing from the drink. Does that possibility (peels/seeds/pulp) compensate for the 0 percent juice?
2. Does it matter if the lemonade has no juice in it?

SPOTLIGHT: *Food, Inc.*

There are other issues centering on Business Ethics and food. One has to do with justice and fairness in food production. Each step in the process can raise ethical concerns. The documentary *Food, Inc.* (2008) looks at some of the discrepancies in agribusiness around meat production. This includes small farmers versus agribusiness and the impact of powerful corporate interests. It's an unsettling study.

We see downer cows on the way to slaughter and chickens crammed together in dark metal containers, unable to move freely and surrounded by their own excrement, not to mention dead ones all around. *Food, Inc.* brings up health concerns that result from these practices. It raises questions about the gap between the multinationals using their considerable power against small farmers.

Those who are most disadvantaged, the small-time farmers, are like David against the Goliath of agribusiness. They stand little chance to survive without acquiescing to the demands and policies forced upon them. We see some driven to poverty fighting lawsuits against companies, such as Monsanto, that want strict controls over seeds they have patented.

Those who put moral duty at the center of their moral reasoning would call for changes that would support both individuals and businesses. They would praise those businesses that take seriously the moral obligations they have toward the farmers and customers that their practice depends upon.

CASE STUDY 3: Salmonella and Foster Farms' Chickens

It's not always easy to say you're sorry, especially when your company causes a salmonella outbreak that made hundreds of people sick. But on October 18, 2013 Foster Farms president Ron Foster uttered those words. Mind you, he waited a month to do so. But when sales plummeted after consumers got food poisoning from Foster Farms' chickens, an apology seemed prudent.

It wasn't a pretty picture. The salmonella strain in the chickens was very strong, showing resistance to antibiotics. As a result, there was a high rate of hospitalization among the consumer-victims. In fact, the CDC said 42 percent of the victims were hospitalized—double the regular rate (Pierson and Hsu, 2013).

Initially, Foster Farms refused to recall any of their chickens. President Ron Foster said, "We are committed to ensuring the safety of our products, and our family-owned company has maintained an excellent food safety record during its near 80-year history." Unfortunately, as the consumer response indicated, not all were convinced. As of January 19, 2014 the number sickened with salmonella rose to 430 (Farrow, 2014).

It looks like another apology is in order: On January 8, 2014 the USDA closed the Foster Farms plant in Livingston, CA. The chickens weren't the focus—it was a cockroach infestation this time. Two other facilities were threatened with closure because of unsanitary conditions. Plant officials once again tried to assuage the consumers' fear and disgust:

Food safety is Foster Farms' highest priority and the company took action immediately upon learning of any concern. This is an isolated incident; no other company plants are affected. Today's treatment is expected to fully resolve this incident (Pierson, 2014).

We might wonder what consumers should do. Staying informed is clearly a good idea. So might be lobbying the USDA for a few changes. For example, *E. coli* triggers a recall, but Salmonella does not. *Here's why:* Salmonella is not considered an adulterant like *E. coli*, says Smith DeWaal of the Center for Science in the Public Interest. Evidently, "health officials have been lobbying the USDA to change that, arguing more dangerous strains of salmonella resistant to antibiotics have emerged in recent years" (Pierson and Hsu, 2013).

A Deontological Ethicist would look at this sorry state of affairs and ask, "What is our moral duty here? What ought we do? What is our obligation to consumers when it comes to public health and safety?" One answer is holding businesses and regulatory agencies responsible so they have procedures in place and quickly respond when problems arise. This is especially the case when product safety and public health are involved. Reassurances only carry weight when they are grounded in reality—and morality.

The very idea that it is legally permissible to market chicken infected with antibiotic-resistant Salmonella tells us that it's time for changes in the law. As for vermin such as cockroaches or rats; well, that calls for tighter controls over sanitation and hygiene. Both the public and businesses suffer when such protections are not in place. In that sense, public health and corporate stability—financial and otherwise—go hand in hand.

ETHICS CODE: Dole Foods

Dole foods (producers of fruits and vegetables) has a nicely-worded seven-point Deontological code of ethics. You can see it at http://www.dole. com/~/media/Files/Documents/Code%20of%20Conduct/DoleCode_EN_Public_2013.ashx

Exercise

Think about Foster Farms' chickens and cockroaches, and then read over Dole's code and see how it could act as a framework for addressing the sort of abuses is disclosed in the Foster Farms case.

Works Cited

Buder, Leonard, "Beech-Nut Is Fined $2 Million for Sale Of Fake Apple Juice," *New York Times*, November 14, 1987, http://www.nytimes.com/1987/11/14/business/beech-nut-is-fined-2-million-for-sale-of-fake-apple-juice.html (accessed December 20, 2014).

Dolan, Maura, "Disgraced Journalist Stephen Glass Unlikely To Ever Be Lawyer," *Los Angeles Times*, January 28, 2014, http://articles.latimes.com/2014/jan/28/local/la-me-ln-stephen-glass-lawyer-ruling-20140128 (accessed December 20, 2014).

Dole Food Company, Inc., *Code of Conduct*, http://www.dole.com/~/media/Files/Documents/Code%20of%20Conduct/DoleCode_EN_Public_2013.ashx (accessed December 20, 2014).

Farrow, Deke, "Number Sickened By Foster Farms Salmonella Outbreak Rises To 430, Government Reports," *Merced Sun Star*, January 19, 2014, http://www.mercedsunstar.com/2014/01/19/3449660/number-sickened-by-salmonella.html (accessed December 20, 2014).

Greene, Bob, "How Beech-Nut Betrayed A Trust," *Chicago Tribune*, June 22, 1988, http://articles.chicagotribune.com/1988-06-22/features/8801090674_1_beech-nut-apple-juice-bottles (accessed December 20, 2014).

Kant on the Web, http://www.hkbu.edu.hk/~ppp/Kant.html (accessed December 20, 2014).

Keating, Douglas J., "Restaging A Staged Quiz Show In The 1950s, An Ex-contestant Of *Twenty-one* Revealed That The Show Was Rigged. A New Play At The Annenberg Tells His Story," *Philly.com*, May 27, 1991, http://articles.philly.com/1991-05-27/news/25799000_1_herb-stempel-quiz-show-scandal-quiz-show (accessed December 20, 2014).

National Public Radio, "This is NPR, Our Guiding Principles," http://ethics.npr.org/ (accessed December 20, 2014).

Neil, Martha, "Disgraced As Journalist, Stephen Glass Faces Skeptical Calif. Supreme Court In Law-License Bid," *American Bar Association Journal*, November 6, 2013, http://www.abajournal.com/news/article/disgraced_as_journalist_stephen_glass_faces_skeptical_state_supreme_court (accessed December 20, 2014).

O'Neill, Onora, "A Simplified Account of Kant's Ethics," in Tom Regan, (ed.), *Matters of Life and Death* (Philadelphia, PA: Temple University Press, 1980).

Pierson, David, "USDA closes Foster Farms Plant over Roach Infestation," *Los Angeles Times*, January 8, 2014, http://articles.latimes.com/2014/jan/08/business/la-fi-0109-foster-farms-cockroaches-20140109 (accessed December 30, 2014).

Pierson, David and Tiffany Hsu, "Salmonella Outbreak In Chicken Shows Resistance To Antibiotics," *Los Angeles Times*, October 8, 2013, http://articles.latimes.com/2013/oct/08/business/la-fi-mo-foster-salmonella-20131008 (accessed December 20, 2014).

Traub, James. "Into the Mouths of Babes," *New York Times*, July 24, 1988, http://www.nytimes.com/1988/08/28/magazine/1-into-the-mouths-of-babes-589788.html (accessed December 20, 2014).

Welles, Chris, "What Led Beech-Nut Down the Road to Disgrace," *Business Week* (February 22, 1988), in Marianne M. Jennings (ed.), *Business Ethics: Case Studies and Selected Readings*, (Minneapolis, MN: West Publishing, 1993).

Wood, Donna J. and Alden Detwiler, "Beech-Nut's Apple Juice," 2007, http://docslide.net/documents/case-beech-nut-apple-juice-case.html (accessed December 20, 2014).

2.4

Moral Character
Virtue Ethics

Spotlight: *Erin Brockovich; Roger & Me; Salmon Fishing in the Yemen, Food, Inc.*
Case Studies: Kellogg's and Michael Phelps; The European Horsemeat Scandal
Ethics Codes: GM's Corporate Citizenship; Kellogg's "K Values"

> *Erin: I don't know what I think I'm going to do for these people. No matter what I do, it won't be enough. We can get these people. With a little effort, I really think we can nail their asses to the wall.*
> *Ed: Oh, you do? With all your legal expertise, you believe that?*
> *Erin: Don't you ever just know? ... Look, I admit I don't know shit about shit. But I know the difference—between right and wrong!*
> —Erin Brockovich

Erin Brockovich didn't realize how her life would change when she took a job at a law firm. She had no qualifications and her brash manner along with her sexy tops and miniskirts caused a bit of a ruckus. Not in her wildest dreams did she picture how a low-paid secretarial job would turn into something so important and wide reaching. Nor did she envision that her environmental activism over contaminated water in Hinkley, California would lead to a $333 million settlement. *Erin Brockovich* (2000) tells the story of the woman and the town that started it all. It is a testimony to civil action, to working together in community and taking a stand. When you smell a rat, it's time to get involved.

Brockovich had no degrees, other than a DUMOT (Determined Unemployed Mother of Three). But a spark was lit when she uncovered evidence that something was very wrong in Hinkley and it could be traced to toxic chemicals in the water. She devoted herself round the clock to

Business Ethics Through Movies: A Case Study Approach, First Edition. Wanda Teays.
© 2015 John Wiley & Sons, Ltd. Published 2015 by John Wiley & Sons, Ltd.

digging deeper. We follow along as the evidence mounts and the locals get behind her.

Effecting change is always a challenge. And when your opponent has billions of dollars, it's definitely an uphill battle. The ominous threat didn't stop her: "You should watch your step. A young lady like yourself with three young children." Yes, she was disturbed by it. But no, she did not throw in the towel. "I'm not gonna quit 'cause of one creepy phone call."

Erin had the courage and perseverance needed to take on a class action case. She was willing to call it as she saw it and expected others to do the same: "People are dying, Ross. You've got document after document, right under your nose, ... and you haven't said word about it. I wanna know how the hell you sleep at night." Tact was not one of her strong suits, but honesty was.

She single-handedly persuaded hundreds of people to sign on so the lawsuit could proceed. If there's one ethicist who would lift his hat to her it is Aristotle. As it turns out, so would Judge Simmons, who ruled that the lawsuit against PG&E could proceed and said, "On a more personal note, as a resident here in Barstow, which is not far from Hinkley, I am... appalled that, not only was Hexavalent Chromium used, but your clients actually sent these residents pamphlets telling them it was good for them."

Aristotle asks us to look at what makes for a meaningful life and what it means to be a virtuous person. His approach forms the basis of this chapter. As we will see, Confucius also considers virtues to be central to his ethical theory. We will apply Virtue Ethics to *Erin Brockovich*, *Roger & Me*, *Salmon Fishing in the Yemen*, and *Food, Inc.* (Chapter 2.3). Our two cases focus on Kellogg's and Michael Phelps and, secondly, the European horse-meat scandal. For ethics codes, we will turn to GM and Kellogg's. Let's start with our framework.

Ethical Framework: Virtue Ethics

Aristotle is a man who values moral character. That is his ethical focus. Not moral duty or end goals. His eyes are on the qualities—the ethical traits—needed to get there from here. For him being virtuous is the path to a well-lived and meaningful life, one he calls "*Eudaimonia.*"

Let's start with his view of the soul. Aristotle says when we look into the soul we see passions, faculties, and states of character. His view of *passions* may be in sync with *your* view. He includes joy, fear, hatred, longing, appetite, confidence, and the feelings we get from pleasure or pain. *Faculties* are the vehicles for feeling those passions (of becoming angry, feeling pity, being in pain, and so on). The third thing we'd see looking into the soul would be *states of character*; these connect us to our passions and indicate how we stand in relationship to them.

Our goal should be moderation. For Aristotle, the extremes (e.g., rage and apathy) are undesirable states, so we should avoid them. "Seek the middle path," he'd tell us. We don't judge people good or bad on the basis of their passions. It's what you *do* that counts. The fact you are scared or as mad as a hornet doesn't make you a good or bad person. That's where rationality comes in. We have passions and are moved by them, thanks to our natural faculties. Then the reaction kicks in. We can be even-tempered or either overreact or underreact. This is a matter of self-control (or lack of it). So for Aristotle, our states of character are the propelling force behind our dispositions.

Overview of Aristotle's Ethics

Aristotle's approach is quite distinct. In contrast to the two major theories—Teleological Ethics (ends-focused) and Deontological Ethics (duty-focused)—his is more people-centered and focused on living a purposeful life. His emphasis is on moral character and the core characteristics of a virtuous life.

How *do* we have a life of meaning, knowing that what we do matters? The answer lies in the intellectual and moral *qualities* that knock our lives into shape. Don't ask, "What are my moral obligations?" or "What objectives should guide me?" Ask, "What kind of person do I want to be?" Getting to the person I want to be requires me to practice certain virtues on a regular basis, as a matter of habit. For Aristotle, the intellectual and moral virtues set the foundation for moral development.

At the heart of Aristotle's Virtue Ethics are *intellectual* virtues and *moral* virtues.

Aristotle's Intellectual Virtues

Aristotle's Intellectual Virtues

- Creativity
- Logical Reasoning
- Practical Wisdom ("Street Smarts")
- Philosophical Wisdom (Thinking about the big questions of life)
- Understanding and Comprehension (evaluating and making judgments)

Face it: We would thank our lucky stars to have two or three of those intellectual virtues, much less all five. But if we *did* have all five, we'd be creative/artistic, analytical, practical, philosophical, and able to make judgments about the dilemmas we face. That's an amazing range.

The question is: Did Aristotle leave anything out? Would mathematical and scientific reasoning fit under Logical Reasoning? How about topographical knowledge of the earth and space? Would musical knowledge count in the Creativity category? Would knowledge of languages and cultures be a type of Practical Wisdom or would a sixth Intellectual Virtue be required?

And what about technological skills and computer literacy? Being able to work with hardware differs from a facility with software. This could be useful for a business or any other organizational system centered on education, knowledge, and skills. We might want to think through the Big Five, given it is so useful to us and could be a powerful guide for business. We can see this in Table 2.1.

Aristotle's Moral Virtues

The intellectual virtues are clearly a dynamite combination for developing professional skills, building a career, running a business, or starting a new job or project. The other part of the package is Aristotle's set of *moral* virtues.

Most of his moral virtues are geared to keeping things on an even keel. Not too hot, not too cold. But not too tepid either. A primary virtue is courage—knowing when to stick your neck out, take a stand, climb out on a limb, or take a flying leap. Some situations call for a response that has a spine to it; such as indignation or even outrage. Generally Aristotle recommends a path of moderation, as we see in the listing of his 12 moral virtues (Table 2.2).

Each of Aristotle's desirable moral traits is the mean between extremes. One has the quality in short supply and the other has it in excess. Neither extreme would ordinarily cultivate moral character.

Utilitarians ask, "What is your goal?" "How can you maximize benefits and get the most for the most? Their advice is, "Always try to do what is best for the society as a whole, the majority." Deontologists ask, "What is your moral duty?" Their advice is, "Be true to your moral obligations." Even if "the truth hurts," we should support individual rights and uphold our moral duties.

Aristotle would tell us to focus on moral character. Set a direction and the virtues will keep us on track. Aristotle's moral virtues work with the intellectual virtues to shape the person we become. He would tell us to be neither cowardly nor foolhardy; be courageous. Be neither not stingy

Table 2.1   Aristotle's Intellectual Virtues Applied to Business

Intellectual Virtue	Business Version	Example
Creativity	Innovation, brainstorming, expansive thinking	Use of graphics & aesthetic marketing—e.g., Apple's marketing, *Got Milk?* Ads, Nike's swoosh logo.
Logical Reasoning	Clear, well-ordered processes, and systems of organization	Clear communications, use of statistics to support points, detail as necessary to educate consumers—e.g., clearly written manuals, tech support
Practical Wisdom	Listening "from below," recognizing the working knowledge of others	User-friendly products, paying attention to consumer surveys and social media in terms of trends and general interests per demographics, providing healthcare and hygienic conditions, safe products—e.g., beef recalls due to *E. coli*
Philosophical Wisdom	Putting things in perspective, balance, thinking *big* as well as precise, more focused knowledge	Conveying to the public and to employees the values and beliefs underlying the organization—e.g., strategies for growth, corporate ethics codes and codes of conduct
Understanding & Comprehension	Synthesizing & evaluating, sifting evidence to determine what's worthwhile, what needs to be eliminated, identifying problems	Responding quickly to problems and to addressing issues (safety concerns, public fears, concerns of injustice and the like)—e.g., Tylenol's response to the cyanide poisoning

(tight-fisted) nor wasteful; be generous. Be neither self-deprecating nor self-promoting; be unpretentious, humble. And be neither callous nor sentimental. Be compassionate.

Table 2.2 Aristotle's 12 Moral Virtues

Moral Virtue		
TOO LITTLE: *Moral Deficiency*		*TOO MUCH:* *Moral Excess*
Cowardly	**Courage**	Reckless
Self-denial	**Self control**	Self-indulgent
Stingy	**Generosity**	Wasteful
Surly	**Amiable**	Fawning (Clinging)
Petty	**Honorable**	Vulgar/Gross
Humorless	**Witty**	Buffoon
Self deprecating	**Pride/Ambition**	Self-promoting
Apathetic/Wimpy	**Even-tempered**	Hot-headed
Gullible	**Integrity/Sincerity**	Arrogant
Callous/"Cold fish"	**Compassionate**	Sentimental
Shameless	**Modesty**	Shy
Malicious	**Righteous Indignation**	Envious

Decide how you want to live your life, pursue goals that are challenging, and develop your strengths. Aim high, but not so high that you'll be defeated. Take time to reflect on your progress and look within at your moral strengths and shortcomings. A periodic moral inventory helps keep us honest.

Confucius and Virtue Ethics

Aristotle is not the only proponent of Virtue Ethics. Confucius also sees the importance of a life of virtue. He continues to have great influence in China and elsewhere in the world. Ethicist Cecilia Wee (2014) says, "According to Confucius, there is one true path ('the Way') that all humans should try to follow. Its crucial component is the cultivation and development of the appropriate inward attitudes and feelings towards others, which are then expressed in appropriate outward behaviors." She notes that Confucians emphasize the roles we play in relationship to others, especially family members:

Confucians hold that the appropriate attitudes and behaviors towards others should be subject to gradations. In general, these should differ according to the relation to the person in question. Confucianism is well known for emphasizing the importance, indeed the primacy, of the family.

More generally, what is accorded to any given person would depend on the *role* one inhabits with respect to that person: what is appropriately accorded to one's father, elder brother, friend, political leader etc. would thus be quite different (Wee, 2014, p. 252).

As with Aristotle, Confucius emphasizes a range of virtues as the path to get there from here. Any hope of attaining "moral sagehood" rests on the virtues we possess. Asian Studies Professor Edward Slingerland observed that, "Modern Westerners tend to stress the importance of creativity and thinking for oneself—to borrow from Apple, we all want to *Think Different*. If the Confucians were to adopt a competing marketing motto, it would be *Think Ancient"*(2014, p. 71).

Wee looks at the issue of virtues and notes:

> There are of course certain general virtues or attributes that Confucius and his followers thought the ethical person should possess and make an effort to cultivate. These virtues would include sincerity (*cheng*), trustworthiness (*xin*), conscientiousness (*zhong*)—and especially benevolence (*jen*). Benevolence is held to be the key or overarching virtue, without which one cannot be an effective political leader or attain moral sagehood.
>
> These attributes or virtues may be expressed in different behaviors... depending on the role that one occupies in respect of the person in question. There are also virtues that tend to be role-specific; for instance, the virtue of filiality (*xiao*) obviously applies specifically to sons and daughters (2014, p. 2520).

As with the Feminist Ethicists (see Chapter 2.5), Confucians argue that our sense of self has relational components that show our interdependence. This differs from the Western view that we are each independent, autonomous beings, free to make choices.

> The Confucian conception of the self... sees the self as relational, and as embedded within a set of social, and more especially, familial relations... Confucians see themselves primarily as a part of a larger whole(s). They are *members* of a particular family, a particular institution, and a particular society. They are, thus, embedded in a wider network of specific relationships. It then behooves them to cultivate the appropriate internal attitudes and outward behaviors in respect of each of these roles (Wee, 2014, p. 252).

This view has direct consequences for Business Ethics. Confucians hold the view that in professional ethics, as Wee notes, "an action, at least to some extent, is regulated by the specific role that she has undertaken as a professional" (p. 252). Of course, most of us have to navigate around boundaries and roles within our work setting. Consequently, paying close attention to roles and relationships is advisable, regardless of our connection to Confucian Virtue Ethics.

SPOTLIGHT: *Roger & Me*

Roger and Me (1989) zeroes-in on moral character and how our decisions and actions can affect others. It shows the *many* attempts on the part of filmmaker Michael Moore to get General Motor's CEO Roger Smith to come to Flint, Michigan. He wants Smith to see how decisions made at General Motors had wide-reaching consequences. GM's decisions to close the Flint plant resulted in devastation to the lives of GM's autoworkers.

Prosperity in business is rarely a straight line. There are ups, downs, and stops in-between. Sometimes this is not any one person's fault; the factors may be many and multilayered. But how we react to the cycles of success and failure tell us a great deal about our moral character. How we face adversity—especially adversity we had a hand in creating—puts our moral fiber to the test.

For Aristotle, this is the "center of gravity" of a movie. In his view, how we react to crises, what we do under pressure is like a weather gauge for the soul. Both Jeffrey Wigand (*The Insider*) and Erin Brockovich (*Erin Brockovich*) faced pressures that put them to the test. Neither gave up.

In *Roger & Me*, Moore holds CEO Roger Smith accountable for the hardships that rocked Flint following GM's cutbacks. He wants Smith to see the fallout with his own eyes. Flint was the birthplace of GM, "the largest corporation in the world" (at one time, anyway)—and now looks like it's in its death-throes.

Flint went from boomtown to ghost town. It went from a time "when every day was a great day" to one where great days were a pipe dream. On November 6, 1986, GM closed its plant in Flint. This was a loss of 30,000 jobs. Factories in the US were replaced by their clones in Mexico, where non-union employees worked for a fraction of the cost. Moore rails against such outsourcing:

MICHAEL MOORE: So this was GM chairman Roger Smith. And he appeared to have a brilliant plan: First, close 11 factories in the U.S, then open 11 in Mexico where you pay the workers

70 cents an hour. Then, use the money you've saved by building cars in Mexico to take over other companies, preferably high-tech firms and weapons manufacturers. Next, tell the union you're broke and they happily agree to give back a couple billion dollars in wage cuts. You then take that money from the workers, and eliminate their jobs by building more foreign factories. Roger Smith was a true genius.

Moore seeks to interview CEO Roger Smith, but faces roadblocks at every turn. Smith's handlers effectively limit access to their boss. Moore goes to GM headquarters and is rebuffed. Ditto at the private club where Smith is a member. And so on. Moore doesn't give up. His mission to meet Smith in person isn't diminished one iota by his failure to get close to Smith.

We see how appalled Moore is by what happened to the Flint workers and their families after the plant shut down. His confrontational style goes with the territory, but the empathy Moore shows for the currently unemployed comes through loud and clear. His disdain is palpable.

Moore's *righteous indignation* would likely get a nod from Aristotle, as the human tragedy here is undeniable. For instance, we learn that the rat population surpassed the human population by 50,000—testimony to the fact that "things were beginning to look bleak," as Moore put it. The movie shows how hollowed out, how transformed is this once vibrant city.

The pictures of Flint are heartbreaking. This includes tenants too broke to pay rent getting unceremoniously evicted. Desperation is written on the faces of the victims. No surprise that *Money* magazine crowned Flint the worst city in the US to live in. However, this dishonor (= infamy) infuriated the town's citizens, who set the magazine on fire in a demonstration of burning-the-magazine-in-effigy. Shoot the messenger! Clearly, they dread to think that Flint has gone to the rats and the people are the ones on the losing side.

Along the way Moore interviews a bunch of luminaries and injects a touch of dystopian humor into the film. We see this with blast-from-the-past singer Anita Bryant, who encourages Flint's unemployed to "take it one day at a time." She offers a few pearls of wisdom: "Cheer up America, because you live in a great country, a free America." Nothing like a positive attitude! If only there were the fuel to sustain the optimism.

Singer Pat Boone is next, overflowing with words of praise for Flint and encouragement for its woeful residents. "In a free society, in a capitalist society... things change... the key becomes the attitude." Boone throws in, "And do cheer up." Attitude *does* matter, both singers are right. But attitude is not enough to turn-around the Flints of the world.

The third dignitary is an Amway spokeswoman. Another optimist, she opined, "If you have a dream and go after your dream, …You can make a lot of money." We watch her give color advice to a roomful of women seeking to perfect their personal style. That the women may have no income to invest in their appearance was not brought to her attention, but it's hard for *us* to ignore.

One of the tearjerkers of the movie is a segment on a woman selling rabbits out of her yard. They can be either pets or meat (you pick). We see the caged rabbits (very cute, particularly the long haired black-and-white ones!). We watch her nonchalantly grab a rabbit and skin it as fast as you can say, "Tastes like chicken." That this "business" brings her in an extra $10–15 a week lets us know how tenuous her life has become.

Moore finally gets to interview Roger Smith.

MICHAEL MOORE:	Mr. Smith, we just came down from Flint where we filmed a family being evicted from their home the day before Christmas Eve. A family that used to work in the factory. Would you be willing to come up with us to see what the situation is like in Flint, so that people…?
ROGER SMITH: [CUTTING HIM OFF]	I've been to Flint, and I'm sorry for those people, but I don't know anything about it, but you'd have to… What can I do? What do you want me to do about it?

Well, what *can* he do? That question cuts to the quick. "What do you want *me* to do about it?" What do we want the CEOs and power brokers to do when cities turn into shantytowns? It's a vital question and Roger Smith has laid it out there plain and simple. What *can* he do?

We need to answer such questions; they are not incidental by any means. Quite the contrary, as Moore knows. When he finally gets close enough to pepper Roger Smith with questions, he points out that people are being evicted from their homes. And so he tries again:

MICHAEL MOORE:	Could you come up to Flint?
ROGER SMITH:	No I cannot, I'm sorry.

"I failed to bring Roger to Flint," admits Moore and observes that this is the dawn of a new age. As far as his interview style goes, Moore has a way of pushing buttons. Indeed, GM spokesman Tom Kay finds Moore a source of irritation. "Well, if you're espousing a philosophy, which apparently you are, that the corporation owes employees cradle-to-the-grave security, I don't think that can be accomplished under a free enterprise system." Ironically, Kay himself ended up laid off, as was noted on screen.

Nevertheless, Kay raises an important question: What does a corporation owe its employees? What sort of security is within bounds? Kay turns the question—and it is a legitimate question—into a straw man fallacy. This he does by pushing it to an extreme with the terms "cradle to grave." At that point it seems indefensible, allowing him to skirt the issue of the corporation's own moral standing.

The movie still has a lot of punch. It shows us that the human costs of downsizing is an important topic for our study of Business Ethics. Moore mixes pathos with satire, with a sense of humor out of the Theatre of the Absurd. "I'm proud to be an Amer-i-can" sings Pat Boone as the movie wraps up.

ETHICS CODE: GM's Corporate Citizenship

Times change and the big three automakers are back in the business. GM's website speaks of success and taking care of just about everyone who matters. Let's look at their statement on corporate citizenship. As will soon be apparent, it's a far cry from Flint, Roger Smith, and Tom Kay. You can access it at http://www.gm.com/vision/community_education/corporate_citizenship. print.html.

GM asserts: "Our actions are guided by our values. Our values are not only our road map for corporate responsibility; they are the drivers of all our decisions and activity in all countries. They are, in essence, our code of conduct, our character as a company and what sets General Motors apart."

Exercise

1. Research the 2014 massive recall by GM of millions of its vehicles due to a faulty ignition switch.
2. Set out the basics of the case and where ethical issues came to the fore.
3. Finally, assess GM's actions in light of their ethics code.

Aristotle on Friendship   Aristotle considers friendship to be of fundamental importance to a meaningful life. Business Ethics in general and ethics codes in particular acknowledge the importance of community—and collegiality. This reflects a value that Aristotle would share. Relationships matter. And this is more than establishing a network or "Good Ole Boy" system.

Aristotle's Three Kinds of Friendship

- *Friendship of Utility:* Useful for achieving our goals
- *Friendship of Pleasure:* Great for relaxing, having fun
- *Friendship of Virtue:* Mutual respect and integrity

Friendships of utility are probably the most typical kind of relationship found within a business context. We are encouraged to establish a network of useful relationships, as with *Linked In* and related professional networking.

Friendships of pleasure have their place, too, as we know from the proverb "All work and no play makes Jack a dull boy." However trivial that sounds, it is not without meaning.

Friendships of virtue go beyond the level of useful relationship or enjoyable companion. Friends of virtue offer encouragement and support, empathy and help. They give us a reality check when we need one. They help clarify our sense of purpose and direction.

Philosopher Richard Kraut (2010) points out that virtuous friendships are based on equality, in contrast to unequal relationships like that of a parent and a child. The ideal friendships are those of moral equals, where we consider friends to have good character, so we hold them in high regard and respect them. These are inherent to friendships of virtue.

Aristotle and Friendship in Film   It would be remiss of us not to include a look at the work environment, the community, and the way the workplace fosters or hinders our relationships with our colleagues and co-workers. Aristotle provides a useful tool for looking at one aspect of community—*friendship*. We can see that in three insightful movies—*The Insider*, *The Company Men* (examined in more detail in the next chapter), and *Salmon Fishing in the Yemen* (2010).

There we see the highest level of friendship. You know the kind—"true blue" friendships, held together by mutual respect and integrity. For Aristotle, these are friendships of virtue. We see this with Jeffrey Wigand and Lowell Bergman in *The Insider*, Gene and Phil in *The Company Men*, and Sheik Muhammed and Fred Jones in *Salmon Fishing in the Yemen*.

The Insider　When Wigand came forward as a whistleblower he faced one obstacle after another, including death threats. As the toll on his family mounted and his wife took the children and hit the road, Wigand's life spiraled downward. Bergman saw it and made it clear that, yes, he cared. After he learned that providing expert testimony against Brown & Williamson might land him in jail, Wigand was beside himself. Bergman reached out to him. "Maybe things have changed," he said. No, "Nothing's changed"—"Fuck it. Let's go to court," Wigand declared. At that moment things fell into place—a moment of values clarification. He saw what needed to be done.

Friends of virtue do that for us, by asking questions or merely listening as we sort things out. Just being there means everything, silently beside us while the inner turbulence settles and things become clear. Such moments of friendship, of empathy, are invaluable.

The Company Men　The second case involves old time friends Gene and Phil. Both had gotten sacked in their company's downsizing. Gene expresses his anger about the actions of GTX, the company. As far as he was concerned, GTX head honchos acted hastily and unjustly. Aristotle would commend Gene's righteous indignation, given the top brass got bonuses while others got the axe. He would also appreciate Gene's compassion and his humility. Basically, Gene has a strong batting average when it comes to Aristotle's moral virtues.

Gene runs into Phil at a bar and is alarmed at how depressed he seems. He reaches out to Phil, just being there, caring about him. As it turns out, Phil's wife doesn't want the neighbors to know that Phil lost his job. So she coerced him into donning a suit, grabbing his briefcase and pretending to go to work every morning. That leaves Phil with chasms of time looking for another job, or sitting it out at a bar, as now. Phil tells Gene, "You know the worst part? ... The world didn't stop. The newspaper still came every morning, the automatic sprinklers went off at six. Jerry next door still washed his car every Sunday. My life ended and nobody noticed."

Things hit bottom. Phil might as well be invisible. Gene lets Phil know that *he* notices. He suggests they go to an afternoon movie, to no avail. Phil is sinking into despair. Gene can see his friend is not making a good job of handling unemployment or the pretense of his wife. When things go from bad to worse, we see Gene's concern for his friend.

Salmon Fishing in the Yemen　The third case illustrates how one type of friendship can evolve. Dr. Alfred ("Fred") Jones is a Scot with an attitude who works for the U.K. government as an expert in fish and fishing. He is world renown for his beautifully constructed flies used for fly fishing (trout, salmon, etc.) in rivers, lakes, and streams. Only under threat of losing his job does he agree to take on a most unusual assignment—to assist a Yemeni Sheikh who has buckets of money and a vision. Sheikh Muhammed, an avid fly fisher, wants to bring water and salmon (lots of salmon) to Yemen. He has a dream and wants Fred to come on board.

Initially Fred has no more interest in bringing salmon to Yemen than camels to Scotland. The very idea strikes him as ludicrous. Fred pooh-poohs the project until the screws are put into him (help the Sheikh or sign up for unemployment). He opts for the former and becomes a friend of utility along the way. He tries his darndest to get the fish to the Yemen and keep his job in the bargain.

The charming and sincere millionaire not only sets a spark inside the very crusty Fred, but he awakens in him a renewed appreciation for life and for helping others. He shows Fred the value of believing in yourself and in having faith that even wild-crazy ideas may actually work.

We watch as the business relationship evolves to a friendship—yes of utility, but a friendship nonetheless, as the fish are airlifted from Scotland to the Yemen. We watch, too, as the friendship of utility transforms and deepens into a friendship of virtue. Thanks to the lessons he learned, and changes in his values and view of the world (and people too), Fred is not the same man we met back there at the British fisheries office.

Friends of integrity are not merely a source of entertainment. They are a source of enrichment, guidance, and moral clarification. They help us live right. And when we err, as sometimes we do (!), they help point the way out of the darkness, stand by us as we dust ourselves off and start anew, and are our companions as we move forward. At times they have to take us to task, to point out our mistakes, to help keep us honest by holding us accountable.

And when there's a network of such friends, as in the last scene of *The Company Men*, all can benefit. Together they instill in themselves and in one another the value of practicing the moral and intellectual virtues. It makes for character. Businesses that foster such relationships build communities that last.

Aristotle and Business Ethics Law professor Lorie Graham (1995) notes that Aristotle's Virtue Ethics provides a helpful guide for those in the legal profession—and we can extend that to business as well. Look for role models. "A person learns virtues by imitating good people and good actions ... After a while the habit of acting in a good way become one's own...and when he or she then reflects upon the nature of the good actions he or she can understand the virtuous character (Robert Condlin, noted in Graham, 1995).

As Graham observes, understanding moral principles requires *imitating* the actions of others. Aristotle emphasizes "the virtues we get by first exercising them" (*Nicomachean Ethics*). In other words, a student of virtue develops an ethical disposition by performing virtuous acts. We learn by doing—and by watching others and looking to others for advice. This is an important part of the process of acquiring knowledge and building moral character.

Those who are public figures, supervisors, teachers, and those in positions of leadership often serve role models. We look to them for evidence of a developed moral character. So whenever someone shows moral flaws and fails to serve as a good role model, we need to take action. This includes stripping an athlete of awards if they are guilty of using banned performance-enhancing drugs. That's not all, as the next case shows.

CASE STUDY 1: Olympian Michael Phelps and Kellogg's

American swimmer Michael Phelps made a big splash at the 2012 Olympics. He won medal after medal after yet another medal. We like winners and he was certainly that. The Kellogg company signed him to put a face on their cereal—functioning like a spokesman for the company.

That looked like a sure thing for the company, given all the attention Phelps received. Just about everyone who ever took swimming lessons envied those long arms, big feet, and ability to move through water like a sea otter. And then things took an unexpected turn: A video surfaced on YouTube that cast a shadow on Phelps' moral standing. It showed him smoking from a "bong." Evidently it was marijuana, which was not a legal substance at the time, and (at least from Kellogg's perspective) not the sort of thing children should see. This presented an ethical dilemma for Kellogg's. What do you do when things veer off course?

Exercise

1. To what degree do we expect athletes to be moral role models? Can you give any examples?
2. Phelps issued an apology and stated, "I engaged in behavior which was regrettable and demonstrated bad judgment" (Papa, 2012). Was that enough? Once tarnished, is there a way to recover?

3. Was Kellogg's right to reject Phelps as a spokesman? Was there another option that Kellogg should have pursued? Share your thoughts.

ETHICS CODE: Kellogg's "K Values"

Kellogg's ethics code is in line with Aristotle's Virtue Ethics. Look over the code and see to what degree Aristotle's virtues are integrated here in the K Values. You can access them at http://www.kelloggcompany.com/en_US/our-values.html.

SPOTLIGHT: *Food, Inc.*

For Aristotle, character development and finding a sense of purpose requires both intellectual and moral virtues. These are traits developed over time and require a degree of consistency in the decisions we make. This puts the value on moderation and finding the mean between the two extremes. Aim for the middle path, avoid excess, and steer clear of deficiency.

At times, moderation is *not* the right thing to do. Some actions are so ghastly or vicious that our response should be outrage, not tolerance. Movies like *Food, Inc.*, for example, show us disturbing practices around food production. As we saw in the previous chapter, we can look at the movie from a Deontological perspective. Aristotle would also have a few words to say about the moral issues that come to the surface.

One of those interviewed in the film is Joel Salatin, farmer, environmentalist, and author. He reflects, "We have learned how to plant, fertilize and harvest corn using global positioning satellite technology, and nobody sits back and asks, 'But should we be feeding cows corn?' ... We're all into the how of it and nobody's stepping back and saying 'But why?'"

We may be disturbed to learn that, "In 1972, the FDA conducted approximately 50,000 food safety inspections. In 2006, the FDA conducted 9,164." That's not all. Note also: "The meat packing industry for years prevented country-of-origin labeling. They fought not to label genetically modified foods; and now 70% of processed food in the supermarket has some genetically modified ingredient."

Not all of this—and maybe none of this—should sit well with us. Some of the practices of the food industry are not as transparent as they should be. That our response may *not* be moderate is justified in Aristotle's eyes in such circumstances. *Food, Inc.* indicates the need to address these issues. Salatin conveys this concern:

> A culture that just uses a pig as a pile of protoplasmic inanimate structure, to be manipulated by whatever creative design the human can foist on that critter, will probably view individuals within its community, and other cultures in the community of nations, with the same type of disdain and disrespect and controlling type mentalities.

We can speak up and work for change. Would it work? The movie says *yes*; there are grounds for optimism. Just listen to the Vice President of the American Corn Growers Association: "People have got to start *demanding* good, wholesome food of us, and we'll deliver; I promise you. We're very ingenious people, we will deliver."

Aristotle would likely agree with Salatin that we need more integrity and a stronger moral base in food production. He'd also favor a foundation of mutual respect between the various businesses and their customers. The failure on the part of the meat packing industry to properly—honestly—label the ingredients in the meat sold to consumers sends a signals of a flawed morality. It tells us that the customer does *not* come first. That can change.

Let's look now at a case that also calls for honesty in product labeling and in consumer relations.

CASE STUDY 2: The European Horsemeat Scandal

November 2012 was not a good month for either horses or beefeaters. *Here's why:* Horsemeat was found in frozen lasagnas and other products supposedly containing beef in England, Ireland, France and Sweden (Public Radio International (PRI), 2013). *The Guardian* (UK) reported that,

> The Food Safety Authority of Ireland tested a range of cheap frozen beefburgers and ready meals from supermarkets last November for the presence of DNA from other species which were undeclared. It found horse DNA in over one-third of the beefburger samples, and pig in 85% of them (Lawrence, 2013).

Non-edible horsemeat was passed off as edible, adding to the fraud. The U.K.'s Environment Secretary, Owen Paterson, was not pleased.

"It is unacceptable that people have been deceived in this way." Furthermore, "There appears to have been criminal activity in an attempt to defraud the consumer. The prime responsibility for dealing with this lies with retailers and food producers" (PRI, 2013). Yes, Paterson is right to point that out.

Of course, safeguards should be in place to test ingredients. Consumers should be able to trust that the meat they buy is correctly labeled. From the Costco tainted berries case (Chapter 1.3) we know the problems that can crop up if the label is ... misleading. Processed foods like ground beef are especially important to monitor, given any one hamburger patty could contain meat from a number of countries! For example, some of the beef sampled had horsemeat from as far away as Poland (Lawrence, 2013). What we think we're eating and what we are *actually* eating may not be one and the same.

Paterson remarks on this fact: "We take different types of meats and different types of materials from all over the world," he says. "They'll come across many different continental borders. And they end up in a processing factory, and then on a supermarket shelf." It is "close to impossible" to find out where that material came from in the first place, he notes (PRI, 2013). Whatever the benefits, there are shortcomings that center on product safety. Equally unsettling, what is labeled "beef" may not be from a cow. Some beefeaters would be horrified to find out their "beef" contained pork—given some religions prohibit pork consumption. Even if you like pork, it seems only fair to know that's what you're eating.

An economy beef burger that you get in England "can legally contain as little as 47% beef" (Lawrence, 2013). Come again? Forty-seven percent. That means *less than half* of the econo-burger may be beef! Or, to put it another way, 53 percent might not be beef at all. Do the math: less than half of the burger is beef—the more than half remaining is a non-beef concoction!

Exercise

1. If econo-burgers need only contain 47 percent beef, would it be objectionable if the remaining 53 percent contained pig? Or horsemeat? Could other meats be used without listing them? Is that of a different order from 53 percent being soy, corn, or other fillers?
2. Is it just a labeling problem to add in *edible* horsemeat (or pig or...)? So long as companies listed other meats being ground together with the beef would that be morally acceptable? Is transparency the only issue?

3. Let's forget about the horsemeat and pig for a second. Is there any problem in ground beef containing beef from multiple sources? What if those sources are in different countries—so one burger could be a mixture of ground beef from the U.K., Argentina, and the US, for example? Should it be a requirement to list the source(s) of the meat? Share your thoughts as to the moral parameters that should be brought in here.

Ethical Reflections

The lack of transparency in meat production and packaging is deplorable, as the horsemeat scandal illustrates. We also see it in a stomach-churning moment in *Food, Inc.*, when we are shown the unsanitary and inhumane conditions in chicken production. The memory of hundreds, if not thousands, of chickens (both living and dead) crammed together surrounded by excrement in near darkness inside a gigantic metal container is impossible to erase after the credits roll.

It's painfully obvious that there is room for improvement. Virtue Ethics has a lot going for it and could definitely be put to use when we're ready to tackle issues such as those raised in this chapter. From trying to protect the Hinkley residents to seeking redress when they are harmed, to trying to ensure that consumers are aware of the sources of the meat-blends they buy at the grocery store—the circumstances can vary widely. And yet there we are. The test of moral character appears in many forms and in many times and places.

Works Cited

Aristotle, *Nicomachean Ethics*, http://classics.mit.edu/Aristotle/nicomachaen. html (accessed December 21, 2014).

Boylan, Michael, *Basic Ethics*, (Upper Saddle River, NJ: Prentice Hall, 2000).

Condlin, R.J., "Clinical Education in the Seventies: An Appraisal of the Decade," *Journal of Legal Education*, Vol. 33, No. 4 (December 1983), pp. 604–612, http://www.jstor.org/discover/10.2307/42897908?sid=2110549354157 3&uid=70&uid=2&uid=4&uid=3738032&uid=2129 (accessed December 21, 2014).

General Motors, GM's Corporate Citizenship, http://www.gm.com/vision/ community_education/corporae_citizenship.print.html (accessed December 21, 2014).

Graham, Lorie, "Aristotle's Ethics and the Virtuous Lawyer: A Study on Legal Ethics and Clinical Legal Education," *Journal of the Legal Profession*, Vol. 20,

p. 5, 1996, http://papers.ssrn.com/sol3/papers.cfm?abstract_id=991661 (accessed December 21, 2014).

Kellogg Company, Kellogg's "K Values," http://www.kelloggcompany.com/en_US/ our-values.html (accessed December 21, 2014).

Kraut, Richard, "Aristotle's Ethics," *Stanford Encyclopedia of Philosophy*, May 1, 2001, revised April 21, 2014, http://plato.stanford.edu/entries/aristotle-ethics/ (accessed December 21, 2014).

Lawrence, Felicity, "Horsemeat Scandal: The Essential Guide," *The Guardian*, February 15, 2013, http://www.theguardian.com/uk/2013/feb/15/ horsemeat-scandal-the-essential-guide (accessed December 21, 2014).

Papa, Anthony, "Michael Phelps: Greatest Olympian Ever (Who Also Happened to Smoke Pot)," *Huffington Post*, August 3, 2012, http://www.huffingtonpost. com/anthony-papa/michael-phelps-greatest-o_b_1737863.html, (accessed December 20, 2014).

PRI, "Europeans Dealing With Dual Horse Meat Scandals In Food Chain," Public Radio International, February 13, 2013, http://www.pri.org/stories/ politics-society/government/europeans-dealing-with-dual-horse-meat-scandals-in-food-chain-12975.html (accessed December 21, 2014).

Slingerland, Edward, *Trying Not to Try*, (New York, NY: Crown Publishing, 2014).

Wee, Cecilia, "Confucianism and Killing vs. Letting Die," in Wanda Teays, John Stewart-Gordon, and Alison Dundes Renteln (eds.), *Global Bioethics and Human Rights: Contemporary Issues*, (Lanham, MD: Rowman & Littlefield, 2014).

2.5

The Caring Community
Feminist Ethics

Spotlight: *The Company Men; Erin Brockovich; Out of the Clear Blue Sky*
Case Study: Film Recovery Systems, Inc.
Ethics Code: Microsoft

> **HR Director:** *I'm confident all these dismissals will stand up under legal scrutiny.*
> **Gene McClary:** *What about ethical scrutiny?*
> **HR Director:** *We're not breaking any laws, Gene.*
> **Gene McClary:** *I guess I always assumed we were trying for a higher standard than that, Paul.*
> —The Company Men

They say losing a job is right up there with a death in the family and a heart attack. And no wonder—it can be devastating and life-changing. We see how much this is the case in *The Company Men* (2009).[1] It follows three mid-level employees, Gene McClary, Bobby Walker, and Phil Woodward, whose lives radically alter after the axe falls. Most of us know that there's not much preparation to cushion the pain of being terminated or to distance yourself so it just bounces off of you.

The very terms of description (being *fired, axed, terminated, canned, sacked, discharged, given marching orders*) cause visions of crushing blows to come to mind. The movie takes us into this territory in a compelling and touching way. In contrast to *Up in the Air* (Chapter 1.2), which centers on a terminator-for-hire, *The Company Men* centers on the target of such terminators—the employee. We will see how Feminist Ethics gives us tools to study the story that unfolds.

Business Ethics Through Movies: A Case Study Approach, First Edition. Wanda Teays.
© 2015 John Wiley & Sons, Ltd. Published 2015 by John Wiley & Sons, Ltd.

Actor Ben Affleck reflects on playing Bobby Walker, one of the three protagonists. He says,

> In the research I did, particularly for men, it is extremely emasculating to be laid off. Often men lie about it or they try to get another job before anyone finds out. America is founded on the idea that if you work hard, and you play by the rules, you can work your way up. And the idea that one day you're going to move backward, you're going to move down the ladder, it can be excruciatingly embarrassing (*The Company Men*: Special Features).

We watch as Bobby goes from playing golf and driving a Porsche (= wealth, success, leisure time) to being unemployed. It came without warning and, hit him like a two-by-four. His world turns upside-down as he gets sucked into a vortex of desperation, futility, and despair.

It's a downward spiral: Bobby goes from being a Vice President at GTX (his company) to an overqualified job seeker. Thirty-seven years old and frustrated do not make for a winning combination. He's angry that others don't recognize his talents or appreciate the indignity of what he's going through. The lack of sympathy only adds to his misery. This much is obvious: Bobby has a rough road ahead. We watch as he deals with the challenges and struggles to get back on his feet.

In this chapter we will look at Feminist Ethics as a moral framework. Our films here are *The Company Men*, *Erin Brockovich*, and the 9/11 documentary *Out of the Clear Blue Sky*. We will also examine a Business Ethics classic, the Film Recovery Systems case. It resulted in homicide charges against key management personnel. Our ethics code for this chapter is that of Microsoft. Let's start with ethical theory.

Ethical Framework: Feminist Ethics

Feminist Ethicists agree with Aristotle that we should lead a life of virtue and avoid vice, and develop our moral character. However, they would say that Aristotle should include the way *relationships* influence moral reasoning and take a more expansive look at moral agency.

As with Teleological and Deontological Ethics, Feminist Ethics takes different forms. Ethicist Rosemarie Tong points out that, "Some emphasize issues related to women's traits and behaviors, particularly their caregiving ones." Others emphasize "the political, legal, economic, and/or ideological causes and effects of women's second-sex status" (Tong and

Williams, 2014). Those in the second group also look at moral status and personhood.

Traditionally, ethicists have focused on *rationality* as central to moral agency. As we remember, moral agency has two parts: First, the moral agent must be competent (=rational) and, secondly, the moral agent must have free will (not acting under coercion or duress). The first characteristic, competence, is seen as crucial for grasping the difference between good and evil. The second characteristic, free will, is seen as crucial for holding people responsible for their actions. Without the freedom to act on their own volition, it's hard to hold them accountable. Feminist Ethicists think it problematic to prioritize rationality, that other properties are important. That doesn't mean any *one* criterion isn't important. The issue is whether there are more to consider. In addition, the extent that our free will is really "free" determines culpability.

One proponent of a wider view is philosopher Mary Anne Warren. Her work in ethics is interesting and enlightening, and has had considerable impact. She explains why moral status is worth contemplating:

> There are many reasons why we might want a concept of moral status. In the worst case, we might want only to rationalize the power and priv-ilege of our group… But despite this danger, human beings badly need shared standards and principles of moral status, based upon arguments that most people can understand and accept. There are *two obvious facts* about human beings as a species that help to explain why we have this need, and why it is particularly acute at the present time (1997, p.10, my emphasis).

The "two obvious facts" that she points out are:

- Human beings "are clever and opportunistic creatures who have recently come to possess an awesome capacity to do harm."
- "We have a natural capacity to care about other living things, both human and nonhuman—and sometimes about things that are evidently lifeless, such as stones" (pp. 12–13).

Warren believes that philosopher David Hume was right to argue that such moral feelings constitute the essential and instinctive foundation of all human morality. She contends that, "Upon this foundation we con-struct moral concepts, rules, principles, and theories" and strengthening that natural capacity is in our own interest both as individuals and as mem-bers of social communities (p. 13).

Relational Properties

Warren thinks *relational properties* need to be factored into the equation. Look beyond the individual to our links with others. Consider the different ways we are connected to one another. Being a parent, a sibling, a citizen, or a friend would not be possible without others in the world.

For that reason, Warren sees *relationships* as relevant to moral status and to moral reasoning. As we remember from Chapter 2.3, one of Ross's moral duties is gratitude. One form this takes is *loyalty* to friends, family, co-workers. Warren would also say that loyalty, among our other ties to others, can play a role in moral decision-making and that it is wise to recognize this fact.

Existentialist Martin Heidegger's discussion of being-in-the-world is also useful. He thinks of the individual against the backdrop of others around us, in society, etc. Warren would agree, though her work is not in or on Existentialism per se. Nevertheless, both contend that relationships with others shape our identity *and* our morality. Heidegger focuses more on the first (identity), Warren more on the second (morality).

Warren recommends examining our moral roots and how we assign moral standing. Which should weigh more? Most people don't value the life of an insect nearly as high as that of a sentient animal. Most don't value the life of any animal as high as that of most persons. It gets trickier when we weigh one human life against *another* human life and assign relative value (moral status). In both law and morality, that can be controversial, and problematic.

For example, an embryo or fetus does not normally have as great a moral status as a person (certainly not in law). However, there is a great divide around whether that ought to be the case. Warren devoted a lot of time and attention to addressing this moral problem and in trying to sort this out.

Warren on Moral Status

Warren was struck by the fact that many highly regarded ethicists emphasize only one criterion in assessing moral status. For Tom Regan it's sentience, but for Kant, Mill, and to some extent, Aristotle, "rationality" stands out as most significant.

Warren points out, however, that Kant grants full moral status only to *rational* moral agents; namely, adults of "sound mind" (= competent). He precludes infants, young children, severely mentally disabled, animals, and plants from having moral status. However, he doesn't require moral agents to be *human*.

Because Kant does not explicitly demand *humanity* to be a criterion of personhood, Warren concludes that a much broader notion follows. She looks at "persons" that are not necessarily human and asks if we should grant them moral rights. Should we assign "personhood" to genetically engineered humans, cyborgs, extraterrestrials, certain animals, and other rational entities? Although Kant did not take up the issue of *corporate* moral status, that doesn't mean it is not valuable to examine it.

In Warren's view, *personhood*—not humanity—is crucial for moral status. She argues that only persons are members of the moral community. She then sets out criteria of personhood. Such criteria, as it turns out, are very useful, but difficult to settle upon. It's not easy to decide what makes someone a "person."

She drew up a list of five criteria and argued that at least some traits were sufficient, but none were necessary.

Warren's Criteria of Personhood

- The ability to reason
- Consciousness and the ability to feel pain
- Self-motivated activity
- The ability to communicate
- Self-awareness

What do *you* think of this list of criteria? If they aren't adequate, then what should we change? Given the importance we attach to what is a legal and moral *person*, a great deal—truly a great deal—follows.

Another concern is how we see the individual with respect to the moral community. Feminist Ethicists like Warren say we are not isolated monads existing in moral vacuums. We are in the world, amongst others and stand in a caring relationship to those others. A great deal also follows from this. Let's see how.

The Role Of Care In Feminist Ethics

Feminist ethicists posit *caring* as a key component of ethics. This is another thing Heidegger would agree with. He thinks we stand in a caring relationship to others. However, his focus is on authenticity, not morality per se, whereas Feminist Ethicists focus more on the way relationships affect moral behavior, and thus go in a different direction from Heidegger's focus on the individual.

Here's where Aristotle comes in. Virtue Ethics is the closest to Feminist Ethics in emphasizing moral character. In addition, such traits as compassion and generosity are shared values between the two theories. One of the biggest differences, however, is the role of rationality: Aristotle gives it more weight than do Feminist Ethicists, who think care has to be given more credence.

Care involves feelings, along with the supposition that we are capable of *empathy* towards others. "Care is not rational, in the sense of being purely intellectual, deductive, or even egoistic," explains philosopher Alison M. Jaggar. "Proponents of care thinking regard it as rational in a broader, honorific sense... that produces morally appropriate action" (1995, pp. 180–181).

Jaggar distinguishes "Care Reasoning" from "Justice Thinking" in this way:

- *Justice thinking*—appeals to rational and universalizable moral principles, applied impartially.
- *Care thinking*—emphasizes responsiveness particular situations whose morally salient features elicit empathy, openness, and receptivity (pp. 180–81).

Some Feminists turn their attention to social and political problems, including race and gender bias and discrimination; others focus on Ethics of Care. This latter group includes Carol Gilligan, Nel Noddings, and Rita Manning. They see empathy, care, listening—all aspects of interpersonal relationships—to be on the moral map. They think rule-based ethics has not served us well. Carol Gilligan was a catalyst here.

Gilligan versus Kohlberg on the Importance of Rules

Gilligan's early work offers an alternative to the rule-bound approach to morality put forward by Lawrence Kohlberg, who sees principled (rule-driven) morality as the highest level we can achieve. In that sense, he agrees with Immanuel Kant and places a relationship-focused morality lower on the moral scale. He sets out three stages (Boylan, 2000, 127):

Kohlberg's Stages of Morality (Highest to Lowest)

1 Post-conventional morality, which ranges from social contract morality to morality guided by abstract, universal principles.
➡ *Principled morality—The highest level of moral awareness.*

2   Conventional morality, which ranges from interpersonal to societal, and is more attentive to the needs of others.
    ➡ *Social morality—The middle level of moral awareness.*
3   Pre-conventional morality emphasizes individual benefits and is focused on self-interest.
    ➡ *Neanderthal morality—The lowest level of moral awareness.*

The idea that abstract moral principles (rules, rules, and more rules) should light the way for all to follow doesn't sit well with Gilligan or other Care Ethicists. Her advice? Factor the *social context* and relationships into our decision-making. That's what strikes her as most important, not a moral hierarchy placing justice and abstract principles at the top of the ladder (Gilligan, 1993).

Kohlberg is simply mistaken, argues Gilligan. Plus, he fails to see the role gender plays in ethical decision-making. Her research led her to conclude that males and females are *not* on the same ethical wavelength. Their approach to moral dilemmas is fundamentally different. Rosemarie Tong and Nancy Williams (2014) explain:

> Gilligan believes that Kohlberg's methodology is male-biased. Its ears are tuned to male, not female, moral voices. Thus, it fails to register the different voice Gilligan claims to have heard in her study of twenty-nine women reflecting on their abortion decisions. This distinctive moral voice, says Gilligan, speaks a language of care that emphasizes relationships and responsibilities.

Not all agree. The notion of a moral divide between men and women rubs some the wrong way. Michael Boylan, for example, considers Gilligan's view much too one-sided. He thinks there are any number of men who are as caring as women; just look at all those in service professions like teaching, nursing, physical therapy, and the like. He does not consider care the purview of females. Think about it.

Exercise

1.   Do *you* think men and women approach morality differently—and end up with conflicting views about moral development?

2. If there *are* differences, what impact does or should this have in Business Ethics—such as in the development of ethics codes?

Rethinking Rules in Moral Theory

Other ethicists have shaped Care Ethics, especially Nel Noddings and Rita Manning. Noddings thinks ethics is about relationships between the '*one-caring*' and the '*cared-for.*' She contends that, "Real care requires actual encounters with specific individuals; it cannot be bestowed from afar upon individuals in general" (Tong and Williams, 2014). Real care requires relationships. It's not something abstract or detached.

Rita Manning also takes a care approach. She posits caring as a central concern of her work on justice and injustice within prisons and detention centers and in the sorts of policies found in US Customs and Immigration (I.C.E.). She sees an urgent need for change, and many others agree. For example, the use of shackling detainees for court hearings has been under fire. The reality has been this:

> People held at detention centers in the San Francisco area are trans- ported to court shackled at the wrists, waist and ankles, attorneys for four immigrants wrote in a federal lawsuit filed in 2011. The shackles are kept on during court hearings, which is humiliating to immigrants and may predispose judges to view them as criminals, the attorneys wrote (Chang, 2014).

Those put in shackles include people who simply couldn't afford bond; thus not "criminals" in the usual sense of the term. The feds were finally persuaded to stop shackling some defendants. This is a move that Manning and other Care Ethicists would applaud (and continue to work for more change).

This emphasis on relationships has value for putting Business Ethics in place. Look at the context of *this* business, *this* place and time, and *this* community. The care that forms a connection between individuals is of fundamental importance and may be definitive in retaining employees, fostering a positive environment, and instilling the values that are essential to a stable and respectful business.

Let's see this in *The Company Men*, which shows how human connec- tions affect the way business is done.

SPOTLIGHT: *The Company Men*

The Company Men explores the impact on three different mid-level employees of one company's downsizing. The movie opens with Gene, Phil, and Bobby putting on the finishing touches of their business attire— adjusting their ties before the mirror, with family photos off to the side. All head off to work; unaware of the fate awaiting them. One by one, they find out that they no longer are employed by GTX. Each one is in shock. We watch how quickly their moneyed existence crumbles, and, with that, all the trappings (a snazzy car, fancy clothes, expensive artwork, school trips to Italy for their children, and so on).

Most of us don't get to ride in a Porsche much less own one. And most of us aren't members of a golf club. However, we can relate to the loss and the pain of being forced to scale down, way down. And we know the embarrassment of telling family and friends that we have entered the *Realm of the Unemployed*. That is something that people of all colors and stripes can understand, and dread.

Remember Elizabeth Kübler-Ross and her five stages of grief? She says those facing death go through the stages of denial, anger, bargaining, depression, and, finally, acceptance. Well, losing a job can hit about as bad as a dire medical prognosis and can certainly cause a truckload of grief. *You know:* You didn't see it coming, you are devastated, and have no idea what lies ahead. Kübler-Ross's stages resonate with many people. We see this with Gene, Phil, and Bobby, although "acceptance" is not clearly part of their grief process. Their last stage bears more resemblance to transformation, which may be a kind of acceptance. But let's see how her grief model plays out with our hapless fellows.

Stage One They and their family members go into denial. We see it most with Phil's wife, who refuses to accept the situation and forces him to play a game of charades pretending he still has a job. But it's Bobby who shows how hard it can be in terms of self-esteem. Initially Bobby thinks he will quickly rebound, but finds that not the case.

Stage Two Anger bubbles up like poisoned frogs in a lake, pushing people to the breaking point. Bobby and Gene demonstrate that. They see themselves as victims of a grave injustice—and are explosive. In contrast, Phil's anger turns inward, an implosion. His is the seething, muttering under your breath type of anger. He falls into despair. The unfairness eats at him like acid. He is furious that those at the top of the corporate ladder don't suffer similarly. He sees this as fundamentally unjust.

Stages Three and Four   The bargaining and depression stages aren't long in coming. Bobby attends confidence-building pep talks for the recently unemployed. He finds them ludicrous at first, but eventually joins the chanting: "I will win. Why? Because I have Faith, Courage, Enthusiasm." This was not easy, given he saw himself as an "unemployed loser."

Having others to commiserate with is instrumental in keeping Bobby from emotional paralysis. He discovered that those in the same boat share the depression, anxiety, and fear of sinking into the Pit of No Return.

Stage Five   We watch as two of the three men get it together and move past depression in a constructive way. We might call that "acceptance," since they acknowledged the drastic changes they suffered. They took hold of the situation and turned it around, no longer victims. Desperate for a job, Bobby reluctantly asks his brother-in-law Jack for construction work. A little humility was injected into Bobby's moral base.

Care Ethicists would commend Jack's show of empathy toward his unqualified in-law. Bobby could no more do carpentry than sprout wings, and yet Jack let him come on board. At one point Bobby actually contemplates continuing in construction, but Jack told him the truth, nicely delivered— that he sucked at carpentry and encouraged him to take a job he could succeed at. Caring does not mean puffing people up; it means being there for them and acting with integrity.

As for Gene, he expresses no small amount of indignation. Feminist Ethicists would agree with Aristotle that outrage was justified. They'd also seek to change the way decisions were made with the favoritism at GTX. Eventually Gene gets in touch with an earlier reality, one where companies create things that can be seen and touched—like ships, buildings, and cars. He drew from that vision to move forward, while keeping his commitment to help other workers who lost their jobs. From that base, he created a company rooted in a community with shared values.

An ethical business treats its employees and the public with respect and dignity. Gene sees this and seeks to put it into effect. And he makes this much clear: Business practices that are ruthless or indifferent to the human costs of its operation should be tossed out like rotting fish.

Success is not a matter of money, though money counts. As we see with the new company at the movie's end, it is possible to operate with a different model. Business Ethics can be relational in its moral principles and practices. And it can recognize that moral status does not have to revolve around rationality or abstract principles to be applied without acknowledging the human dimension.

Exercise

What should be done when making money is an obsession? On January 23, 2014, a series of letters to the editor of *The New York Times* grappled with that question. Read the views expressed below and share *your* thoughts—and how you'd respond:

- *Bill Stewart:* "During my career... I was aware that in New York, there was a particularly strong obsession with excessive wealth, and that this obsession was culturally acceptable, even desirable and beneficial to society."
- *David Geller:* "During more than 25 years as a wealth manager, I saw many clients who are caught up in the same mind-set... that more money equals a better life... [but] they were not happy and proved to me the fallacy of the accepted equation in our society that Money = Happiness."
- *Eileen M. Howard:* "Once upon a time, great wealth often produced great philanthropy and political intent for the common good of our country. Now it seems as if there are large swaths of our society that re intent upon accumulating an ever-increasing pile of money, no matter how it affects others, while trying to avoid even the slightest responsibility for the good of our country as a whole."

Let's now look at a classic case in Business Ethics where care was in scant supply.

CASE STUDY: Film Recovery Systems and Corporate Homicide

Film Recovery Systems, Inc. in Elk Grove, Illinois, recovers silver from used X-ray film processed in large vats containing water and sodium cyanide. Stefan Golab worked on this procedure and had been suffering the effects—constant headaches, dizziness and vomiting—during the month and a half he had been working there. He asked to be transferred to another department, but his request was denied by Charles Kirschbaum, plant manager at Film Recovery Systems.

A week later, on February 10, 1983, Golab died working over these vats. His death resulted in charges of murder, reckless conduct and involuntary manslaughter of three key figures of the company. Film Recovery Systems claimed it was not doing anything remarkably different from any other business.

The Context

Jay C. Magnuson, Cook County prosecutor in the State of Illinois, investigated the death and was appalled.[2] He charged Steven O'Neil, Gerald Pett, Charles Kirschbaum, and Daniel Rodriguez (the President, Vice President, Plant Manager, and Plant Foreman) with murder and reckless conduct. Pett was found not guilty, but O'Neil, Kirschbaum and Rodriguez were convicted of murder and 14 counts of reckless conduct.

It's a landmark case. It was the first time corporate officials were charged with and convicted of killing an employee through unsafe working conditions. The case was appealed and the convictions were reversed, but not without making a mark.

To support a murder conviction in the state of Illinois, it is not necessary to prove intent. Prosecutors need only show that the person voluntarily and knowingly acted in a way in which death or great harm was a *probable result*. Magnuson's argument rested on plant conditions; lack of adequate safety equipment; knowledge and attempts to deceive on the part of the defendants; and the Illinois State definition of murder.

The Case for the Prosecution

The day Golab died police officers and firemen found such a strong, foul odor in the plant that they choked and gagged, and felt nauseated. They said there were no lights on in the plant and no perceivable ventilation, that, it was filled with a yellowish-orange haze.

Phillip J. Mole, Director of the Cook County Department of Environmental Control, testified that, "tests in an Elk Grove Village factory where a worker died of cyanide poisoning showed the air had levels of cyanide that 'could be detrimental to workers' health'" (Gibson and Unger, 1985). Workers never knew they worked with cyanide. Film Recovery Systems could have used a system with hoods to draw off the cyanide vapors from the vats, but chose not to. O'Neil and Kirschbaum both admitted that none of the equipment had any effect against cyanide gas. Basically the safety equipment at Film Recovery Systems consisted of cloth gloves and sometimes cotton masks. Some workers wore rubber boots. The police officers saw only cloth masks and short sleeve shirts. There were no eye goggles available.

It was testified that, when people came by from different agencies, the plant was cleaned up, windows opened and, in one case, workers wore special plastic and glass face masks during the inspection, but afterwards they were taken away. There were other instances of flagrant deception about the use of cyanide and its dangers.

Magnuson did not claim intent; he argued that all of the defendants knew of the plant conditions, the hazards of working with cyanide, and the totally ineffective safety gear available to workers.

Government Agencies

When the Occupational Safety and Health Agency (OSHA) came after Golab's death, they cited Film Recovery Systems with 17 violations. Prior to February 10, 1983, there was no testing of internal air quality— not by OSHA or any other governmental agency. "A chemical worker's much-publicized death from cyanide poisoning at a Chicago-area plant owned by Film Recovery Systems Inc. occurred after an OSHA inspector, using the 1982 guidelines, chose to forgo a full safety inspection after checking the company's accident records" (Burroughs and Lubove, 1986).

Film Recovery Systems had never registered with the Cook County Department of Environmental Control; consequently, the facility had not been inspected. There was no evidence that the company was in compliance with OSHA's standards. Furthermore, "There is evidence that plant workers were not informed they were working with cyanide. Nor were they informed of the presence of, or danger of breathing, cyanide gas" (*People v. O'Neil*, 1990).

Magnuson faced considerable hurdles in pursuing a murder charge. Barry Siegel (1985) reports,

> For many years, courts rejected the idea that corporations and their executives could be charged with a crime. The reasons were several. A corporation has no mind, so cannot be said to have intent. A corporation has no body, so cannot be imprisoned. Fines levied against corporations usually hurt consumers and innocent shareholders the most. The complex fashion in which a corporation is usually organized and run make it difficult to point fingers at individuals. Finally, corporate officers did not look like criminals and were not thought of as such.

And so:

> The prosecutor looked to another article in the criminal code that defined what constituted a voluntary act. He found what he needed. A voluntary act, the section read, "includes an omission to perform a duty which the law imposes."

General Considerations

Undocumented workers suffered the highest degree of exposure to the cyanide. They generally have little power or status in the workplace and, so, have little recourse when problems arise. Workers didn't realize how dangerous were the plant conditions. There were skull and crossbones on the cyanide drums and some "veneno" ("poison") signs, but the workers didn't know they were working with cyanide. Evidently, the skull and cross bones sign is not a universal symbol, so they wouldn't necessarily know what it meant. For example, it reportedly signifies *high voltage* in Poland, as Harold Henderson (1990) indicates.

Applying the Ethical Theories

A Utilitarian would assess the ethical choices in terms of consequences. They would undertake a cost–benefit analysis to decide what would bring the greatest good for the greatest number. Unfortunately, as we saw in the Ford Pinto case, this kind of reasoning can lead to short-term benefits rather than long-term gains, resulting in potentially disastrous consequences.

One limitation of Utilitarianism is that it is weak on distributive justice. In addition, as Philosopher Robert Solomon (1984) notes, (a) there may not be time to calculate all of the consequences beforehand; (b) we don't usually know enough to calculate the consequences; (c) different kinds of consequences may be difficult to compare; and (d) the consequences of an act may be positive but the act still be wrong (p. 24).

Not all decisions, however, lend themselves to a rule formulation. We see this with Kantian attempts at universalizing decision-making: Sometimes equally worthwhile moral choices are feasible and one must take precedence. *And let's not forget:* Decisions made in the abstract don't always work in the real world.

Feminist Ethicists contend that moral choices are ones that must be *lived,* as well as worked out rationally. Kant's duty-based framework is hard to apply to situations that are messy or with conflicting aspects. His Categorical Imperative and Humanitarian Principle provide guidelines, but don't indicate *priorities* or how to resolve conflicts. Also, there are times when purely rational choices are difficult to put into action.

The Virtues of Feminist Ethics

For Feminist Ethicists, a moral perspective requires that we look at the context and the specific details. This includes expectations about interpersonal acts, such as how to treat one another. In the Film Recovery Systems case, the vulnerable group of undocumented laborers couldn't easily challenge plant officials or report problems. Who would they call? Whenever there's an imbalance of power, measures should be in place to ensure a safe environment. Plus, clear channels should be in place with respect to relevant regulations, procedures, safe working conditions, and adequate safety gear.

Principles must inform our actions. But the principles alone are hollow if our values and relationships are not factored in, Feminist Ethicists argue. This applies to corporations as well. They, too, are embedded within a social context and, so, must balance the different interests. A morally-defensible relationship requires that care be manifest in the actions we undertake and the principles and policies we follow. This applies on both personal and professional levels.

Film Recovery Systems and Moral Agency

One issue of corporate decision-making is pinpointing the moral agent. Is management solely responsible in matters of Business Ethics? There is *responsibility* and there is *accountability*. We need to bring in more than managers into the realm of corporate responsibility. We need to throw a wider net.

Part of our responsibility as concerned citizens, members of organizations, voters, stockholders, and customers, is to support the efforts of corporations to act ethically, and run their businesses so workers are valued and safeguards are in place. That calls for an ethos of caring and responsibility.

In the case of Film Recovery Systems, plant officials were in a position to do something, but they didn't. They saw problems, but failed to act. These included inspectors from Home Insurance who gave FRS a rating of "fair" after seeing problems, but did not insist on changes. These also included governmental departments that didn't even know Film Recovery Systems existed, along with fire inspectors who didn't come by the plant in the two years before Golab's death.

Law professor Alan Dershowitz says the case calls for a new category of crime: "We should have one that specifically reflects our condemnation of this sort of behavior without necessarily assimilating it into the most heinous forms of murder" (Siegel, 1985). We need to determine who should reside in the circle of responsibility and how to hold them accountable. What *is* the morally correct response in such cases as this one?

The New York Times (1986) contends that Americans are reluctant to hold corporate officials responsible for disasters. Yes and no. Since 1986 a lot has happened to reshape that attitude. We now see that business, labor, and government can bring about positive change. Teams can work for good, and many businesses do just that. Others veer off course and lose sight of their responsibility to others. That's why whistleblowers and activists are still vital, as we'll see next.

SPOTLIGHT: *Erin Brockovich*

In the last chapter we looked at Erin Brockovich and how Aristotle would view her moral character. She realized something was afoot, that people living in Hinkley, California, had suffered a disproportionate number of health problems, such as cancer, that shortened their lives.

Her response was not to walk away or throw her arms up in the air. Instead, she started doing research—hours, days, and weeks of research. She conducted interview after interview, building enough trust with the wary residents to see the links between the water they drank and bathed in and the health problems they suffered.

Aristotle would label her courageous. Feminist Ethicists would note that she put others' needs above her own. She cared when no one else seemed to give a hoot. She worked day and night amassing evidence, getting to the bottom of the case. She was threatened, but did not stop. She saw that something very big and ominous was behind this and, if no one else would be an advocate for the victims, she would.

Although she wasn't a lawyer or scientist, she had native smarts, strong passions, persistence, perseverance, and determination. And remember how Rosemarie Tong pointed out that Feminist Ethicists are especially concerned to help the oppressed and address injustices suffered by vulnerable minorities? Erin certainly had that value motivating her.

Kohlberg would place her at Level Two ("Conventional morality") of his three stages. She had a deeply felt commitment to the needs of others, as well as a conviction that these others (the 600+ plaintiffs from Hinkley) had suffered an injustice through no fault of their own.

Gilligan claims that morality needs to be done "in a different voice," one sensitive to those who care and are cared-for and attuned to different perspectives (Gilligan, 1993). In the Hinkley case, like the Film Recovery Systems case, the poor and the powerless had no advocate, or not until Erin Brockovich took it on. Doing so was at a cost to her children, who were left with others while she pursued the case. She had to balance caring for them and caring for the Hinkley defendants. It was not an easy juggling act.

Our final spotlight film shows another example of caring—that of the CEO of a firm devastated on 9/11.

SPOTLIGHT: *Out of the Clear Blue Sky*

The documentary *Out of the Clear Blue Sky* focuses on the human losses of 9/11 by the company Cantor Fitzgerald, a Wall Street investment firm. The film relays events after the firm lost 658 out of 960 employees, the most of any company with offices at the World Trade Center. It was almost double the loss suffered by the New York Fire Department (=343) on 9/11. The firm's offices were on floors 101–105 of the North Tower, and when the planes hit there was little hope for those on upper floors. Of the 9/11 casualties, Cantor suffered 24 percent (almost one-fourth) of the entire number of lives lost to the catastrophe.

Howard Lutnick, Cantor CEO, could be seen as a symbol of grief. His emotional response on public TV riveted the nation. But when he stopped the paychecks of the deceased employees in an attempt to save the company, he was fried in the media. Roasted and toasted! Stopping the paychecks was seen as a heartless, ruthless, and unforgiveable act. It was a very difficult time with very difficult decisions to be made. There was no easy path for Lutnick to take. Iris Mann (2013) reports,

> "People in the first week," [filmmaker Danielle] Gardner said, "would ask me, 'Why isn't Cantor doing this?' and, 'Why isn't Cantor doing that?' And I was thinking, 'There's a tremendous disconnect here. There is no Cantor. There's a couple of people sitting in a living room frantically trying to figure out who's alive.' I remember thinking, 'There's no office. There are no people. I don't know where you guys have been.'"

Things are rarely as simple as they seem. It wasn't long until Lutnick was able to return to the good graces of those who lost loved ones. He was a model of generosity and caring for the families. First was the 10-year guarantee of healthcare for the family members of those who were killed by the terrorist attack. Then Lutnick offered to give 25 percent of Cantor Fitzgerald's profits to the families for the next five years (starting in 2002). This amount came to $180 million. A Cantor Relief Fund was also organized to gather donations and provide support groups and other help for the families.

The movie gives an inside look at a company in crisis and under pressure to make decisions in a constrained time framework. To open for business the day after the attacks on 9/11, Cantor had to borrow $70 *billion*. The New York stock market re-opened for business six days after the attacks. This left very little time for the company to act, particularly given that they had just lost 658 of their 960 employees (= 69 percent).

The movie looks long and hard at the way relationships—human connections—affected the reactions to the crisis and the decisions that were made. The people we see on the screen and the raw emotions expressed are true to life. Feminist Ethicists would consider it an excellent example of moral reasoning being intertwined with interrelationships and a desire to do the right thing—even though there were many obstacles. The resulting movie is a compelling vehicle for seeing a man and a community trying to put an Ethic of Care in action.

ETHICS CODE: Microsoft

When you think of computers and software companies, you may not think of Feminist Ethics. But the values discussed in this chapter are ones that many corporations recognize as vital to a well-run business—care, justice, and diversity. Care improves job performance. Justice furthers a collegial work environment. Diversity—in the different voices and ways of thinking and seeing—leads to innovation. Microsoft indicates that in its ethics code, which you can see at http://www.microsoft.com/en-us/legal/compliance/Buscond/default.aspx#standards.

→ Also consider the CEO's goals set out below.

Letter from Microsoft CEO Steven A. Ballmer

Microsoft CEO Steven A. Ballmer states his goals in a letter to "Fellow Employees." Read the excerpt below and see how it fits the Feminist Ethical model.

Dear Fellow Employee:

Microsoft aspires to be a great company, and our success depends on you. It depends on people who innovate and are committed to growing our business responsibly. People who dedicate themselves to really satisfying customers, helping partners, and improving the communities in which we do business.

People who are accountable for achieving big, bold goals with unwavering integrity. People who are leaders, who appreciate that to be truly great, we must continually strive to do better ourselves and help others improve.

We must expect the best from ourselves because who we are as a company and as individuals is as important as our ability to deliver the best products and services. How we manage our business internally—and how we think about and work with customers, partners, governments, vendors and communities—impacts our productivity and success.

It's not enough to just do the right things; we have to do them in the right way. ...

A Look at Ballmer's Use of Language

- Note the verbs: They range from "aspires" and "depends on you" to "innovate," "grow responsibly," "dedicate," "help," and "improve."
- Ballmer calls for employees to be "accountable," have "unwavering integrity," and become "leaders" who "strive to better ourselves and help others improve."
- Note also that the letter ends with: "who we are as a company *and* as individuals" is as important as the ability to deliver products. This indicates that Ballmer is not a Consequentialist. "It's not enough to just do the right things." Rather, "we have to do them in the right way," affirming means and obligations, bettering ourselves and helping others.

To help others we must care about them and care *for* them in some basic ways. It means holding each other accountable.

Works Cited

Boylan, Michael, *Basic Ethics*. (Upper Saddle River, NJ: Prentice Hall, 2000).

Burrough, Bryan and Seth H. Lubove, "Credibility Gap: Some Concerns Fudge Their Safety Records," *Wall Street Journal*, December 2, 1986.

Chang, Cindy, "ICE Agrees to Stop Shackling Some Defendants for Court," *Los Angeles Times*, January 23, 2014. http://articles.latimes.com/2014/jan/23/local/la-me-ff-immigrant-shackles-20140124 (accessed December 21, 2014).

Gibson, Ray and Rudolph Unger, "Cyanide Hung in Air at Plant, Official Says," *Chicago Tribune*, April 26, 1984, http://articles.chicagotribune.com/1985-04-26/news/8501250316_1_cyanide-film-recovery-systems-film-chips (accessed December 30, 2014).

Gilligan, Carol, "Letter to Readers, 1993," *In a Different Voice*, (Cambridge, MA: Harvard University Press, 1993).

Held, Virginia, "The Ethics of Care: Personal, Political, and Global," in Julie C. Van Camp, Jeffrey Olen, and Vincent Barry, (eds.), *Applying Ethics* (Boston, MA: Wadsworth, 2011), pp. 47–51.

Henderson, Harold, "Murder in the Air," *Chicago Reader*, June 14, 1990, http://www.chicagoreader.com/chicago/murder-in-the-air/Content?oid=875834 (accessed December 21, 2014).

Jaggar, Alison M. "Caring as a Feminist Practice of Moral Reason," in Virginia Held (ed.), *Justice and Care*, (Boulder, CO: Westview Press, 1995).

Mann, Iris, "Little-Known Stories Live Large On Screen," *Jewish Journal*, 6 Sep 2013, http://www.jewishjournal.com/fall_preview/article/little_known_stories_live_large_on_screen (accessed December 21, 2014).

Manning, Rita C., *Speaking From the Heart*, (Lanham, MD: Rowman & Littlefield, 1992).

Microsoft, *Standards of Business Conduct*, Available at http://www.microsoft.com/en-us/legal/compliance/Buscond/default.aspx#standards

People v. O'Neil, 550 N.E.2d 1090 (Ill.App. 1990), http://www.sagepub.com/lippmanccl2e/study/features/11peopleVoneil.pdf (accessed December 30, 2014).

Siegel, Barry, "Officers Convicted: Murder Case a Corporate Landmark," *Los Angeles Times*, September 15, 1985, http://articles.latimes.com/1985-09-15/news/mn-23348_1_corporate-officers (accessed December 21, 2014).

Siegel, Barry "Trial Makes History, Stirs Controversy," *Los Angeles Times*, September 16, 1985, http://articles.latimes.com/1985-09-16/news/mn-22032_1_hydrogen-cyanide (accessed December 21, 2014).

Solomon, Robert C., *Morality and the Good Life*, (New York: McGraw-Hill, 1984), p. 24.

Tong, Rosemarie and Nancy Williams, "Feminist Ethics," *The Stanford Encyclopedia of Philosophy* (Fall 2014 Edition), http://plato.stanford.edu/archives/fall2014/entries/feminism-ethics/ (accessed December 21, 2014).

Warren, Mary Anne, *Moral Status* (Oxford: Oxford University Press, 1997).

Notes

1 Not to be confused with *In the Company of Men*—a quite different film.
2 Thanks to Jay Magnuson for providing me with information on this case.

Unit 3

Moral Reflection: Thorny Questions

3.1

Finding the Balance
Addressing Environmental Disasters

Spotlight: *Civil Action; Local Hero*
Case Studies: W.R. Grace Co.; West Virginia Chemical Spill; Exxon Valdez
Ethics Code: Exxon Mobil Corporation

> *Jerome Facher: What's your take?*
> *Jan Schlichtmann: They'll see the truth.*
> *Jerome Facher: The truth? Oh. I thought we were talking about a court of law. Come on, you've been around long enough to know that a court-room isn't a place to look for the truth. You're lucky to find anything here that resembles the truth.*
> —Civil Action

> *Townsman: I thought all this money would make me feel different.*
> —Local Hero

We see the strange looking water and where toxic chemicals were dumped. We see teenage boys having fun lighting matches and watching flames leap in the air. We see the lawyer walking along the creek, his shoes muddied by we-don't-know-what. We see the children wasting away as cancer gains an upper hand. We conclude that no good can come of this—and we're right. Lives were lost, relationships strained, a community torn apart as questions bubbled to the surface about the industrial waste in the well water. *Civil Action* (1998) tells the story of the sad and gripping case. Assigning culpability and making it stick is another matter. There's a reason it is classified a "legal thriller."

In May 1979 two wells supplying drinking water to East Woburn, Massachusetts were found contaminated with industrial solvents

Business Ethics Through Movies: A Case Study Approach, First Edition. Wanda Teays.
© 2015 John Wiley & Sons, Ltd. Published 2015 by John Wiley & Sons, Ltd.

(chlorinated hydrocarbons) used for degreasing metals. Eight children died. The parents sued W.R. Grace & Company and Beatrice Foods, the two corporations suspected of allowing the industrial waste to seep into the soil. Their attorney was Jan Schlichtmann, the protagonist in *Civil Action*.

In this chapter we will look at businesses and the environment. To some degree Environmental Ethics and Business Ethics share common ground. Corporations and environmentalists must work together to protect the land, the sea, the animals, the plants and the interdependence of one to the other. Both *Civil Action* and *Local Hero* show us why companies must guard against environmental hazards and be prepared when disaster strikes. We'll look at the W.R. Grace case involving tainted well water in Massachusetts, the West Virginia chemical spill in 2014, and the Exxon Valdez oil spill off of Alaska in 1989. We'll also look at Exxon Mobil Corporation's ethics code. We'll start with *Civil Action*.

SPOTLIGHT: *Civil Action* and CASE STUDY 1: The W.R. Grace Case

We watch the snappy looking bachelor–litigator walking toward us. We see his Porsche and how he keeps getting speeding tickets. He lives life in the fast lane—and likes it! Things take a right angle, however, when he's a guest on a radio show. Caller Anne Anderson accuses him of ignoring her phone messages. His embarrassment is obvious and we can tell they're about to connect.

As it turns out, Anne and her family live in East Woburn, a small industrial town north of Boston. Within a six-block radius of their house eight children got a rare form of leukemia (acute lymphocytic leukemia) and died between 1969 and 1982. In time, more deaths ensued. The families' drinking water came from two wells, known as G and H. When Anne starting asking questions and shared her concerns about the water (off color, bad taste), she was not taken seriously. But then,

> Five years went by. City, state and federal officials ignored them. Then a breakthrough— In 1979, the *Woburn Times*, a local newspaper, reported that 184 buried barrels that had contained chemicals had been discovered near to the site where the City of Woburn had drilled two wells, G and H for drinking water...
>
> The wells were tested. But the chemical in the barrels didn't match. However, the officials did find something else—dangerous levels of

Trichloroethylene, TCE, and other chemical solvents. TCE is a common groundwater pollutant known to cause neurological disorders, cell mutations, liver damage and cancer in laboratory animals (Seattle University School of Law).

At that point Anne contacted Schlichtmann. She helped unite the families in a class action suit against the two companies (W.R. Grace and Beatrice Foods) suspected of dumping chemicals into the well water. The Woburn wells G and H were closed in 1979, but the damage had already been done. By the time Schlichtmann filed the lawsuit, two of the children affected, including Anne's son, Jimmy, had died.

We see how difficult it is to launch a class action suit—or any suit against a company regarding environmental catastrophes. Establishing causation can be tricky. If there are competing or additional causal connections, the case is weaker, so setting out the causal chain is crucial. Of course, it could be just be considered bad luck, a mere coincidence that children got leukemia in this small town. Anne didn't buy it. In her view the idea that it was mere "chance" that the children got leukemia was a pile of hooey. Something must have caused this cancer "cluster" and the most likely culprit was in the water they drank.

In his opening statement, Schlichtmann pointed to the chemicals in the drinking water and argued causation. He drove it home that,

> These chemicals are on the EPA's priority pollutant list. These chemicals are toxic. These chemicals can destroy cells. These chemicals can be toxic to the heart muscle, to the heart tissue, to nerves, to mucous membranes, to the gastrointestinal system, to the skin, and they can affect the body's ability to fight disease. These chemicals can cause cancer (Seattle University School of Law).

In the case of a disease like leukemia, it may be hard to pin the cause on a particular event, entity, or substance. An added complication is that *proving* it could incur considerable expense and that may be outside the reach of the families (the plaintiffs) or the law firms that represent them.

Defense attorney Jerome Facher, representing Beatrice Foods, successfully argued that the evidence didn't stick. Throughout the film he makes pithy comments and offers Schlichtmann words of advice. The interchange between the attorneys and the ways in which numbers are tossed around like ping pong balls is an eye opener. As UCLA law professor and author of *Reel Justice* ("The Courtroom Goes To The Movies"), Michael Asimow (1999) put it:

> Can the adversary system determine whether toxins dumped by these companies made the children sick? According to the new film *A Civil Action*, the answer is a resounding no. As defense counsel [Facher] sagely observes, truth lies at the bottom of a bottomless pit—depths the trial process cannot hope to plumb. Relying on the adversary system and lay juries to find the truth simply compounds the disaster and creates more tragedy... The film dramatizes the human side of the litigation, while presenting the realities of complex tort litigation more successfully than any other film.

It's a gripping story, and even more so since it's based on an actual event. One of the many touching scenes in the movie is when one of the plant workers conveys his regrets to Anne. His heartfelt, "I am so sorry about your son" shows that you don't have to be in a position of leadership to feel responsible or to share in the grief of the families.

That's the thing: Moral culpability may rest on one person's shoulders. However, often it is not a solo act. Rather, it rests on a series of actions and decisions that ripple out, drawing others in and they, too, take part in the direction and choices that later get made. That's why whistleblowers are so important.

Given the case is presented from the perspective the plaintiffs (the families, the victims), we get a sense of the human costs of environmental disasters (human-caused or acts of God). We also see how well-intentioned people can try to bring about restitution. Arriving at a just resolution is often difficult, as obstacle after obstacle may be encountered on the path. It may take both determination and perseverance to hang in there and face the challenges ahead.

We see this with Jan Schlichtmann. When we first meet him, he comes across as slick (as when he hands out his business card to a man in a car accident). He later shows a determination that borders on an obsession. He is driven to win the case so the families get their due and expects his colleagues to make the necessary sacrifices for that to happen.

In a telling scene, Beatrice counsel Jerome Facher says to Schlichtman, "We are like kings. We *are* kings." That's a striking claim. We picture kings sitting in their counting house (or castle!), counting out the money. And that's exactly what comes across when Facher pulls out a $20 bill and sets it between the two men. He makes an offer: Add six 0's to that 20. We do so in our mind's eye— $20,000,000. It sounds like a lot of money. But is it enough? Schlichtmann wastes little time in brushing the offer aside, but later comes to regret it when Beatrice Foods gets out of the lawsuit. Schlichtmann's colleague, the number cruncher, tells him, "We're floating on credit without a net." As we know, an excess of credit and the absence of a safety net make for a bad combination. Not all cases come to the resolution we hope for. And this one is no different:

> The jury returned a verdict in July, 1986. They responded that there was insufficient evidence against Beatrice; that W.R. Grace had negligently contaminated the wells. However, the jury could not determine when W.R. Grace chemicals had contaminated the wells. Eventually, Grace settled with the plaintiffs for approximately $8 million, although the company denied any wrongdoing. Phase one had lasted 78 days. The trial never proceeded beyond this phase. But the case was not over (Seattle University School of Law).

You've got to hand it Schlichtmann. He didn't give up. His partners flew the (barren) coop, having suffered losses from the case. It's hard to blame them, given the price they paid to be involved over the span of time from start to finish.

But Schlichtmann can't let it go. Given what we've seen of this man's will-to-win, it's not surprising that he doesn't give up. One day it hits him: Maybe, surely maybe, someone saw something and that someone could provide the evidence needed for an appeal. He found this in a trucker for J.R. Riley tannery, a subsidiary of Beatrice Foods. As it turns out, he had been told to clear contaminated land. Take it down to the topsoil and thus cart off incriminating evidence. At last!

Schlichtmann filed an appeal in 1987, after learning of a drilling report that had not been given to him by Beatrice attorneys. He argued that this report could have affected the outcome of the case, but he failed to convince the Court of Appeals on this issue (Seattle University School of Law).

Eventually the tide turned and the EPA got involved, the J.R. Riley tannery and W.R. Grace both saw plants closed and money—the largest sum in New England history—put to an environmental cleanup.

It's an engrossing case and a riveting movie. As it turns out, the Woburn case isn't the only one involving W.R. Grace; sadly enough there are others. One involves asbestos contamination causing 200 deaths and 1,000 illnesses in Libby, Montana in 2009 resulting in $130 million in cleanup (CNN, 2009).

The case, and the film, has had considerable impact on how the judicial system works. It is testimony to the role environmental watchdogs and agencies like the EPA can play in helping prevent environmental tragedies such as this one.

CASE STUDY 2: West Virginia Chemical Spill in 2014

January 9, 2014 was a bad day for West Virginia. That was the day that locals called authorities about a weird smell—sort of like licorice—coming from an industrial site north of Charleston. Upon arriving, state inspectors found one of Freedom Industries' storage tanks had ruptured. The Elk River, the water supply for 300,000 people, was contaminated with a chemical called MCHM (*a.k.a.* 4-methylcyclohexane methanol, notes David Zucchino). They were advised not to drink it or bathe/shower in it. Residents were beside themselves with anxiety and anger.

Over 7,500 gallons leaked from the storage tanks into the Elk River. The company's lax response in failing to stop the leak or alert officials made things worse. Surprisingly enough, no agency made regular inspections of the tanks. And we certainly can't blame residents who were "puzzled and outraged" (Zucchino, 2014).

Charleston mayor Danny Jones made his thoughts clear: "I can't believe there is not a law against what they did, ... [The chemical company is] a bunch of renegades who have done irreparable harm to this valley. ... Quite frankly, somebody needs to go to jail."

The reaction of Freedom Industries was *not* modeled after Johnson & Johnson in the Tylenol crisis. There, CEO James Burke took affirmative action and came across as the model of responsibility. Not so, here. West Virginians have been left to scratch their heads and worry. From one crisis manager's perspective, the typical response is pathetic:

> "Mostly what organizations do in these kinds of moments is duck," says Davia Temin, a New York-based crisis manager. "They do not come forward. They do not put their CEO forward. And they do not work out of the playbook of good crisis management, probably because they don't have anything good to say" (Mufson, 2014).

Mind you, just how much the EPA should do by way of protections is a contentious issue. For instance, West Virginia state senator Joe Manchin III is opposed to a strong regulatory role on the part of the federal government (with the EPA). He argues, "Coal and chemicals inevitably bring risk—but that doesn't mean they should be shut down." He adds, "Cicero says, 'To err is human.' But you're going to stop living because you're afraid of making a mistake?" For some, the lax protections and slow response on the part of Freedom Industries falls in the category of *negligence* rather than a mistake.

Senator Manchin points to the state motto: "Mountaineers are always free." The implication is that the state has a long history and deep commitment to individual liberty. The result is a "hands-off" view of outside interference. On the other hand, the state of West Virginia "has also been the scene of five major accidents related to coal or chemicals in eight years" (Gabriel, Wines and Davenport, 2014). This reality suggests that not all freedoms can be unbounded.

On February 4, 2014 a Federal Grand Jury was launched to look into the West Virginia chemical spill. On December 14, 2014 the grand jury indicted four owners and operators of the company. Each was charged with violating the Clean Water Act, which bars discharges of pollutants without a permit. The indictment stated that Freedom Industries, and its owners and managers, did not meet a reasonable standard of care to prevent spills. Gary L. Southern, the company's president, was one of those indicted; he was also charged with making false statements under oath, wire fraud and bankruptcy fraud (Wines, 2014).

Exercise

1. How do we strike a balance between the rights of a company to run its business and the duties of regulatory agencies to minimize harms (to the environment, humans, and animals)?
2. How should we weigh penalties when businesses fail to take adequate precautions around the storage, handling, and distribution of dangerous/toxic chemicals?
3. If *you* were the CEO of Freedom Industries—or hired by the company to deal with the many concerns on the part of the 300,000 Charleston residents, what would you do? Set out the steps you would take to address the crisis.

SPOTLIGHT: *Local Hero*

Felix Happer heads up Houston-based Knox Oil and Gas. He has buckets of money and a love of astronomy. When we meet him, he's thinking about building an oil refinery in a remote area of Scotland. He sends his trusty, eager-to-please employee Mac MacIntyre to seal the deal.

Arriving in Scotland, Mac is met by the local Knox representative, a much less business-minded man, Danny Oldsen. Oldsen wastes no time in falling for a beautiful oceanographer with the fitting name of Marina. She has much more eco-friendly ideas for the land and sea, indicating that a refinery is a disastrous idea. Mac and Danny head up to the seaside village of Ferness. Mac hopes to persuade the inhabitants to sell their entire village so the refinery can be put in place.

True enough, the thought of getting more money than you ever dreamed possible would be hard to resist. Who wouldn't appreciate an infusion of large sums of cash? The residents of Ferness get on board—almost all of them. There's a holdout in the form of one old codger, Ben Knox. Ben has no more intention of parting with his land than selling his kidneys on the black market. The cult classic *Local Hero* (1983) tells the tale.

Mac never loses sight of the goal to acquire the land for the refinery, but Danny doesn't get with the program. Rather, he comes to see the beauty of the land and the charms of the people, not the least Marina. Meanwhile, Happer's interest in astronomy is piqued as Mac reports on his progress and on the night skies of Scotland.

We see the difference a little clarification of values can make. The "why" behind decisions doesn't always float to the surface; some stay submerged until we come upon them in ethical dilemmas. As we know, moral character develops over time. One action, even a courageous action, can't define a person's moral character. Our morally good and desirable qualities reveal our moral fiber, our strength of character. They are the traits that we respect in others, such as integrity, humility, an even temperament, and self-control.

Local Hero illustrates the value of finding a balance between competing interests. It shows us the benefits of asking, "Where can we see the benefits, of the various options we face, the choices? What good came about (or will come) as a consequence? How about the downside of decisions? Are there any negatives or ethical pitfalls that we should examine?"

- Once he arrived in Scotland and saw the site of the proposed oil refinery, Felix Happer understood why Ben Knox refused to sell his property. The environmental benefits of *not* proceeding with the oil refinery outweighed any financial gains that would come from such a project.
- The maxim "Do no harm" to the environment moved to the forefront as the story unfolded. As a result, the principle of maximizing profits (or even the social goods of lower priced oil) became less significant as a factor in the decision-making. *Local Hero* shows the process of reassessing the end goals.

- We would gain by finding the best path for developing our moral character. We can take this suggestion to the film and ask what moral qualities we see in the characters—what moral traits are exhibited. In our moral assessment we might ask how many of these were in place at the beginning of the film and how many developed, or eroded, as the plot unfolded.
- Three characters help us weigh moral traits.

  First is Mac MacIntyre who followed the company plan. Mac doesn't question the underlying values that put capital gains above the beauty of the land and the sustainability of the eco-system. He could not see alternative energy sources that did not have such a drastic ecological effect.

  Second is Danny Oldsen who had no qualms about dispensing with the original vision. His openness to the options took him down a different path; one that CEO Felix Happer saw and appreciated.

  Third is Felix Happer. He had the moral fortitude to find out why there was a holdout on the land acquisition and was able to weigh competing interests and shift direction. He saw for himself that the benefits of a refinery in Ferness could not justify the loss to the land and destruction of the unique ecostructure.

Focusing on moral character and strengthening our moral qualities is a powerful way (whether in film or in business) to do an ethical inventory of the dilemmas we face. We can then decide what to zero-in on for a more detailed assessment and, thereby, sort through the moral dilemma and put things in order. We can then construct, deconstruct, and evaluate moral reasoning.

Moral Assessment

We can approach ethical decision-making from the standpoint of reasoning and morality and use both perspectives to clarify goals and weigh the options. Both are crucial tools, as Aristotle shows with his intellectual and moral virtues. The other ethical theories can also be put to use, as we saw in Unit 2.

Moral *development* should not take second place to moral *assessment* says philosopher Robert Solomon (1992). His discussion on the benefits of Virtue Ethics is insightful and interesting—as well as useful! He sees six ways Virtue Ethics applies to Business Ethics. These are:

- Community
- Excellence

- Role Identity
- Integrity
- Judgment
- Holism

Let's see how each one has value in the workplace. From Solomon we can infer:

- *Community* means that yes we are individuals, no question of that. But we find our identity in community, including businesses and institutions (p. 75). Who we are as persons is inextricably linked to our co-workers and to our work life.
- *Excellence* means we can't simply follow the dictums "do no wrong" and "avoid making mistakes." We need also demonstrate benevolence by doing good. Have high standards of excellence by which we can gauge ourselves. This means strive to do our best, and not just fall in line and "keep our noses clean" (pp. 75–76).
- *Role identity* means accepting the particular obligations that come with the job and a sense of loyalty to our employers. All ethics is contextual, so don't think about Business Ethics in the abstract. Look at a specific company or corporation and try to figure out where the employees fit in the structure (p. 76).
- *Integrity* is the heart of the moral beast. Think of it as the hub to which all other virtues attach—or as Solomon says "the key" (p. 76). Without integrity, the moral edifice would collapse. Normally integrity entails being in sync with the standards and values of the company, but not blindly so. If those standards or values fall short, then we can rely on our sense of integrity to get us back on track. In that sense, integrity may require us to speak up against a policy or workplace norm that is morally remiss or short-sighted.
- *Judgment* is the outcome of evaluation. Think of the evaluative terms "shows good judgment" or, alternatively, "shows bad judgment." This is the ability to weigh factors and make the right call. It isn't just a matter of applying rules or principles to particular situations (p. 77). Making a "judgment call" means that we look at the options, weigh the relevant factors, and make a decision based on what seems right, fair, or just. Conversely a "bad judgment" occurs when there's a disconnect in weighing the factors and making a decision.
- *Holism* keeps all the pieces in place. This is the role of the big picture. Try to see how the moral parts of our lives are interconnected, not fragmented. Furthermore, we should be careful not to compartmentalize

Business Ethics as inherently different from the ethics we practice in the rest of our lives. Try to see how the professional and the personal are linked on the ethical level. The virtues of business are not isolated from the virtues of the rest of our lives (pp. 78—79).

Some employers would replace us with robots if they could and others don't flinch about downsizing or outsourcing jobs. On the other hand, there are plenty of employers that do care *and* employees who are deeply loyal.

Ideally we should integrate the different roles we play. As Solomon puts it, good employees should also be good people! Of course who we are at work and who we are at home aren't always a perfect match. However, if the gap between our work self and our personal self is like night and day— like Dr. Jekyll and Mr. Hyde—then it's time for a little moral inventory to see if there's a way to build on the similarities.

Moral Assessment: Local Hero

Local Hero presents us with a moral conflict after Felix Happer sends Mac to Ferness, Scotland, is to buy out the entire village so that it can be converted to a refinery. When one of the locals, Ben Knox, refuses to sell, residents try to convince him to trade his land for money. They do not succeed. Mac's loyalty to Happer locks him into a way of thinking and seeing the world. He's so fixated on the refinery plan that he can't see the environmental riches of the area.

Here's where Solomon's points about excellence and good judgment come into play. He would look at MacIntyre and say he falls short on both of these. First, he's too concerned with "toeing the line." Secondly, he misses the big picture and fails to question the wisdom of the entire project. Thirdly, he doesn't take seriously competing values. He is single-minded in trying to get the signatures of all the residents so the refinery can move forward. But he takes it too far. Let's not forget: *Single-minded doesn't mean narrow-minded!* Wanting to please your boss should not take precedence over weighing the facts and thinking for yourself.

As it turns out, Happer did *not* appreciate Mac's blind loyalty. This is made evident by Happer sending Mac back to Houston, Texas and keeping Danny to work with him on innovative and environmentally friendly alternatives to a refinery.

Mac doesn't show good judgment in this respect, because he doesn't consider the impact a refinery would have on the ecosystem. Nor does he spend a millisecond on possible alternatives to a refinery, as did Danny and

Marina. Mac's rigidity and loyalty gets in the way of his good sense and good judgment. We see this in the following interchange with two of the locals who take him to meet holdout Ben Knox:

MAC:	Where's the door here?
URQUHART:	There is no door. Just knock on the window.
MAC:	How do you do business with a man who has no door?
VICTOR:	The ethics are just the same.

Mac takes his mission too much to heart. Perhaps he over-identifies with his job. Sure we should throw ourselves into our work. Sure we should do the best job we can, while keeping our integrity intact. Quality of performance is not a collection of suitable end goals, but meeting those goals and obligations within the bounds of our values.

We should not have to surrender our reasoning skills and independence of thought as a term of employment! Aristotle would offer this advice: In the *Poetics*, he talks about practical wisdom as one of the intellectual virtues. This is the foundation of good judgment. It functions like "street smarts" or "horse sense"—seeing how it works from the ground up.

Local Hero shows the limitations of dreaming up projects that rely on people and places around the globe, far from the origin. Too much distance can be as harmful as too little. What looks good in the abstract or planning stages may not be feasible (or desirable) in the final analysis. Ideas on paper don't always work or should work when we start to implement them. MacIntyre didn't see that, but Happer did. He had no trouble letting go of the idea of a refinery once he understood what was at stake. He was able to balance the competing values and use his good judgment.

ETHICS CODE: Exxon Mobil Corporation

It is instructive to look at the ethics policy of Exxon Corporation, an *actual* oil company, in contrast to Knox Oil and Gas in the movie. You can see it at http://corporate.exxonmobil.com/~/media/Miscellany/2004/investor_governance_ethics.pdf.

Exercise

How would Exxon's ethics code give insight into the value put on caring for the pristine environment as we see in *Local Hero*?

nuclear explosion or natural catastrophe. Read about one man's solution and then answer the questions below:

Carved into the permafrost of a remote Arctic mountain, a "doomsday vault" housing samples of the world's most important seeds is taking shape to provide mankind with a Noah's Ark of food in the event of a global catastrophe... An enormous freezer measuring 5,200 cubic meters (6,800 cubic yards), the vault will preserve some 4.5 million batches of seeds from all known varieties of the planet's food crops.

The hope is that the vault will make it possible to re-establish crops obliterated by major disasters. "It's a cheap insurance policy," says Cary Fowler, executive director of the Global Crop Diversity Trust, the project's mastermind (*Terra Daily*, 2007).

Paul Smith, head of the Millennium Seed Bank, points out that, "This is a utilitarian drive, not a bunny-hugging one. The vast majority of modern medicines have their basis in plants. Yet only one-fifth of plant species have been screened for pharmaceutical use." Smith adds, "Who knows what miracle cures might be out there waiting to be discovered? But we are already losing species" (as noted by Lovell and *Climatewire*, 2010).

1. Do you think the "Doomsday Vault" is an effective way to provide a fail-safe for massive crop loss?
2. Can you envision using this model to apply to other sorts of disasters (e.g, loss of animal life)? If so, how might it be employed?
3. Another potential use of the vault is to preserve seeds that have not been genetically engineered. Can you think of ways that might come into play in the years ahead?

Works Cited

Asimow, Michael, "In Toxic Tort Litigation, Truth Lies at the Bottom of a Bottomless Pit," *Picturing Justice*, February 1999, http://usf.usfca.edu/pj/articles/Civil_Action-Asimow.htm (accessed December 26, 2014).

CNN, "Asbestos Cleanup 'Emergency' Declared In Montana Town," June 17, 2009, http://www.cnn.com/2009/US/06/17/montana.asbestos/index.html (accessed December 26, 2014).

Environmental Protection Agency, "Exxon Valdez Oil Spill Profile," January 16, 2014, http://www2.epa.gov/emergency-response/exxon-valdez-spill-profile (accessed December 26, 2014).

Exxon Mobil Corporation, *Code of Ethics and Business Conduct*, http://www.exxonmobil.com/corporate/files/corporate/investor_governance_ethics.pdf (accessed December 26, 2014).

Gabriel, Trip, Michael Wines and Coral Davenport, "Chemical Spill Muddies Picture in a State Wary of Regulations," *New York Times*, January 18, 2014, http://www.nytimes.com/2014/01/19/us/chemical-spill-muddies-picture-in-a-state-wary-of-regulations.html?hp&_r=0 (accessed December 26, 2014).

Lovell, Jeremy and *Climatewire*, "Researchers Rush to Fill Noah's Ark Seed Bank While Politicians Bicker," *Scientific American*, July 7, 2010, http://www.scientificamerican.com/article/researchers-rush-to-fill-seed-bank-while-politicians-bicker/ (accessed December 26, 2014).

Mufson, Steven, "One Week After W. Va. Toxic Spill, New Owner Of Freedom Industries Puts Firm In Bankruptcy," *Washington Post*, January 17, 2014, http://www.washingtonpost.com/business/economy/new-owner-of-freedom-industries-must-face-fallout-of-west-virginia-chemical-spill/2014/01/17/77b1a572-7df2-11e3-93c1-0e888170b723_story.html (accessed December 26, 2014).

Saundry, Peter, "Exxon Valdez Oil Spill," *Encyclopedia of Earth*, June 9, 2010, updated February 20, 2013, http://www.eoearth.org/view/article/152720/ (accessed December 27, 2014).

Seattle University School of Law, Anderson v. W.R. Grace, http://www.law.seattleu.edu/centers-and-institutes/films-for-justice-institute/lessons-from-woburn/about-the-case (accessed December 26, 2014).

Solomon, Robert, "Corporate Roles, Personal Virtues: An Aristotelian Approach to Business Ethics" (1992), in Thomas Donaldson, Patricia H. Werhane, and Margaret Cording, (eds.), *Ethical Issues in Business: A Philosophical Approach*, 7th edn. (Upper Saddle River, NJ: Prentice Hall Publishing, 2002).

Sorkin, Andrew Ross, "Imagining the Worst in BP's Future," *New York Times*, June 7, 2010, http://www.nytimes.com/2010/06/08/business/08sorkin.html?_r=0 (accessed December 27, 2014).

Terra Daily, "Norway: Noah's Ark of Seed Samples Tucked into Arctic Mountainside," *Terra Daily*, http://www.terradaily.com/reports/Norway_Noahs_Ark_of_seed_samples_tucked_into_Arctic_mountainside_999.html (accessed December 26, 2014).

Wines, Michael, "Owners of Chemical Firm Charged in Elk River Spill in West Virginia," *New York Times*, December 17, 2014, http://www.nytimes.com/2014/12/18/us/owners-of-chemical-company-charged-in-elk-river-spill.html?_r=0)accessed December 26, 2014).

Zucchino, David, "West Virginia Puzzled, Outraged Over Chemical Leak, *Los Angeles Times*, January 16, 2014, http://www.latimes.com/nation/la-na-chemical-danger-20140117,0,7792964.story#axzz2qoB1oF00 (accessed December 26, 2014).

3.2

Going Postal
Addressing Workplace Violence

Spotlight: *John Q; Polytechnique; Murder By Proxy: America Goes Postal*
Case Studies: Gunman at LAX; The Montreal Massacre; Virginia Tech Rampage
Ethics Code: Los Angeles World Airports (LAWA)

> *Mitch Quigley: This country man; can't go anywhere without gettin'*
> *mugged, or murdered or stabbed. Kids killin' their classmates, drivebys,*
> *ya know, I won't even go into a post office any more.*
> *Steve Maguire: Shut up, Mitch.*
> *Dr. Raymond Turner: No, you shut up. I hate the little bastard but*
> *he's right. You know how easy it is to get a gun in the country? In five*
> *minutes, boom, gun show.*
>
> —John Q

> *They treat the machines better than they do the people… and they say*
> *you have no rights. When people don't feel there's any alternative, it's*
> *a simple fork in the road to go—violence toward others or violence*
> *toward self.*
>
> —Murder By Proxy

John Quincy Archibald's son needs a heart transplant, but John's health insurance is inadequate for such high-priced surgery. His wife has reached the end of her wits with all of his promises that fail to materialize. It's a perfect storm for desperation—which rarely leads to positive results. And this much is true: Rarely do good things come out of a desperate state of mind.

Face it: What would *you* do if your child was at death's door and only a heart transplant could send the Grim Reaper back to where he came from?

Business Ethics Through Movies: A Case Study Approach, First Edition. Wanda Teays.
© 2015 John Wiley & Sons, Ltd. Published 2015 by John Wiley & Sons, Ltd.

You try to reason with your employer. You try to get another job (over-qualified!!). And you throw yourself on the mercy of hospital administrators whose altruism shriveled up ages ago. John's desperation is like a lobster in a pot of boiling water. We are only a little bit surprised when he yanks out a gun, chains the ER door shut, and takes hostages. Among them is the cardiologist who would do the transplant if John's insurance covered the cost.

Remember the phrase, "Going postal"? That reached the vernacular after a number of murderous incidents involving post office employees going berserk and shooting co-workers. Of course, it's not just postal workers who lose it and kill others in the workplace. Even though he is a sympathetic character, John could be said to have "gone postal" when he pulled his gun, took hostages, and demanded a transplant for his son.

In this chapter we will look at a disturbing workplace safety issue—violence. Violence includes overt and covert behaviors —anything from aggressiveness to verbal harassment to murder (*Nursing World*). Three films illustrate ways it occurs—*John Q* (hospital), *Polytechnique* (school), and *Murder by Proxy: America Goes Postal* (workplace). As an issue for Business Ethics we may want to pass by this thorny problem, but it is unwise to do so. The ethics code here is that of the Los Angeles World Airports. We will also get some insight into the creation of this code. We'll end with a look at federal regulations regarding workplace violence.

Workplace Safety and Workplace Violence

Two forms of workplace safety warrant our attention. One is *safe conditions* (= workplace safety) and the other is *violence* (= workplace violence). Both are important.

Workplace Safety

Most companies do not treat workplace safety as an *ethical* issue. That does not mean they do not care about it. However, ethics codes tend not to mention the conditions under which employees must work. One exception is the code of the American Staffing Association (ASA). Among its duties is:

ASA members agree to always strive
To ascertain that employees are assigned to work sites that are safe, that they understand the nature of the work the client has called for and can perform

such work without injury to themselves or others, and that they receive any personal safety training and equipment that may be required.

No job is without risk, but many dangers are preventable or could be minimized. Occupational Safety and Health Administration (OSHA) is a regulatory agency overseeing workplace conditions so they are "safe and healthful." Even so, workers are injured or killed every year on the job.

OSHA reports that 4,405 workers died on the job in 2013. Injuries were in much greater numbers, so it is important that work conditions be addressed. The "Fatal Four" are falls, electrocution, struck by object, and caught-in/between (as in a cave-in or excavation accident). Accidents around construction are the most common, so safety measures are vital. So too is a caring response and proper compensation for work-related injuries and disabilities.

Workplace Violence

"Nearly 2 million American workers report having been victims of workplace violence each year," reports OSHA. Moreover, "The truth is, workplace violence can strike anywhere, anytime, and no one is immune." That means you, me, and that guy over there.

You may never have raised your voice in your entire life and are cool as a cuke. That doesn't protect you at the airport, shopping mall or your favorite restaurant when someone goes over an edge, or the local gangsters shoot up the place, or you-name-it. The National Center for Victims of Crime (2013) gives us a sense of the magnitude of this problem:

> Millions of workers experience violence or the threat of violence in their workplaces every year. These crimes range from physical assaults to robbery and homicide. Although the numbers of such crimes have significantly declined in recent years, *workplace violence is the second-leading cause of occupational injury* (my emphasis).

In addition,

> Workers in certain occupations—such as nurses, utility workers, taxi drivers, letter carriers, and especially those who work alone or at night— are particularly vulnerable. Unlike other crimes, the greatest proportions of these crimes are committed by strangers. ... Decreasing the occurrence of these crimes is a growing concern for employers and employees nationwide.

Between 1997 and 2010, 79 percent of workplace homicides were shootings. Other homicides (the remaining 21 percent) were due to stabbing; hitting, kicking, and beating; and assaults. That is a staggering percentage: Nearly four-fifths of workplace homicides are gun-related.

Note also how prevalent violence is in particular types of jobs. For example, in 2009 "more than 50 percent of emergency center (EC) nurses had experienced violence by patients on the job and 25 percent of EC nurses had experienced 20 or more violent incidents in the past three years," reports the Emergency Nurses Association (American Nurses Association). They note that no federal standard requires workplace violence protections. This will leads to a lot of challenges.

When a determined gunman or terrorist group arrives with weapons, most businesses are caught off guard (as in the mall rampage on September 21, 2013 in Nairobi, Kenya). So, Let's first look at a 2013 real-world case, the takeover of Terminal 3 at LAX.

CASE STUDY 1: Guns in the Airport (LAX)

Consider this scenario: A Transportation Security Administration (TSA) officer has been shot and others wounded at the Los Angeles airport (LAX). As the shooter makes his way toward the gates, terrified passengers run, hide, or fall to the floor. Airport officials and the LAPD close the roads into the airport, so anyone coming or going must do so on foot. There is widespread terror and chaos.

Here's the nitty gritty: On November 1, 2013 a single gunman walked into Terminal 3 armed with a military-grade assault rifle not designed for civilian use. Paul A. Ciancia, the 23-year-old shooter and unemployed motorcycle mechanic, killed the TSA officer and wounded others before being stopped by four bullets.

The suicide note in his pocket reveals a beef with the government and especially the TSA. "Black, white, yellow, brown, I don't discriminate," the note read, says a law enforcement official (Reeve, 2013). In short, Ciancia went to the airport with the intent to kill. It's unsettling to think that one shooter could close down one of the biggest airports in the United States.

Senator Diane Feinstein, who favors gun restrictions, brought attention to the rifle that the shooter used. In a November 3, 2013 interview on *Face the Nation* she said, "The weapon was a .223 MP-15, where the MP stands for military and police" and "Clearly designed not for general consumption, but through practice now for general consumption—same gun that was used at Aurora." She was referring to the rampage in Aurora, Colorado where 12 people were killed and 70 injured at the opening night of the Batman movie, *The Dark Knight Rises*.

Feinstein is not optimistic about changing the gun laws. "I think there's a hammerlock on the Congress by the gun owners and the gun people, and it doesn't matter," she observed (McMurry, 2013). There are considerable obstacles to tightening-up access to guns and restricting the types of weapons that can be sold.

Addressing Violence

There are several steps to addressing workplace violence.

- *First* we need to address weapons acquisition. As Senator Feinstein indicates, the average person (here, a 23-year old) can acquire an assault weapon designed for military use. That brings up important issues about access to guns, waiting periods, and security checks.
- *Second* is the need to address the weapons themselves. This is the issue of what sorts of guns are available for purchase to be used for purposes other than military or law enforcement.
- *Third* is to address restrictions. This includes background checks, waiting periods, prohibitions as to who cannot legally purchase a gun; e.g., mentally ill, ex-cons, those on probation for violent crime or with current restraining orders or on a terrorist watch list, etc.

Anyone who gets hold of an assault rifle can kill a dozens of people in a matter of minutes, if not seconds. That reality shapes both security and safety issues in the workplace, at schools, and at other institutions. and yet ethics codes tend not to address workplace violence. Perhaps violence is thought to be too rare and unpredictable to register when devising or modifying ethics codes. Nevertheless, workplace safety—and that includes workplace violence—merits our attention.

Workplace Chaos: Lessons from LAX

Sometimes life imitates art. Take the shooting at LAX. "It was like a science fiction movie, like the *Day the World Ended*," said Schalon Harrison Newton, a businessman trapped for nearly eight hours at the Tom Bradley International Terminal after arriving from Japan. "Thousands of people were on the street and there were no vehicles except police cars. It was a very strange experience," he said (Weikel and Nelson, 2013).

Airport officials declared that *public safety* was their first focus when gunshots broke out. However, there are secondary concerns when thousands of people are affected by an act of violence. There needs to be *contingency plans* and *clearly defined procedures* for crisis management. If there were such policies, they weren't put into effect. People were running in all directions. They then faced restrictions (including canceled flights) that continued for much of the day. and many travelers were held for hours in the Bradley terminal, with limited access to food and water and few updates from LAX staff (Weikel and Nelson, 2013). Furthermore,

"There was a communications breakdown after the shooting," said Marshall McClain, an airport police officer and president of the Los Angeles Airport Peace Officers Assn. "The airport website was down. The airport radio station had been closed and passenger contact with employees was weak. People were just told to use Twitter."

Of course Twitter requires phones or Internet access. Those who told people to "use Twitter" made a few assumptions, not all warranted. As LAX remains a top target for terrorists, Los Angeles Councilman Mike Bonin says that there is a need to minimize the fallout and "improve information sharing, evacuation procedures and care for stranded passengers."

If there was an *evacuation plan*, no one seemed to know it, or follow it. For example, Red Cross officials set up a sleep center just north of the airport, expecting up to 300 passengers. Sandwiches and bottled water were waiting, but only one person showed up. This gave rise to questions about whether the *shelter* was properly publicized.

"Really, no one knew anything," said Andy Dulman, an airline passenger who was transported from Terminal 3 to another terminal after the shooting. "It felt like someone told the buses where to take us, and that was it. It really seemed like we were on our own" (Weikel and Nelson, 2013).

ETHICS CODE: Los Angeles World Airports (LAWA) Code of Ethics

In the Preamble to its *Code of Ethics*, LAWA states that it subscribes to six core values. "These values are honesty, integrity, respect and collaboration, responsibility, public trust, and citizenship." Access the code at: http://www.lawa.org/welcome_LAWA.aspx?id=690.

Exercise

Georgianna Streeter, the team coordinator for the writing of the LAWA ethics code answered questions about the process (below). Read her remarks and note what two or three things stand out—and could help other companies develop an ethics code.

1. **Who participated in writing/creating the LAWA ethics code?**
   The LAWA Code of Ethics was written with the assistance of the ethics office ... There were 16 members plus an advisor from Human Resources and the three ethics office employees. We wanted a broad scan of employees with a good number of managers and line employees involved so it addressed the worldview of as many employees as possible.

2. **What process was used?**
   It was a very productive and creative process using an in-house team described above over a three-month period meeting once or twice per week on set days. ...Through our weekly meetings we identified the values we wanted, worked through the meanings and expressions and examples. We then looked at areas of functionality or operations that we thought deserved some reference to in terms of what philosophical approach would be helpful in decision-making ...

   Once the team designed the structure, a couple of us were the scribes and we put in the actual language and then took that back to the team for review and approval. ... Once those approvals were garnered, we took the Code (after getting it printed) to the full Board and they passed a resolution adopting the code.

3. **Was there a particular ethicist or ethical theory that you used as a model or guide?**
   Absolutely—since I was the main coordinator of the project and one of the main writers, I used Aristotelian thought when and where possible. One of the refrains I made often was discussing the notion of excellence as in *arête* [the quality of excellence toward which we strive in our daily conduct in society (Vassalo, 2004)] I wanted to convey the concept of excellent work, not just measured by the output but by the thought and decisions that went into it as well.

4. **Have you found this a workable code—or would you add or subtract anything?**
   I think it is a very workable code. With that in mind, we also wrote it with the knowledge that it should be changed or updated over time as the needs and world-view of the Airport Department also changed.

… Given that we are a government agency we live by lots of rules already, but rules are what define behavior and purpose most of the time too.

CASE STUDY 2: Guns in the Classroom— The Montreal Massacre

On December 6, 1989 another lone gunman with an axe to grind loaded a mini-14 rifle and brought along a hunting knife and headed into L'école Polytechnique in Montreal, Quebec. Twenty-five year old Marc Lepine had one goal in mind. He wanted to kill as many "feminists" (women) as he could.

When Lepine first arrived at the school, he went in a classroom and ordered the men to leave (they did). He then proceeded to shoot all nine female engineering students in the room, killing six. He then moved from classroom to classroom and on to the cafeteria. By the time he took his own life, fourteen women were dead. Another ten women and four men were injured. Lepine's suicide note blamed feminists for ruining his life. The tragic event has come to be known as the "Montreal Massacre."

On the National Day of Remembrance on December 6, 2006, the prime minister of Canada said, "The motive behind the Montreal Massacre was hatred of women." The National Day of Remembrance was a call for action. Our goal, said the prime minister, should be "to eliminate all forms of discrimination towards women and to bring together women and men in the name of equality" (Canwest News Service, 2006).

Looking back at the gendered violence of that rampage, it's worth noting that many people took steps to effect change. For example, Stanley G. French, Director of the Humanities PhD program at Montreal's Concordia University was a catalyst for scholarly work on violence against women.

Unfortunately, there has been case after ghastly case of gunmen walking into schools and taking the lives of students, faculty, and staff. We devote time to pore over the shooter's pathology. We lament the deaths of innocent people in the line of fire. We tally the results—the numbers of victims, the rising body count. But we haven't been able to prevent such senseless killings. More work is required.

Conflicting Values

The conflicting values of "do no harm" and "protect innocent lives" versus "uphold the right to bear arms" and "preserve gun ownership" make for a heated debate. When the dust settles, gun owners still have guns and schools, hospitals, airports, and workplaces are open territory for a determined shooter. It's hard to conclude that we've made much progress. Even attempts to restrict entry have failed. As we saw at Sandy Hook Elementary School in Newtown, Connecticut, 26 people were killed (20 children) after the lone gunman "shot his way in, defeating a security system requiring visitors to be buzzed in. Moments later, the principal was shot dead when she went to investigate the sound of gunshots" (Barron, 2012).

Many argue that gun ownership is a fundamental right. This view has to be given careful consideration. That it has resulted in the unnecessary loss of human life is regrettable, but is not seen by of the vast majority of law-abiding gun-owning citizens as the root of the problem. Explanations like "guns don't kill people, people kill people" carry a lot of weight for a portion of the population. Is this morally acceptable? Maybe so, maybe not, depending on your politics, religion, or values.

But one thing is certain: Workplace safety is not just about equipment malfunction. It's not just about toxic chemicals that workers are exposed to (as in the Film Recovery Systems case in Chapter 2.5). It's not just about poorly maintained ventilation systems (as with the 1976 Legionnaire's conference in Philadelphia that killed 29 people and sickened others). It's not just about inadequate safety gear (as nurses and doctors faced in the 2002–03 SARS outbreak that took 44 lives in Toronto). And it's not just about shooters on a rampage. The concerns regarding workplace safety range from proper hygiene to the protection of human life.

Workplace Violence in Film

In addition to *John Q,* two other movies look at workplace safety. One is the gripping *Polytechnique* (2009), which chronicles the Montreal Massacre. It is an unflinching look at the way hatred reaches expression. The second is *Murder By Proxy* (2010), about a former employee who goes into the Royal Oak, Michigan post office on November 14, 1991 and kills four supervisors and wounds five others before taking his own life. Because of such killings, the term "going postal" has become part of the English language.

However many differences there may be between them, the movies have common threads. There's the desperate father (*John Q*), the woman-hater (*Polytechnique*), and the disgruntled ex-postal employee (*Murder By Proxy*). Each one is at a boiling point. And each one takes his frustration out on others. All three films pinpoint the vulnerability of businesses and institutions to acts of violence.

Let's start with *Polytechnique*. That the film is labeled both "Drama" and "Horror" is an indication of its disturbing aspects. Nevertheless, it is a powerful movie about an important and troubling issue.

SPOTLIGHT: *Polytechnique*

The movie centers on three protagonists—two engineering students, Lisa and Jeff, enrolled at L'école Polytechnique, and a determined killer, Marc Lepine. The movie opens with Marc getting things in order, including a suicide note. It's wintry, snow is on the ground and he has to wear a heavy jacket to keep warm.

We don't yet know his intent but all signs suggest this isn't a happy fellow. Cut to Lisa and Jeff. Given their ease with each other, we infer that they're good friends. This fact makes it hard for Jeff when Marc orders the men to leave the classroom, and even harder when Jeff looks through the classroom window and realizes the fate awaiting the women. Marc has gone to the school to kill as many women as possible.

This much is true: Marc has no trouble bringing his rifle into the school and making his way into the classroom without any impediments or interruption. The only security guard we see is downstairs, away from the classrooms, unaware of what is transpiring. It is Jeff who runs to get help, urging the guard to call the police, telling him that girls are being held hostage in the classroom. Jeff does not know what more to do. But it's clear he wants to do something to stop this. For that reason, he moves from room to room trying not to get shot while attempting to help the victims.

Lisa is among the women segregated and then shot. We follow as she tries to go for help, but she can only drag her bloody, injured leg along, barely able to do more than stagger. Because she can't move quickly, she's in danger of being shot again. We understand why she re-enters the classroom and curls up on the ground. Maybe she can survive by playing dead; maybe the gunman won't finish her off. The tension grips us with fear and empathy.

We see how quickly lives can change. It's hard not to identify with Lisa, who was in the wrong place at the wrong time. It could have been you or me, that's how random was the violence. It is also hard not to identify with Jeff: He doesn't run off, trying to get to safety like many of the others. He sees what's happening and wants to do something to stop the bloodbath.

But he has no way to confront the killer (With what? He doesn't even have a book to wave at him).

And yet he can't leave. He's too sickened by what is happening; too alarmed to leave. He can see that it's women who have been targeted and tries to help those who are still alive. That he is able to do so, though at considerable risk, speaks of his courage. He doesn't see that—but we do.

Later, when Lisa is being wheeled out on a stretcher, Jeff apologizes for having left the room when the gunman ordered the men to leave. Lisa doesn't blame him, but he can't hear her; his guilt is too great. When all is said and done, the killer has taken his own life, but Lisa survived. Life returns to some semblance of normalcy. It's not easy to pick up the pieces. We see the toll the violence has left on her. How could it not? That's the thing about violence—it affects everyone—the victims, the shooters, the ones who see but can't help, those who do help, those who run to safety, those who lose a son or daughter, friend or mere acquaintance—everyone.

The movie never reveals what drove Marc Lepine to have such hatred of women. His brutality, his cold demeanor is frightful. It is hard to watch and yet deeply compelling. There is no erasing what happens; there's a reason victims are called *survivors*. Samuel Beckett's novel *The Unnamable* speaks to such determination: "I can't go on. I'll go on." Lisa goes on.

Jeff is not so resilient. Although he did not suffer a *physical* injury in the massacre, the psychological harm has him in a stranglehold. He saw death up close and could do nothing to stop it. Any attempt would likely have resulted in being killed, and yet Jeff can't shake it. He entered Dante's circles of hell and couldn't escape. The movie vividly shows us how tenuous life is, how fragile.

We should note that the Columbine high school massacre in 1999 put school violence on the map. Its horrific toll is etched in our collective memory. Michael Moore responded with a film on the fascination with guns and what he sees as a culture of violence in the US This is *Bowling for Columbine* (2002), for which Moore received many awards.

Exercise Round One

You are head of security at a university with close to 30,000 students. It's a bit of a sprawling campus, with dorms at one end of the campus and classroom buildings towards the other end. It is 7:15 a.m. on April 16, 2007 and you've just been notified that two people were shot and killed in one of the dormitories across campus.

Think About It
1. What should you do in terms of the first response? In what order?
2. What do you communicate to students, faculty, and staff?
3. What ethical issues do you face, given the shooter has not yet been apprehended?

Exercise Round Two

Two and a half hours have passed since the two people were killed in the dorms. You figure those killings are due to a domestic dispute and the killer will be found soon. You didn't lock down the campus or send out a campus alert, since it seemed an isolated incident. As it turns out, the killer left campus and returned—this time to the classroom building, and, after chaining the doors shut, he killed 30 more. You are still in charge of security so once more are called to respond.

Think About It
1. What should you do in terms of this second response? In what order?
2. What do you communicate to students, faculty, and staff?
3. What ethical issues do you face, given the shooter has taken his own life? Later you find out that the killer was a student there too. How does that fact impact the ethical issues raised?
4. What changes should be made in terms of security at the university?

You may realize that this is the Virginia Tech massacre. The university was eventually found negligent in terms of their response. As a result of what happened, there was likely some pretty serious soul-searching (CNN Wire Staff, 2012). In any case, changes to security protocol came big time to the college(Virginia Tech).

Addressing School Violence

What mechanisms need to be put in place before we can rest easy (if we will ever be able to rest easy)? The truth is that when people set out to harm others at the worksite, we've got a problem. It's difficult to find the right balance. On one hand, we don't want the workplace to become a fortress. Nor do we favor extensive or intrusive personal checkpoints á la the security checks at airports. On the other hand, the worksite has to be a safe environment—one with protections in place. This was a major concern at Virginia Tech after that fateful day.

When we think about schoolplace violence, Columbine may be the first to come to mind. This is the carefully planned school massacre resulting in the death of twelve students and one teacher at their Colorado high school on April 10, 1999. The two student-gunmen eventually took their own lives. Since that time there have been numerous similar incidents, each leading to measures taken to try to prevent other "school rampages." There are no indications that we've seen the last.

The fact that Adam Lanza shot his way into Sandy Hook School in Connecticut on December 14, 2012 indicates that barriers only block some perpetrators, but not all. The Newtown shootings were the second-worst school rampage in the US In first place is Virginia Tech, where in April 2007 another lone gunman killed 33 students and faculty before taking his own life, as did Lanza and as did Lepine in Montreal.

In the Virginia Tech case, a state panel sharply criticized decisions made by the university before and after the shooting massacre, saying "university officials could have saved lives by notifying students and faculty members earlier about the killings on campus." The report makes it clear that mistakes were made:

> "There does not seem to be a plausible scenario of a university response to the double homicide that could have prevented the tragedy of considerable magnitude on April 16," the report said. "Cho had started on a mission of fulfilling a fantasy of revenge."
>
> "But if the university had issued an alert earlier or canceled classes after Mr. Cho shot his first two victims, before moving on to shoot the rest in a classroom building, the death toll might have been lower, the report said. It found that even after university officials had learned the full scope of the massacre, their messages to students played down the unfolding emergency as a "routine police procedure" (Urbina, 2007).

The truth is that schools are vulnerable, as we have seen. Ditto airports and hospitals. Our next spotlight movie suggests that the post office and other workplaces can be dangerous places too. It seems like nowhere is safe—underscoring how important it is for this issue to be addressed.

SPOTLIGHT: *Murder By Proxy: America Goes Postal*

Incidents of employees who kill co-workers are a cause for concern—for both employers and employees. *Murder by Proxy* zeroes in on the 1992 rampage in Royal Oak, Michigan. There a former postal employee became "mad as hell" and couldn't take it any more. Some who are mad as hell count to 10 and eventually calm down and go on, never to look back. And then there are those who are mad as hell and decide to show the world just how mad they are. Sometimes they can be stopped from hurting others, but not always.

The movie focuses on Thomas McIlvane, a postal worker who has been fired—unjustly, he feels. His ex-colleagues voice the view that the workplace environment is hard on the employees. They suggest that McIlvane was treated unfairly by his supervisors and, having no effective channels of recourse, internalized the anger that would eventually explode.

Criminal Justice professor James Alan Fox observes that shooters tend to be treated as mentally defective, but that we need to examine the workplace *environment*. "All too often it's not the employee—it's the job," he argues. The very conditions of disempowerment on the job plant the seeds of alienation and frustration. That does not justify killing others, but may help us understand the catalyst.

Experts and employees note that this incident is but one of many: Across America, workers are often subjected to harsh working conditions and demeaning and disrespectful treatment. Here are some of the opinions expressed in the film.

- "We like to believe it's just a few bad apples. No one has ever and can ever come up with a profile that's sufficiently predictive."
- "It's easier for people to see it as one crazy guy who's snapped than to see the larger picture of how American people are treated."
- The alienation of the instigator tells us that we need to look at what's toxic in the workplace and look at those issues.

There was a time where violence in the workplace was unthinkable, but no longer. "We are not talking about America's streets; more and more it's the workplace," a news anchor observes. "It's another case of rage in the workplace."

Addressing Contributing Factors

Employers have to address hostile environments, working conditions, as well as relations between employees, customers, and other businesses. Many businesses have already done so, with positive results from their proactive practices and policies.

When such steps haven't been taken employees may feel disempowered, frustrated, or on their own to deal with problems. No good can come of that. "Individual workers can never stand up to an owner," says a commentator in *Murder by Proxy*. Many workers who are bullied or humiliated have little recourse. Unions have been weakened or are gone. Salaries have stagnated and workers have less security.

The filmmaker presents the argument that, since the early 1980s, economic forces favor the employer, the owners, and the businesses. In contrast, workers are left without the recognition or support that might prevent the outbursts and killings that seem to mount as the years go by. We are left with the message: Change is definitely in order.

Determining Accountability for Workplace Violence

The US Department of Labor points out that, "No employer is immune from workplace violence and no employer can totally prevent it." In addition, "The cost to organizations is staggering. It is impossible to overstate the costs of workplace violence, because a single incident can have sweeping repercussions."

There are two contrasting views on assessing the case of individuals who go over the edge and kill others in an act of rage.

Look at the Individual On one hand, any competent adult is responsible for their choices and actions. Whatever the pressures, the despair, hardships, or disappointments, we can't blame anyone else for our behavior. When reflecting on what we've made of our lives, we should not try to pass the buck. Individuals must be held accountable when they cross the line.

Look at the Work Environment On the other hand, we have to look at the context and the community and not simply focus on the individual. A worker may not have the power to confront problems, to change an oppressive or hostile environment. The workplace must be assessed when individual workers cross the line.

By the first line of reasoning, if we've got a problem, we need to do something about it. It is not okay to take out anger or frustration on anyone else—and shooting innocent people is simply unconscionable. By the second line of reasoning, if we don't look at the context within which workers operate, problems will arise and fester. We need to address work conditions and ensure fairness, as well as channels of redress, and reasonable workloads.

"Lean and mean" may be good for investors but not for workers. Should we admire and revere those who succeed, even if they lack compassion for others? What message does that send? An inflated view of "success" at any cost will pit workers against workers. The result, according to *Murder by Proxy*, is a form of social Darwinism where only the strong survive. The more you buy, the more you've got to lose. Economic insecurity washes over people like ocean waves: "How do I make it?" "I'm in debt up to my eyeballs."

The movie asserts that all is not as it should be in the workplace. We as a community and as a society should waste no time in turning things around. Individual workers have neither the power nor the authority to transform the status quo (or not usually). Such change requires a concerted effort of like-minded people. That very fact fuels the frustration laying the groundwork for acts of violence. Consequently, we need to put our heads together and find ways to bring about change.

First Steps (Before Things Escalate)

It's good to have a few tips on dealing with volatile situations at work. Given that a conflict can lead to something more problematic—even explosive—dousing the flames is to be recommended. The question is in the *how*. At the *Harvard Business Review* (*HBR*) they say, "Stop being so nice."

Denial and avoidance may be the norm when conflicts arise, but this drives the problem underground, not away. The fact we don't talk about it doesn't mean the problem ceases to exist. Here are three tips to confront conflict in the workplace. They are inspired by *Harvard Business Review*'s management tips (see e.g., Ashkenar and Bodell, 2013).

Tips on Dealing with Conflict in the Workplace

1   Know Thyself
    Do a self-inventory to determine if you held back from speaking ("kept your tongue") in order to avoid a conflict. Then ask yourself if it would have been better to speak up. Not all silence is equal, or a good idea. Look for patterns in what conflicts you avoid—and what that says about you.
2   Reality Checks Have Their Place
    Rilke, or was it Camus, or maybe another famous writer once said, "The face of a friend is a reflection of your own face in a distorted (foggy?) mirror." The idea is that we see ourselves in our friends—and they see us too. They may see our patterns of aggression or avoidance, of speaking up or staying silent. Those perceptions may be invaluable (and help us Know Thyself). Ask for feedback; it may be the catalyst you were looking for!

3 Stick Your Toes in the Water
Let's face it: You're not going to be transformed from Wimpy Willy to Smooth Silvio overnight. Nor should you. Gradual change is often to be preferred (not always, but often). That said, it is wise to find ways of addressing conflict. It may be in the form of speaking up to the offender (or adversary). Or it may be in the form of speaking to an appropriate other (a supervisor). The wheels of transformation are set in motion by the action you take.

These tips carry us only so far: Some conflict *should* be avoided. Think about the most effective way to express a concern or address a conflict. Remember the movie *Ghost Dog*? The protagonist tries to think like a Samurai warrior before taking any action! We might also think of projecting ourselves far enough ahead to forestall conflict.

Similarly, martial arts master Ip Man in *The Grandmaster* visualizes in his own mind what moves to make *before* lifting a finger. "Let the objectives shape the means." That doesn't mean that the end *justifies* the means, but that the end helps us determine the *tools* we'll need. If the end is a brick wall, then we need to know something about mortar. If the end is a watercolor painting, we better be able to handle a paintbrush. And so on.

We can understand why this issue has gotten the attention of the federal government. Let's turn now to their guidelines.

Federal Recommendations Regarding Workplace Violence

There seems to be no end in sight to school shootings. They are many other businesses and institutions where individuals have vented their anger or frustration on others. Action is required. The question is, "What do we do?"

On the US Department of Labor (DOL) website are strategies to create a calm and cool workplace. Read through the recommendations with a view to how best to create a positive work environment and, as much as possible, keep workplace violence to a minimum.

The US Department of Labor

Work Environment
The best prevention strategy is to maintain an environment which minimizes negative feelings, such as isolation, resentment, and hostility among employees. Although no workplace can be perceived as

perfect by every employee, there are several steps that management can take to help create a professional, healthy, and caring work environment. These include, but are not necessarily limited to:

- Promoting sincere, open, and timely communication among managers, employees, and union representatives;
- Offering opportunities for professional development;
- Fostering a family-friendly work environment;
- Maintaining mechanisms for complaints and concerns and allowing them to be expressed in a nonjudgmental forum that includes timely feedback to the initiator;
- Promoting "quality of life" issues such as facilities and job satisfaction; and
- Maintaining impartial and consistent discipline for employees who exhibit improper conduct and poor performance.

Clearly, this issue requires careful thought and action. There's no reason to think it's going away any time soon, so we need to reflect on how best to work for change. One of the objectives of doing Business Ethics is to find a way to work for change so that all workplaces are able to keep violence to a minimum and have as preventative measures in place.

To accomplish this we need to make as few assumptions as possible. Keep an open mind. Examine ethical dilemmas from diverse points of view, with empathy for the relevant parties. Treat others with respect and dignity. Have procedures and policies for a just and fair workplace. Confront problems and improper conduct in a timely way. Be willing to look at the hard questions. And don't give up.

Works Cited

American Nurses Association, "Workplace Violence," *Nursing World*, http://nursingworld.org/workplaceviolence (accessed December 27, 2014).

American Staffing Association, ASA Code of Ethics and Good Practices, *American Staffing*, http://www.americanstaffing.net/members/code_of_ethics.cfm (accessed December 27, 2014).

Ashkenar, Ron and Lisa Bodell, "Nice Managers Embrace Conflict Too," *Harvard Business Review*, October 16, 2013, https://hbr.org/2013/10/nice-managers-embrace-conflict-too/ (accessed December 27, 2014).

Barron, James, "Nation Reels After Gunman Massacres 20 Children at School in Connecticut," *New York Times*, December 14, 2012, http://www.nytimes.com/2012/12/15/nyregion/shooting-reported-at-connecticut-elementary-school.html (accessed December 27, 2014).

CNN Wire Staff, "Virginia Tech To Review Negligence Verdict In 2007 Shooting Rampage," *CNN News*, March 15, 2012, http://www.cnn.com/2012/03/15/justice/virginia-virginia-tech (accessed December 27, 2014).

Los Angeles Times, Associated Press, "Murder Ranks 2nd as Cause of Postal Workers' On-Job Deaths," *Los Angeles Times*, July 10, 1995, http://articles.latimes.com/1995-07-10/news/mn-22439_1_postal-worker (accessed December 27, 2014).

Los Angeles World Airports, LAWA's New Code of Ethics, http://www.lawa.org/welcome_LAWA.aspx?id=690 (accessed December 27, 2014).

The National Center for Victims of Crime, Information and Statistics, Available at http://www.victimsofcrime.org/library/crime-information-and-statistics/workplace-violence (accessed December 27, 2014).

McMurry, Evan, "Sen. Feinstein on LAX Shooting: Gun Groups Have 'Hammerlock' on Congress," *Media-ite*, http://www.mediaite.com/tv/sen-feinstein-on-lax-shooting-gun-groups-have-hammerlock-on-congress/ (accessed December 27, 2014).

Reeve, Richard. "Paul Ciancia is Identified As LAX Shooter, Authorities Say," *ABC News*, November 1, 2103, http://www.wjla.com/articles/2013/11/-paul-ciancia-is-identified-as-lax-shooter-police-say-96298.html (accessed December 27, 2014).

Urbina, Ian, "Virginia Tech Criticized for Actions in Shooting," *New York Times*, August 30, 2007, http://www.nytimes.com/2007/08/30/us/30school.html?pagewanted=all (accessed December 27, 2014).

U.S. Department of Labor, Commonly Used Statistics, Occupational Safety and Health Administration, https://www.osha.gov/oshstats/commonstats.html (accessed December 27, 2014).

U.S. Department of Labor, "DOL Workplace Violence Program," http://www.dol.gov/oasam/hrc/policies/dol-workplace-violence-program.htm (accessed December 27, 2014).

U.S. Department of Labor, "Workplace Violence," Occupational Safety and Health Administration, https://www.osha.gov/SLTC/workplaceviolence/index.html (accessed December 27, 2014).

Vassallo, Philip, "The Virtues, Arête," *Philosophy Now*, https://philosophynow.org/issues/45/Arete (accessed December 27, 2014).

Virginia Tech, "Safety and Security," *VT Alerts*, Available at http://www.alerts.vt.edu/alerts-security.html (accessed December 27, 2014).

Weikel, Dan and Laura J. Nelson, "Passenger Chaos After LAX Shootings Brings Official Scrutiny," *Los Angeles Times*, November 5, 2013.

3.3

Stand By Me
Addressing Workplace Inequities

Spotlight: *Matewan; Made in Dagenham*
Case Studies: UAW and H&M on Pay Equity; The Fast Food Workers
Strike; H&M and Child Labor; Marriage Equality
Ethics Code: H&M

> ***Rita O'Grady:*** *When did we, in this country, decide to stop fighting?*
> *I don't think we ever did. But you've got to back us up. You've got*
> *to stand up with us. "We" are the working classes—the men and the*
> *women. We're not separated by sex, but only by those who are willing to*
> *accept injustice...*
> —Made in Dagenham

> ***Joe Kenehan:*** *You think this man is the enemy? Huh? This is a worker!*
> *Any union keeps this man out ain't a union, it's a goddam club! ...*
> *There ain't but two sides in this world— them that work and them that*
> *don't. You work, they don't. That's all you get to know about the enemy.*
> —Matewan

Rita O'Grady is one of those spunky women who may not know what fork
to use for the salad, but can handle husband, children, and making automobile seat covers in Dagenham, England. It didn't rub her the right way
that the women got paid less than the men for doing work at a similar skill
level. No, that didn't set well with Rita. Nor did it set well that she wasn't
taken seriously when she pointed out the disparity.

Some people look at injustice and feel defeated. Others speak up and set
the wheels of change in motion. Rita is in the latter group. We follow
along as she takes on the system—a very big system, the Ford Motor
Corporation.

Business Ethics Through Movies: A Case Study Approach, First Edition. Wanda Teays.
© 2015 John Wiley & Sons, Ltd. Published 2015 by John Wiley & Sons, Ltd.

Let's face it: We might feel overwhelmed at how perilous a journey it could be. We might be inclined to cut our losses and throw in the towel. Not Rita O'Grady. She did not give up. Of course she saw that her female co-workers took risks to back her up and that the men joining forces with the striking women put their jobs on the line. She also saw that the corporate honchos weren't going to give in without a fight. But she figured out that the right thing to do would be to see that justice was done. *Made in Dagenham* (2010) tells the tale.

It's an inspiring story of workers uniting to effect change. There aren't many movies about the working class and the struggles they face; you can count them with a dozen eggs. In this chapter we will look at two films, *Made in Dagenham* and *Matewan*, which show individuals, unions, and communities seeking to address pay and other inequities. They show us that we are not powerless; that we can make a difference. They also show us the role of the community in sustaining justice in the workplace and in institutions—and the government as well.

Both films illustrate the power of collective action, with or without a union. There is a range to consider when thinking about discrimination in the workplace, as we'll see. We will also examine the case of the use of child labor by retailer H&M, as that raises some important issues for those in the West. Finally, we'll turn to the issue of marriage equality.

Existentialism gives us useful tools for framing the discussion. It serves as a valuable ethical framework.

The Moral Framework of Existentialism

Existentialism is so named because it is a philosophy of individual existence. Its centers on being-in-the-world and on what it takes to reach our potential. We don't choose our parents or where and when we were born. But we *do* choose what to make of ourselves, what kind of person we want to be. We are defined by what we do: Actions, not words, give shape to our lives.

Existentialist Jean Paul Sartre put it this way: "Man is the sum of his acts." Or, as Phil Connor put it in *Groundhog Day*, "You make choices and you live with them." We have the freewill to decide for ourselves—a good thing. But we are then responsible for what we do. Don't blame anyone else, Sartre would advise us.

Existentialists look at us as individuals in all our uniqueness. We live here and now, in this place and time. We understand who we are by jumping into the stream of life, by engagement. Life in context reveals the boundary conditions that throw us back on ourselves and call us to reflect on what we are doing with our lives, what sort of person we are becoming.

Consider what it is that gives our lives meaning. At the heart of the journey, say Existentialists, is *authenticity*. This means being honest with ourselves about who we are. Consider why we do the things we do and our relations with others (co-workers, acquaintances, friends and family, community, society). This is framed by choice and responsibility. As noted in the *Harvard Business Review* (2013),

> Authenticity — what is it, who has it, and how do you get it? Most people associate authenticity with being true to oneself — or "walking the talk." But there's a problem with that association; it focuses on how *you* feel about *yourself.* Authenticity is actually a relational behavior, not a self-centered one. Meaning that to be truly authentic, you must not only be comfortable with yourself, but must also comfortably connect with others (Su and Wilkins).

One of the foremost twentieth-century Existentialists is Martin Heidegger. He believes authenticity is central to being-in-the-world and his views on the subject have been very influential. He speaks of authentic people as being grounded, true to their own values, and able to get a handle on what's happening around them. They think for themselves. Self-deception is *not* the mark of an authentic individual; being honest with yourself and standing up for what you believe is. Those who are authentic show that they mean what they say. They think on their feet and don't cave under pointed questions. They are able to set out their point of view, but to reassess it when it seems warranted.

Within a work setting—or most any setting—the ability to stand back and look at what we're doing is vital. Otherwise, we could be blindsided. Plus, an essential aspect of integrity and authenticity is humility. This allows us to subject our own values and behavior to the bright light of self-scrutiny. There's a balance between caving under pressure and thinking we can do no wrong.

To be authentic means we are self-motivated, independent thinkers, who are conscientious in dealing with others. Personal integrity is the bedrock of authenticity. It is shown in a variety of ways; such as, good character, virtue, decency, fairness, scrupulousness, sincerity, truthfulness, and trustworthiness. This is a person who aims for the right thing, the fair thing, in any given circumstance.

In contrast, the inauthentic person lacks personal integrity, is neither scrupulous nor sincere and fair. Don't count on an abundance of honesty either. The everyday manifestation of inauthenticity Heidegger calls the "they-self," because inauthentic people are not self-defined. They turn to others for validation and want others to set the direction and make the decisions. They look outward, not inward, when forming their values and can't be trusted to put virtues on the front burner.

Such people are prone to gossip ("idle talk"), to being busy bodies ("idle curiosity), and tend to be unfocused and easily distracted (mental fog of "ambiguity"). You know the type—they prefer gossiping about others to speaking the truth or staying silent. They poke their nose into other people's business, but not because they care to help out. "Empathic" is not a label you'd slap on a "they-self."

That said, inauthentic people *can* get out of their inauthentic state. There's hope for those who have lost their way and don't lead a life of integrity. All we have to do is get in touch with our authentic selves, strip the "in" from inauthenticity, and grab hold of the truth. Heidegger says the "call of conscience" calls to the *self* of the they-self to get back on track. At heart, we know right from wrong and can get a hold of what it takes to live with integrity.

Think about journalist Stephen Glass (Chapter 2.3) who fabricated story after story after story in *The New Republic*. His lies multiplied, until he was in the thick of deception. Not only did the edifice of lies eventually collapse, but by 1998 so did Glass's reputation and career. He went on to study law and eventually ended up in California. Unfortunately, his past came along with him across the country and attempts to have that erased did not succeed. It came to the fore in his quest to practice law in the State of California. As Julie Bosman (2014) reports,

"The applicant failed to carry his heavy burden of establishing his rehabilitation and current fitness," the court said in a unanimous decision... [On January 27, 2014] The court said Mr. Glass had not been forthright in a previous application to the New York bar and had not acknowledged his shortcomings in that effort (he was informally notified in advance that his New York application would be rejected). Many of his efforts at rehabilitating himself, the court wrote, "seem to have been directed primarily at advancing his own well-being rather than returning something to the community."

Let's now turn to our movies, and look at individuals who had the guts to take on an unfair system. They couldn't do it alone, however impressive were their personal traits. They needed others to stand with them in their quest for justice. The combination of powerful leadership skills with the integrity to provide moral weight makes all the difference.

The Power of Collective Action

You may know the classic movie *Matewan* (1987) and its portrayal of the few brave souls who took on the coal mining industry in hopes of putting a union in place. Those with money and power used physical force to crush such efforts. Brutal, even violent, means were deployed to squash union organizers as flat as cockroaches.

That story is set in West Virginia, not England, like *Made in Dagenham*. It is set in 1920, not 1968, like *Made in Dagenham*. Its focus is coal mining, not the auto industry, like *Made in Dagenham*. But they share a common thread: One person with strength and determination and a strong sense of right and wrong, can move mountains. Even if it's one shovel-full at a time, slowly but surely unjust work conditions can undergo a transformation. Without support from the top, there needs to be strong leadership from below. And there must be enough compassion to see the human cost of collective action.

SPOTLIGHT: *Matewan*

In *Matewan*, we follow along as labor organizer Joe Kenehan gradually gets striking miners and "scabs" (blacks and Italians brought in to replace striking coal miners) to work together so a union can be put in place. The movie opens with Joe and the "scabs" arriving on the train; they are met by striking miners. As you might imagine, the miners view their replacements with disdain. This was demonstrated by the angry reception (sticks, stones, punches) they received.

Joe can see that he's walking into a wasps' nest. The tension is palpable. Strikers are furious with the mining company and afraid the blacks and Italians are going to take their jobs. The blacks and Italians are just trying to survive. As one points out, "I didn't come here lookin' for trouble. A man's got to eat." He came thinking there were jobs; that he's a union man himself. Being called a "scab," he says, is worse than the most racist term he's been called.

Joe makes it clear to the men that the union should organize and build support—to work together, blacks and whites. He wants *all* the men to walk out. "All the dagos and the coloreds?" he is asked. "That's what a union is," Joe answers, adding "You better get used to it." To bring about real change racism has to be left behind. Consequently, the task he faces is two-fold. To get an effective union so the pay and conditions at the mine meet the men's goals—a living wage as we'd say today—the miners have to act as a collective, a community. Together they will be more powerful than acting as individuals. And they can't be divided amongst themselves by either race or ethnicity.

We forget how difficult a time it was and how much was needed to succeed. Power backed by physical force is difficult to overthrow, even by the most determined opponent. But Kenehan displays the strength of purpose needed to build a coalition of the willing and determined. He shows that effective leadership must have the backing of a loyal community. Anything else will burn out in the short term and lack the foundation for long-term gains.

SPOTLIGHT: *Made in Dagenham*

Rita O'Grady is such a leader as well, as we see in *Made in Dagenham*. Although she didn't have to stand up to gun-toting thugs, she nevertheless had to confront powerful adversaries, like Norma Rae in the much earlier film (*Norma Rae*) with a similar focus. We watch as *she* builds a coalition of the willing and determined. She also had to convince men to join forces with the lower-paid women. The salary for the women sewing up the seat covers for Ford Motor Company was considerably less than the salaries of men working at a similar skill-level. Ford wasn't open to reassessing their pay scale, so the workers had a tough fight ahead.

One of the ethical dilemmas that Rita faces is how much sacrifice on the part of the strikers was acceptable. A strike meant loss of pay and possible physical risk if things got nasty. And a lengthy strike could wreak even more havoc.

What if a strike dragged on and on, as they often do? What then? Rita had important decisions to make. None were easy. The road ahead was filled with potholes, but she was clear about the cause justifying the risks. Similarly, Joe Kenehan had no doubt that the battle may be difficult but the workers in the mine needed to join forces and form a union to fight the good fight. Both *Made in Dagenham* and *Matewan* help us see that many of the things we now take for granted came about because of the Ritas and Joes of earlier times.

CASE STUDY 1: United Auto Workers, H&M and Pay Equity

First, let's consider a real-life case about justice and fairness. This one has nothing to do with a dockworkers' union or mob bosses—but it does have to do with one of the biggest unions in the United States, the United Auto Workers. Formed in the 1930s, the UAW is still a powerful and very influential union.

The Two-Tier System

A common practice in American automobile plants is to pay new workers at a significantly lower rate than that of "veterans." Is it fair? They aren't the only ones with differential pay for the same or similar work (think of fast food restaurants with salary tiers tied to age). This practice is under examination, as we'll see.

Ben Klayman reports on the UAW's attempts to get rid of the two-tier wage system. What has been in place is a formula whereby new automotive workers are paid at 57 percent of the rate of veteran workers. Norwood Jewell, a top official with the UAW indicates that the time has come to chuck that formula:

> "The international executive board hates two-tiers," he said. "We didn't do two tiers because it's a wonderful thing," he added, saying they were a "financial unfortunate" caused by the weak industry in 2007. "We hate them. We intend to eliminate them over time." Pay of hourly workers at the entry level starts at just under $16 an hour and rises over time to more than $19. Veteran workers are paid just more than $28 an hour.

Jewell said key to eliminating the second-tier wages will be the UAW successfully organizing non-union plants in the US South. "If we don't organize them and bring them up to our standard, we're never going be able to totally eliminate the second tier, " he said (Klayman, 2013).

A two-tier system, as Jewell points out, is not the solution. It was put in place when the economy was in a downturn and now needs to go; the sooner the better from his point of view.

The pay differential means those at the lower tier get 43 percent less than the veterans at the upper tier. Calculated in terms of a 40-hour work-week those at Tier 1 make $640 per week, while those at Tier 2 make

$1120 (= $480 more per week and $1920 more per month). Given how wide is the gap between the two tiers, you can see why Norwood Jewell and the UAW are seeking to get the two-tier system changed.

A Living Wage at H&M

Now let's turn to H&M, one of the world's leading clothing retailers. On December 1, 2013, *The New York Times* took up the issue of a living wage. They commended mega-retailer H&M's public intentions to seek a living wage for its employees. The editorial board of the *Times* pointed out two things: One, the dismal pay and, two, how little has been done to address it. They said:

> Most workers who make clothes for Western retailers in countries like Bangladesh and Cambodia, where H&M's efforts will start, earn too little to cover even the bare necessities of life. Yet most American and European companies doing business in such places have chosen to look the other way or blame weak national governments for the problem.

> H&M's plan is to do this in stages. "Starting with two factories in Bangladesh and one in Cambodia, H&M says it will pay higher wholesale prices for clothes so factory owners can give workers raises. By 2018, H&M said it aims to extend the program to 750 factories employing 850,000 workers and covering 60 percent of its total production (*New York Times*, 2013).

In order to pull this off, "it will have to give fewer big orders to a smaller group of factories and commit to them for years at a time." What this means is bigger orders for fewer factories, thereby strengthening the one selected. This will give factory owners the certainty they need to raise wages, suggests the *Times'* editorial board (*New York Times*).

Not everyone agrees that raising the minimum wage is the best course of action. Economist Douglas Holtz-Eakin (2013) is among the naysayers. He argues that increasing the minimum wage won't solve the problem: "It wouldn't target those hurt the worst: the unemployed and low-skilled, and in fact would build bigger barriers for those without a job." He claims that, "raising the minimum wage, while not destroying jobs, impedes job creation. That means an even slower recovery to full employment."

Not everyone agrees with *that*. Among them are fast food workers who indicated their pay was peanuts and they had had enough.

CASE STUDY 2: The Fast Food Workers' Strike

On August 29, 2013 fast-food workers at McDonald's, Burger King, and other restaurants walked off the job in 60 cities across the US. As reported by *Reuters*, "The striking workers say they want to unionize without retaliation in order to collectively bargain for a 'living wage'" (Abrahamian, 2013).

They wanted $15 an hour (the federal minimum is $7.25). The median wage for front-line fast-food workers is an estimated $8.94 per hour (= $357.60/per week, which is 55 percent of the auto workers at tier one and only 31 percent of the auto workers at tier two—a gap of $1120 – $357.60 = $762.40 a week).

"It's almost impossible to get by (alone)," said McDonald's worker Rita Jennings. She was among about 100 protesters who marched in downtown Detroit Thursday. "You have to live with somebody to make it" (Abrahamian, 2013).

Exercise

1. Assume you are the manager of *Fish-n-Fries* fast food drive-in. You sympathize with workers' complaints that the $8.50/hour wage is too low; but if you pay them more, your prices will have to increase. The question is, "How do you raise salaries and up the cost of the take-out food and drink without losing customers"?

The Question of Trade Offs

Raising the minimum wage would affect some of the choices open to businesses. And though a "living wage" will only benefit those who are *actually* employed, it would help that segment of the population and ripple out from there. We have to weigh the trade-offs. Here's the bottom line: *If we can't have it all, how do we make compromises?* Let's give this matter some thought.

We make trade-offs all the time. For example, we could have better gas mileage, but the trade-off would be driving at lower speeds or driving lighter vehicles. Most of us prefer the trade-off of a faster drive to work to paying less for gas. And we could live longer if we didn't smoke or overdo the junk food or sweets.

Starbucks transformed the take-out coffee market by convincing consumers that $4 or $5 for a cup of coffee was an acceptable trade off, if they could choose between a range of ingredients (kinds of milk, flavored syrups, whip cream on top, spices, and so on) and had nice little tables to sit at.

That's not all. Apple persuaded customers that the quality and aesthetic value of their product was an acceptable trade-off for the cost of their computers, iPads, and cell phones. Cost is just one component in many kinds of decisions.

This is not a minor issue. For example, would we agree to a salary cut of 5 percent if we could guarantee that all infants and children received a minimal level of health care? Would that be an acceptable trade-off? What about schools that stretch the school year to 11 months in exchange for higher levels of literacy? These are decisions that individuals and business leaders have to make on a regular basis. Consider, then, what should guide our thinking. The *Harvard Business Review* (2012) offers a model for decision-making as to acceptable trade-offs. This is what they recommend as a guide:

Trade-Off Model: Guiding Principles

1. Set boundaries
   - *Examine options:* Establish which options are on and off the table.
   - *Narrow the field*: Eliminate choices that aren't worth pursuing.
2. Balance short-term vs. long-term gains ("wins")
   - *Sort and weigh:* Specify what long-term goals are worth short-term sacrifices—and vice versa.
3. Gauge support
   - *Watch your back:* Decide who'll back or oppose your ideas and whose support you'll need.

Arriving at a plan of action requires the clarity of mind and enough perspective take a wider look around. We need to decide what fits with our values and which options are feasible. We have to get a sense of which moral duties should guide our decision-making and what virtues should shape our moral character. Set the boundaries.

Let's consider how this model could be applied to the two-tiered pay scale that the UAW is trying to change (Case Study 1). Klayman (2013) reports that the American automakers say they need the entry-level wage scale to compete on labor costs with Japanese, South Korean and German automakers that have US plants. They are, thus, working with a trade-off that they want the UAW to accept.

We start by setting boundaries with the first step of the model. These are the parameters of what is acceptable and what is not. They are shaped by values—our ethical base. What is on or off the table when it comes to viable options may require moral reflection. The question is, "Just what are we willing to do to reach our objectives?"

Addressing Inequities

When Rita decided to fight the pay inequities at Ford she owned her own power. And when Joe persuaded the miners and the "scabs" to combine forces he owned his own power. That others stood behind them to form an alliance shows how the community can act together and effect change. By becoming a force to be reckoned with, the group's solidarity couldn't be ignored—or not for long!

They showed the will power and personal integrity to take a stand. Each one inspired their co-workers to work together and do the right thing. The power of *one* was then transformed to the power of the *many*—the community. That they succeeded is to be celebrated, but their moral character would be no less impressive had their efforts fallen short of the goal.

There's a reason that businesses and institutions put a high premium on integrity. One way we see it is by the frequency the term appears on ethics codes. To get a sense of the centrality of integrity in Business Ethics, let's look at H&M and see what lessons we can learn. Later (Chapter 3.5) we'll look at the Bangladesh sweatshop disaster.

CASE STUDY 3: H&M and Child Labor

One of the ethical concerns raised about H&M is their hiring policy, Specifically, it is said that they employ workers in Bangladesh as young as 14 years old. In the US this would not be legally permissible. However, not all countries prohibit that practice.

Exercise

1.   Given the concern about exploitation of children, should H&M take the more restrictive path and *not* employ underage workers?

2. What should be the policy regarding hiring minors?
3. Should it follow the laws and values of its country of origin, or does Cultural Relativism win out? Should the norms of the country where work is outsourced guide the moral reasoning here?

The Debate on Child Labor

H&M takes on this issue on their website. There we find the following statement "A Clear Stand Against Child Labour":

> On the few occasions on which we have discovered underage workers at our suppliers we have acted in accordance with our policy. In co-operation with the supplier we have tried to find a solution that is in the best interests of the child. The family is contacted and in most cases the family accepts that the child should continue with *some kind of education* until he or she is 15 years old, or *until the legal working age in the country in question (but not lower than 14 years)*. Wages continue to be paid during the study period so that the family does not lose its income. (emphasis mine).

While it may seem like a "clear stand against child labour," this policy is at odds with the US Department of Labor's standards. On the DOL website we find the following:

> While 16 is the minimum age for most nonfarm work, minors aged 14 and 15 may work outside of school hours in certain occupations under certain conditions. Minors may, at any age: deliver newspapers; perform in radio, television, movies, or theatrical productions; work for their parents in their solely owned nonfarm businesses (except in mining, manufacturing, or in any other occupation declared hazardous by the Secretary); or gather evergreens and make evergreen wreaths.

The child labor guideline in Great Britain is similar. There we find,

> **Full-time work**: Children can only start full-time work once they've reached the minimum school leaving age [approximately 17 years old] – they can then work up to a maximum of 40 hours a week. ... School-aged children are not entitled to the National Minimum Wage. Young workers aged 16 to 17 are entitled to at least £3.79 [=$6.30] per hour. [Once someone reaches 18, adult employment rights and rules apply.] (www.gov.uk).

You can see this is not a clear-cut matter. Corporations based in the West have to decide where to draw the line around the use of children to produce the clothes that so many people want to buy at bargain rates. Similarly, consumers have a role to play here—it's not just a one-way street.

Discrimination in the Workplace

Another type of inequity in the workplace centers on discrimination. As we saw with *Made in Dagenham*, discrimination can take the form of sexism. There's also discrimination based on age, disability, race or ethnicity, sexual orientation, to name a few. They are occasionally dealt with in movies, reminding us that they are not just a thing of the past. There has been progress, but there's ample room for improvement. An overview may be instructive.

Ageism Getting older has its virtues (experience, a bit more wisdom, a greater appreciation of diverse perspectives, social action on issues like poverty, education, and health care). However, the downside includes being less attractive as a candidate on the job market, and subtle or overt discrimination in the workplace. Some cultures revere their elders; others don't.

Movies like *Wall Street* present the wise elder in the form of Lou Mannheim. In contrast, some movies present older employees as being slow on the uptake. We see this with Shelley Levene in *Glengarry Glen Ross* (1992). He is anxious, scattered, financially desperate, and ethically challenged. He is also a target of derision. His moral failings adds to the portrayal of the not-so-wise elder.

Racism Racism in the society and on the job is shown to varying degrees in movies. *12 Years a Slave* is like a guided tour of Hell. There slaves (= unpaid laborers who can be bought and sold and who have few, if any, liberty rights) endure horrors on a regular basis. Historical-dramas *The Help* and *The Butler* offer insights into racism by looking at the underclass—the "help" (maids, butlers, gardeners, and so on). That human trafficking is still a factor of our society signals to us that forms of slavery still exist as business enterprises.

As far as racism in the workplace goes, discrimination we see in society tends to get carried into the corporate world. The one often correlates with the other. We see that racism has not been eradicated as a social problem (in and out of the workplace) and is not a typical subject for blockbuster films. However, it has received attention in independent and foreign films.

From *Do the Right Thing* and *Boyz n the Hood* to *Mississippi Masala* and *Babel*, from *Sleep Dealer* to *District 9*—movies have ventured into the moral territory and prodded us to examine issues of justice and consider the virtues of social action. It might be in a scene (e.g., *Babel's* segment on the Mexican nanny who takes her white charges to a party in Mexico, only to face a nightmare situation trying to return to the US). Or it might be threaded throughout the entire movie (e.g., *Dry White Season*, *Sleep Dealer* and *District 9*).

Disabilities and Special Needs Few movies present protagonists with special needs. The exceptions can be found in TV shows like *Covert Affairs* with its blind tech-savvy agent and *Person of Interest* featuring a genius-mastermind millionaire with disabilities. In March 2013 the show *Switched at Birth* made TV history with an all American Sign Language (ASL) episode. In each of these, the protagonist is presented in a positive light, with talents in excess of the norm. All three show they are successful regardless of any special needs they face.

Of course we know that many of those with special needs *do* face hurdles that others may be oblivious to or don't even think about (such as the location of light switches, access to elevators, doorways wide enough for wheelchairs, and so on). And we can be certain that many have faced prejudice and discrimination on the job. Discrimination against people with disabilities was outlawed in 1990, but that doesn't mean there aren't issues. Remember that seen in *Avatar* when wheelchair-bound vet, Jake Sully, is referred to as "Meals on Wheels" as he made his way right after arriving on the planet Pandora?

To get an understanding of the obstacles facing people with disabilities, a team from the Wharton School of the University of Pennsylvania (2013) did a study. The Wharton team identified three key obstacles to hiring workers with disabilities.

1 *Negative perceptions*—for example, the fear felt by employers that employees with disabilities will create more work for their supervisors.
2 *Lack of external hiring support*—the fact that employers will find very few resources on the outside that are available to help them recruit people with disabilities. In addition, job applicants with disabilities "are often reluctant to self-identify as such, for fear that doing so will make bosses ... less, rather than more, willing to hire them," the policy brief states.

3   *Lack of internal hiring support* —often a budgetary problem arising from the fact that funds don't exist for creating internal expertise in "hiring, accommodating and training people with disabilities.

Regarding Henry (1991) presents an insightful and sympathetic look at a wealthy lawyer, Henry Turner, who suffers serious injuries after being shot in a robbery. The movie traces his recovery and the difficulties he faces, such as the lack of support from his employer. We see this is a life-changing event: Turner is led to reassess his life and what he used to think so important. He discovers how oblivious—and at times uncaring—those without disabilities can be and how much they take for granted—as he once did.

Sexual Orientation   A classic on this topic is *Philadelphia* (1993). It highlights how homophobia can enter the workplace and make life miserable for its victims. The movie centers on a gay attorney with AIDs. After being fired from his law firm he sues for wrongful dismissal.

It's still a riveting movie.

That the more recent *Dallas Buyers' Club* (2013)—also riveting—covers some of the same territory makes it clear that discrimination around sexual orientation (and AIDS) is not a thing of the past. Yet. But there has been considerable progress, as the following case demonstrates.

CASE STUDY 4: Ben & Jerry's and Apple on Marriage Equality

Posted on Ben & Jerry's website is the following statement on gay rights and marriage equality.

Background and History

Ben & Jerry's has a long history of commitment to social justice, including gay rights. This commitment is grounded in our Company's core values, which include a deep respect for people inside and outside our Company and an unshakable belief that all people deserve full and equal civil rights.

In 1989, we extended full benefits to unmarried partners of our employees, including same-sex partners. In 2000, we advocated publicly for our home state, Vermont, to create civil unions as a big step forward for equal protection for gays and lesbians. In 2009, we renamed our iconic Chubby Hubby flavor to support the same sex marriage law taking effect, offering scoops of "HUBBY HUBBY" in Vermont to symbolically show our support. In the UK, we created a special edition flavor called "Apple-y Ever After" in 2012 to urge Parliament to legalize same-sex marriage.

Our Position
Very simply, Ben & Jerry's supports marriage equality for gays and lesbians everywhere. We will continue to work in partnership with relevant nonprofit organizations to:
- Build public support for marriage equality
- Add our voice to the public discourse around marriage equality
- Celebrate the expansion of marriage equality to new states and countries

Ben & Jerry's isn't the only company coming out of the closet on gay rights. In a *Wall Street Journal* opinion piece, Apple CEO Tim Cook (2013) calls for federal action on the issue. He starts out noting the benefits of a more-accepting workplace: "People are much more willing to give of themselves," he argues, "When they feel that their selves are being fully recognized and embraced." That's hard to argue with, however Utopian it sounds.

Cook says of Apple's anti-discrimination policy: "At Apple, we try to make sure people understand that they don't have to check their identity at the door." The issue, as he indicates, is one of justice and fairness. Sounding like a Deontological Ethicist, Cook affirms that, "As we see it, embracing people's individuality is a matter of basic human dignity and civil rights."

Another upside, he notes, is that it's good for business. "It also turns out to be great for the creativity that drives our business," Cook observes. "We've found that when people feel valued for who they are, they have the comfort and confidence to do the best work of their lives," he adds.

So what do we take from his reflections? One thing is that eliminating prejudice on the job is a human rights issue. Plus, it is as important now as in the past. He reminds us that those who do nothing enable prejudice to continue; thus, calling us to take the moral high road.

Cook leaves us with this insight: "So long as the law remains silent on the workplace rights of gay and lesbian Americans, we as a nation are effectively consenting to discrimination against them." He'd say it's time to stand up and be counted.

Where Do We Go From Here?

From the standpoint of self-interest a business stands to gain by addressing the inequities examined in this chapter. From the standpoint of their employees, a business will see long-term benefits in putting a just system in place and doing what it takes to sustain it. From the standpoint of the society and human rights, addressing inequities and injustices in the workplace is the ethically right thing to do.

As Tim Cook said of individuals who stand by and do nothing, so too we could say of businesses—to do nothing is to enable a discriminatory workplace. To do something, to take the steps needed so workers are treated with respect and dignity makes all the difference in the world.

ETHICS CODE: H&M

We saw in this chapter that H&M has a goal of a "living wage" for its employees. How to get there from here is the question. But if it's a value worth striving for, then we need to find a way. For that, the moral guidance of the company's ethics code is vital. So what about H&M's?

The introduction of its Code of Ethics sets out four basic values: *honesty, transparency, integrity,* and *fair play*. Access the code at http://about. hm.com/content/dam/hm/about/documents/masterlanguage/CSR/ Policies/Code%20of%20Ethics%20employees.pdf. There you'll see that employees must sign the code, acknowledging having read it.

Exercise

1. Considering the range inequities we've seen in this chapter, would H&M's four values be all that is needed to address these issues (discrimination, unequal pay, child labor, etc.)?
2. Do you see examples of these values in the movies we've looked at in this text? Cite some.

Works Cited

Abrahamian, Atossa Araxia, "U.S. Fast-Food Workers Protest, Demand A 'Living Wage'," *Reuters*, August 29, 2013, http://www.reuters.com/article/2013/08/29/us-usa-restaurants-strike-idUSBRE97S05320130829 (accessed December 27, 2014).

Bosman, Julie, "California Denies Scorned Journalist Stephen Glass Right to Practice Law," *New York Times*, January 27, 2014, http://www.nytimes.com/2014/01/28/business/media/california-denies-scorned-journalist-stephen-glass-right-to-practice-law.html (accessed December 27, 2014).

Cook, Tim, "Workplace Equality Is Good for Business," *Wall Street Journal*, November 3, 2013, http://online.wsj.com/news/articles/SB10001424052702304527504579172302377638002 (accessed December 27, 2014).

H&M, Code of Ethics, H&M.com, Available at http://about.hm.com/content/dam/hm/about/documents/masterlanguage/CSR/Policies/Code%20of%20Ethics%20employees.pdf (accessed December 27, 2014).

H&M, "Clear Stand Against Child Labour," About H&M, http://sustainability.hm.com/en/sustainability/commitments/choose-and-reward-responsible-partners/code-of-conduct/clear-stand-against-child-labour.html (accessed December 27, 2014).

Harvard Business Review, "Make a Critical Trade-Off," Management Tips, *Harvard Business Review*, September 4, 2012, http://hbr.org/tip/2012/09/04/make-a-critical-trade-off (accessed December 27, 2014).

Holtz-Eakin, Douglas, "Raising Minimum Wage Is Misguided," *New York Times*, December 4, 2013, http://www.nytimes.com/roomfordebate/2013/12/04/making-low-wages-liveable/raising-minimum-wage-is-misguided-policy (accessed December 27, 2014).

Klayman, Ben, "UAW Wants To Eliminate Two-Tier Wage System: Official," *Reuters*, December 17, 2013, http://www.reuters.com/article/2013/12/17/us-autos-uaw-wages-idUSBRE9BG10Y20131217 (accessed December 27, 2014).

New York Times Editorial Board, "A Swedish Retailer Promises a Living Wage," *New York Times*, December 1, 2013.

Rodriguez, Salvador, "Apple's Tim Cook Says Anti-Gay Discrimination Policy Good For Business," *New York Times*, November 4, 2013.

Su, Amy Jen, and Muriel Maignan Wilkins, "To Be Authentic, Look Beyond Yourself," *Harvard Business Review*, April 24, 2013, http://blogs.hbr.org/2013/04/to-be-authentic-look-beyond-yo/ (accessed December 27, 2014).

United Kingdom Government, "Child-Employment," https://www.gov.uk/child-employment/minimum-ages-children-can-work (accessed December 27, 2014).

United States Department of Labor, "Elaws: Employment Law Guide," http://www.dol.gov/compliance/guide/childlbr.htm (accessed December 27, 2014).

Wharton School, "Job Discrimination Against the Disabled: Not Just an Academic Issue," *The K@W Network*, June 18, 2013, http://knowledge.wharton.upenn.edu/article/job-discrimination-against-the-disabled-not-just-an-academic-issue/# (accessed December 27, 2014).

3.4

Enough Already
Addressing Workplace Harassment

Spotlight: *North Country, The Invisible War, Disconnect*
Case Studies: Eveleth Mines; Bullies in the NFL
Ethics Code: Amazon.com

> *Hank Aimes: My name is Hank Aimes and I've been a miner all
> my life. And I've never been ashamed of it until now. You know
> when we take our wives and daughters to the company barbecue,
> I don't hear any of them calling them those names like bitches and
> whores and worse. I don't see anyone grab them by their privates or
> drawing pictures of them on the bathroom walls, it's unspeakable.
> Unspeakable!*
>
> *So what's changed? She's still my daughter! It's a heck of a thing, to
> watch one of your own get treated that way. You're all supposed to be my
> friends, my brothers. Well, right now I don't have a friend in this room.
> In fact the only one I'm not ashamed of is my daughter.*
>
> —North Country

Josey Aimes had no idea when she took a job at the mining company
where her father worked that her life was about to be turned upside down.
When you can't trust the people you work with, you know you're on
shaky ground. We see this in *North Country* (2005), where workplace
harassment is so entrenched that the leadership sees no reason to uproot
it. Women crying foul are treated as either a bunch of ninnies or as if they
had it coming ("nuts or sluts"). We follow along as victims and co-workers
face the harm and fight back.

There are times when you just have to realize, "Enough, already."
When co-workers or supervisors have crossed a moral line around
harassment, abuse, or bullying, an injustice has been done. That's when

Business Ethics Through Movies: A Case Study Approach, First Edition. Wanda Teays.
© 2015 John Wiley & Sons, Ltd. Published 2015 by John Wiley & Sons, Ltd.

an attitude adjustment is in order. As we saw in the last chapter, one individual can be a catalyst to change by drawing upon the community to present a united front. A supportive workplace can be a counterforce when things spin out of control. In fact, the community itself can sort out interpersonal conflicts, build goodwill, set up channels for addressing inappropriate behavior, and establish the policies and mindset to foster decency and fairness.

As you know, change doesn't always happen overnight and good people don't always prevail. Standing up against any form of injustice may not bring about positive results. But it may lay a foundation for systemic change. We saw this with the Civil Rights movement.

Those who are morally deficient may have power not easily dislodged. But perseverance counts, as our next movie demonstrates. It tells the story of a woman who faces one indignity after another. She is not alone, but her peers are reluctant to complain. They aren't about to risk their jobs to protest the conditions at the plant. Support is not forthcoming.

Fear is a big inhibitor, as we see here. Fear of retaliation (being fired, being subject to more or different forms of harassment, etc.) keeps the other victims from speaking up. It took *years* and a class action lawsuit until decent behavior came to Eveleth mines. Let's see how.

SPOTLIGHT: *North Country*

North Country takes us into a hostile workplace. Women are subjected to harassment and abuse ranging from the disgusting (e.g., obscene posters. gross sex "toys") and the intrusive (e.g., groping, grabbing, sexual gestures) to the cruel (e.g., locked in portable toilets that get turned over, covering the woman with excrement) and the shameful (e.g., no union support, indifferent management, no recourse within the company).

The movie centers on Josey Aimes, a single parent who takes a job at Eveleth mines. She has no idea what lies ahead in terms of the harassment she will experience. Josey's own father (Hank Aimes) has worked at the mine for years. He's got his own set of biases to overcome before he can empathize with his daughter. When Josey starting working at the mine he viewed it critically, just short of disdain.

It was "men's work;" women shouldn't be doing such physical work. There's no way Hank supports Josey taking on work at the mine. His bias about gender roles makes it hard for Hank to appreciate her point of view. Basically, Hank was from another era, one where men did manly things like work in mines, go off to war, and carry the financial burden of their families. His was an era of strictly defined roles and stereotypes. This may be why he couldn't easily grasp how much abuse she suffered.

Men he'd known for years were harassing, threatening, and mistreating his daughter. These were men he worked with. These were men he'd trusted his own life with. He finally got it, that this community had veered off course and lost its moral compass. It was time for individual members to do something. The question was, "Could he?"

The pressure to be "loyal" and not squeal on your "homies" is a fact of life. The idea of "ratting out" friends or co-workers goes against deeply embedded norms. And yet conflicts *do* occur and ethical dilemmas *do* rise to the surface. We may have to step up to the plate, even if it means separating from our teammates. *North Country* shows this with Hank and other employees at the mine. We then see that a community can be a force of its own.

When that force is good, it can be transformative. This we see with elections, policy decisions, and professional organizations setting out directives for its members to follow. Look, for example, at Johnson & Johnson's handling of the Tylenol crisis (Chapter 1.2) of Virginia Tech's response to the school massacre (Chapter 3.2). In both cases, business "as usual" was past history, as decisive and definitive steps were taken—with wide-reaching consequences.

So too here in *North Country*. The harassment Josey suffered made it clear that business "as usual" was not okay. Individuals had to confront the culture of abuse at Eveleth Mines. As Josey's friend and lawyer Bill White says, "What are you supposed to do with the ones with all the power are hurting those with none? Well, for starters, you stand up. Stand up and tell the truth. You stand up for your friends. You stand up, even when you're all alone. You stand up."

White makes it clear that entrenched values and actions are not necessarily in the right, or worth preserving. At times we need to speak up. *North Country* is a compelling demonstration of the scope that Business Ethics may take—and change a work culture so all employees can enter without fear of abuse or insult.

CASE STUDY 1: Lois E. Jenson vs. Eveleth Taconite Co.

The movie is based on an actual case—*Lois E. Jenson vs. Eveleth Taconite Co.* It was the first class action sexual harassment case in the US. The plaintiffs include Lois Jenson and other women working at the Eveleth mines.

They were subjected to sexual harassment, threats, stalking, intimidation, sexual pranks, and abusive language, as well as sex discrimination in job promotions according to court documents. The case was filed in 1988 and settled ten years later for $3.5 million. The 1998 settlement came "after a long, tortured, and unfortunate history," as noted by the US Court of Appeals, 8th Circuit.

The work conditions were barbaric, as seen by the mistreatment and indignities many female employees suffered. This could also be seen by the complacency of those who stood by and did nothing—including the union. The Court cited sexually explicit graffiti and posters on walls, lockers, desks, and elevators, as well as in cars, restrooms, interoffice mail, and bulletin boards. It also noted unwelcome touching, grabbing, and frequent generic comments about women belonging at home, not in the mines (Court of Appeals, 8th Circuit). It was nothing less than ghastly.

In a 2006 interview with *The Guardian* newspaper, Lois Jenson conveys what it was like when she began work at Eveleth Mines. It was 1975 and she was but one of a handful of women working there:

> The moment she stepped foot in the processing plant, she sensed the hostility. "It really was like they had never seen a woman before." On her first real day on the job, she was working alone sweeping up dirt in an isolated section when a miner passed by. He waited to speak until he was close to Jenson.
>
> "You fucking women don't belong here. Why don't you go home? That is where you belong," he said. "I realised how vulnerable I was in that little room with no way out. There were 600 men and four women in the mine, and I knew no one. It was intimidating" (2006).

No wonder she considered the experience "intimidating." Those were hellish years for Jenson and her female co-workers. The Court found that Eveleth Mines had created or condoned a sexually hostile work environment and that sexual harassment was "standard operating procedure."

This is a case where individuals, the work community, and the corporation all played a role in sustaining an abusive work environment. The film is a valuable study of moral agency. It gives us insight into the importance of moral integrity of a business with respect to its own employees. As Jenson puts it,

> "This was about sexual harassment and being able to go to work knowing you were going to come home safely, but also that you could go to work

knowing that you would not be grabbed or raped, or have these verbal abuses," she says. "There were times I felt so terrible about myself on the job that I couldn't stand it" (Goldenberg, 2006).

Those days are gone. Since 1998, sexual harassment is on the radar. Alison Neumer Lara of *The Chicago Tribune* (2005) observes that,

"This case was part of a real change in the culture that recognized that sexual harassment was a serious form of, not only unlawful, but deeply destructive discrimination," says Jocelyn Samuels, vice president for education and employment at the National Women's Law Center in Washington. "Employers now understand when they've got a problem. It's no longer such an uphill fight." Workers understand, too: Rules are strict, lines are bright and consequences are severe.

"In the olden days, if it was a senior person or a good old boy, maybe the discipline wouldn't be as harsh," says Thomas Kennedy, president of Chicago-based Human Resource Consultants. "Now the attorneys advise them to terminate them regardless of seniority and regardless of length of service."

The new bottom line is that harassment won't be tolerated—a welcome change for all the women and men who said "Enough, already" to a sexually-abusive workplace.

SPOTLIGHT: The Invisible War

When thinking of the Armed Forces, the images that come to mind are soldiers fighting in a battlefield or dragging a buddy to safety—not sexual assaults. However, *The Invisible War* (2012) makes it abundantly clear that rape, sexual assault, and harassment is occurring throughout all the military—the Army, Navy, and Air Force. The documentary shows the extent of the problem and the difficulties victims have suffered in seeking redress.

As we saw with the corporation leadership at Eveleth Mines, military leadership failed to take the assaults seriously. On December 20, 2013 President Obama declared: "Today, I instructed Secretary [of Defense Chuck] Hagel and Chairman [of the Joint Chiefs of Staff Martin] Dempsey to continue their efforts to make substantial improvements with respect to sexual assault prevention and response, including to the military justice system," Obama continued: "I have also directed that they report back to me, with a full-scale review of their progress, by December 1, 2014" (Miller, 2013).

Working for Change

The movie is not easy to watch and the news accounts are not easy to read. But the reality is that sexual assaults in the military can't be brushed aside much longer. On, December 9, 2013 Congressional (House and Senate) negotiators reached an agreement on a Pentagon policy bill to strengthen protections for military victims of sexual assault. Jonathan Weisman (2013) reports:

> The new measure would prevent commanding officers from overturning sexual assault verdicts, expand a special victims counsel program for the survivors of sexual assault throughout the military and make retaliation for reporting assault a crime.
>
> Significantly, for criminal complaints, including sexual assault, courts of investigation—known as Article 32 hearings—would act more like preliminary hearings looking for probable cause to pursue a court-martial. Under the current system, sexual assault accusers are brought before investigators and grilled in cross-examinations. But commanders will maintain control over the court-martial process.

You may wonder what's wrong with the military handling such complaints. Well, the problem, says military justice expert Eugene R. Fidell (2013) is a possible conflict of interest, with commanders having the power regarding decisions on prosecution. In his view, real reform in the military has been delayed, and more change is needed, as he points out:

> *The Invisible War* put the issue front and center, with on-camera interviews from a number of veterans who came forward to describe their own cases, including retaliation they'd faced for making a complaint—and impunity for perpetrators. The controversy gained momentum when the Defense Department released data indicating as many as 26,000 sexual assault incidents in a year, the overwhelming majority of which did not lead to disciplinary action.
>
> Those numbers certainly suggest that there are far more sexual assaults than is tolerable. The last straw came when a three-star Air Force general set aside a jury verdict in a sexual assault case from Aviano Air Base, in Italy, drawing attention to the fact—unknown to most civilians and legislators—that commanders also have this power.

The numbers *are* significant.

> Reported sexual assaults in the US military increased by over 50 percent in 2013, new data reveals. The boost punctuates a year filled with damning disclosures of a culture that has failed to protect the enlisted from systemic levels of sexual violence (rt com, 2013).
> The Department of Veteran Affairs also found that 85,000 US veterans received medical treatment for sex abuse trauma last year, which indicates that the effects of assault have far-reaching consequences, both financially and emotionally (rt.com, 2013).

One apparent change is this: "Sexual assaults reported by U.S. military troops rose 8 percent in 2014 amid signs that victims are increasingly confident about reporting the attacks" (Alexander, 2014).

These are significant numbers. And they matter. They matter in the military and they matter in other workplaces and institutions. The closed culture of the military makes assault difficult to bring to light and address. But *The Invisible War* and other media attention brought more transparency. And with the passage of the bill and further scrutiny, we can bring about long-needed change.

Addressing a Sexually-Hostile Workplace

You'd think people should be able to go to work or a school, hospital, airport, or whatever without fear of harm or harassment. That seems a no-brainer. It's to no one's benefit when a workplace is not safe to enter without an armed platoon or hefty bodyguard in tow.

You'd also think that all places conducting business would take steps to ensure a safe and healthy environment and take swift action against those who harass, bully, threaten, or otherwise contribute to a hostile workplace. That many *do* take such steps deserves recognition. The goal is to have all on-board.

The bottom line is that businesses—from the mines to the military and all points in between—need to send employees a clear message about sexual harassment and violence. The three basics that all businesses should follow are:

- Educate and inform
- Respond to complaints
- Be proactive

Employees should know what sexual harassment is and know that it won't be tolerated. Businesses need to take complaints seriously and respond in a timely way (= with minimal delay). There should be a process for filing complaints that protects confidentiality as much as possible so they do not fear retaliation. In addition, there should be training sessions, guidelines, and resources as proactive steps.

Structuring a Sexual Harassment Policy

One component of being proactive is a *policy* on sexual harassment. Having a policy is more important to a business that we might realize—for the employer as well as employees.

Andrew Wicks (1992) points out that:

1 A policy reduces the potential for and extent of the liability for incidents of sexual harassment
2 A policy will likely lead to a decrease in harassment and helps protect the company image if such incidents occur
3 A policy helps create a positive work environment
4 A policy is an expression of concern for the integrity of the business and the well-being of the employees and, thus, is the morally correct thing to do.

Model sexual harassment policies are readily available (e.g., on the Internet) for you to examine. Think about what you'd expect to be included in such a policy to really give a clear—and effective—message. Here is the structure of a model policy put out by the state of Vermont:

Components of a Model Sexual Harassment Policy

1 Statement of the importance of the policy
2 Definition of sexual harassment
3 Examples of sexual harassment
4 What the employer will do in response to an allegation of sexual harassment
5 What to do if you think you've been harassed
6 What to do if the employer does not handle the matter in a satisfactory way
7 Where to get a copy of the policy
8 Who to contact if assistance is needed in filing a report of sexual harassment

CASE STUDY 2: Bullying in the NFL

Women aren't the only victims of harassment in the workplace. Just ask Jonathan Martin,

> a 300-pound bruiser, a physical powerhouse playing for the Miami Dolphins football team. Size matters, but it doesn't always protect you from the unwelcome comments or actions of others. In Martin's case, teammate Richie Incognito, another 300-pound bruiser, crossed a line. Reports indicate that Incognito went from prankster to bully.

Young football players often face treatment from older team members, akin to hazing rituals found in fraternities. *The New York Times* (2014) cites examples of rookies being forced to carry the equipment for the older players (= mentors), being expected to sing on command, serve them food, be taped to goal posts, and so on. Supposedly this is funny. It is certainly humiliating. It also creates a culture of the powerful and the powerless—not unlike what Josey faces in *North Country*.

And let's not forget name-calling: Incognito reportedly called Martin "the Big Weirdo," and sent racist and threatening text messages. That would have been bad enough. But Martin and other rookies received this kind of treatment with "the tacit, unsupervised approval of coaches and executives" (Branch and Belson, 2014). The bullying then became culturally acceptable—institutionalized—not unlike other forms of harassment.

Presumably such "pranks" are a rite of passage meant to contribute to building team spirit and strengthening character. As for boundaries: "Players and coaches around the league generally defended the culture of pranks, provided they did not become overly aggressive." Not surprisingly, "Those borders may be impossible to define," say Branch and Belson (2013).

It didn't end well. Martin left the Dolphins, Incognito was suspended, and the Dolphins' management had to confront a public relations' problem. As a result, the incident was a catalyst for change. A special report was commissioned about conditions on the Dolphins, 'we are also looking at the workplace environment and what changes should be necessary,'" said NFL Commissioner Roger Goodell (Belson, 2013). A destructive culture had been put in place and it went downhill from there. Jokes led to pranks. Pranks led to harassment and bullying.

When shifts take place gradually it is not always obvious when things have gone too far and the bounds of decency and fair play have been crossed. True, but that's one of the responsibilities that a business has to deal with. This includes paying attention to the environment itself. Then if it goes toxic, they can act expeditiously, so problems don't fester—or grow.

Addressing the Culture

Evidently, the Miami Dolphins created and sustained a bullying culture that thrived under neglect from the top. As with many situations that deteriorate, behavior that's tolerated or even encouraged may look positively diabolical under the bright light of clear reasoning. And here with the NFL that surely is the case. "What were they thinking?" we may wonder. Ben Shpigel (2014) conveys just how bizarre things got:

> On the Miami Dolphins' practice field, players simulated sexual acts as they taunted a teammate about his sister. In the team's hallways and meeting rooms, racist epithets and homophobic language flowed. One coach gave an offensive lineman an inflatable male doll as part of his Christmas stocking stuffer. Many of the Dolphins knew, but did not say or do anything. The players apparently considered this behavior part of the job. In the wake of it, a young player, Jonathan Martin, quit the team … [He] said he twice considered committing suicide.

The NFL's investigation and subsequent 144-page report on the bullying accusations concluded that the complaint had merit. It asserted that Richie Incognito, John Jerry and Mike Pouncey (all Dolphins players) had "'engaged in a pattern of harassment' toward Martin; another young offensive lineman; and an assistant trainer, including improper touching and sexual taunting." According to the defense lawyer, Ted Wells, hired by the NFL, "The verbal and physical abuse was widespread and even celebrated." (Shpigel, 2014).

Think about it. Attorney Wells brought up these two issues: (1) That the verbal and physical abuse was widespread and (2) that the verbal and physical abuse was celebrated. Indications were that the harassment and bullying was not just accepted, it was encouraged. It had reached the level of a subculture. Here's where cultural relativism rears its head.

Once behavior and its accompanying mindset are widespread *and celebrated*, it can then be sufficiently entrenched that it becomes the status quo. At that point, it takes concerted effort to bring about change.

Although Pouncey reportedly called Martin "a coward for snitch-ing," Dolphins' owner Stephen Ross vowed to take action. Indicating that he was "disturbed by the language used and the behavior" described in the report, Ross said, "I have made it clear to everyone within our organization that this situation must never happen again." He added, "We are committed to address this issue forcefully and to take a leader-ship role in establishing a standard that will be a benchmark in all of sports" (Shpigel, 2014).

Incognito was suspended indefinitely. His lawyer says the report is "replete with errors," denying that Jonathan Martin was bullied by Incognito or any other of Dolphins' offensive line (Shpigel, 2014). Sorting through all the evidence will take time, as it includes allegations of behavior as well as conversations, comments, and text messages.

We are told that, "Martin's sister was also mentioned during a string of five text messages, sent by Incognito on Jan. 6, 2013, that Martin found particularly revolting. Insulting him with homophobic language, Incognito also referred to Martin's sister in sexually graphic terms."

In a forceful commentary, William C. Rhoden of *The New York Times* opined, "Incognito should be barred for at least a season and ordered to seek the help he appears to need desperately." In his view, fellow Miami Dolphin offensive linemen also accused of bullying Jonathan Martin, Mike Pouncey and John Jerry, should be suspended. "If you want to clean up the workplace, clean it out," he said (2014).

If 300-pound football players can be victims of bullying and they can be driven to quit their jobs, you know something's off base. Bullying is not merely a problem for the weak or fragile. Both victims and bullies come in all shapes and sizes. In addition, victims across the spectrum can suffer to the point that their lives will no longer be the same. This is not right. Harassment shouldn't be a workplace hazard.

Cyber-Bullying in Disconnect

In the first unit of this book we looked at the film *Disconnect* (Chapter 1.4). It included a segment on cyber-bullying, which is as much a concern as in-your-face bullying. In the movie, the victim was a teenager, Ben Boyd, and his tormenters were two fellow students from high school.

The bullying started as just a cruel prank. It wasn't long until things escalated and became increasingly nasty and mean-spirited. After Ben emailed a revealing photograph, they seized the opportunity to make his life miserable. That the bullies didn't intend for the situation to go over an edge doesn't relieve them of responsibility.

As a result of the photo being sent to just about everyone at his high school, Ben became a laughing stock. It was a downward spiral from there. What Ben then did makes for a shocking and heart-wrenching scene. It is also a reminder to those of us in the audience that bullying is a serious issue with serious repercussions. As a societal problem, it calls for concerted action.

Addressing Cyber-Bullying at Work

Workplace bullying can be just as devastating as that with peers in schools. As a result, employers can't afford to ignore it or trivialize it. What may seem like a prank may not be experienced as such by the victim.

To get a sense of the prevalence of bullying, we need only look at some statistics. The Workplace Bullying Institute (WBI) posted these key findings of a 2010 survey. You can see that it's not a minor form of harassment; that there are a lot of victims—and bullies—out there.

Key Findings: Survey Results

* 35 percent of workers have experienced bullying
* 62 percent of bullies are men (= 38 percent of bullies are women)
* 58 percent of targets are women (= 42 percent of targets are men)
* Women bullies target women in 80 percent (four-fifths) of cases
* Bullying is four times more prevalent than illegal harassment

Given the extent of the problem, organizations are trying to find ways to deal with workplace bullies. Here is some advice for those on the receiving end, the victims. It is adapted from guidelines set out by *Nursing World*.

Tips for Victims of Workplace Bullying

1 Don't become part of the problem: Fight back, but don't bully back.
2 Be aware of your vulnerabilities and what pushes your buttons.
3 You're not alone: Tell your supervisor or relevant official what's going on.
4 Trust the system: Companies are taking notice and starting to take a hard line against bullies.

5   Help stop others from being victimized: Don't ignore others being bullied.
6   Be proactive: Be aware of how to handle conflict and develop a reflective disposition.
7   Empower thyself: Develop the self-confidence and resilience to deal with what's going on.
8   Confront the situation: Sometimes you can't avoid dealing with conflict.

Because workplace bullying can be devastating to a business and/or its employees, some companies have instituted zero-tolerance policies. Plus, companies with good anti-bullying policies periodically remind employees what workplace bullying is, how to report it, and the consequences for bullying (*Bullying Statistics*). We should hope so!

Just turning the spotlight on bullying and other forms of harassment is good Business Ethics. Not only does it send a message to all that civility is not an outmoded concept, it also lets employees know that they aren't on their own if they are harassed or bullied at work.

Exercise

1. Assume you've been asked to be part of the solution at *your* workplace, sports team, or school—or as a consultant for another company or institution:
    *   Sketch out a list of guidelines you think should be included.
    *   State your ideas for a "No harassment, No bullying" campaign.
2. *Stopbullying.org* sets out a few suggestions for victims. Look them over and see what you think. Does the 3-Step plan go too far? Far enough? Write a 1–2 paragraph response.

The Stop Bullying 3-Step Action Plan
1   *Name it!* Legitimize yourself. The sheer act of naming has healing value.
2   *Take time off to heal and launch a counterattack.* Research state and legal options, look for internal policies, job options, and talk to a lawyer. Gather data as to the economic impact the bully has had on your employer.
3   *Expose the bully.* Make the case that the bully is too expensive to keep. Give the employer a chance to make things right. Tell others about the bully—you have nothing to be ashamed of.

ETHICS CODE: Amazon.com

Amazon.com's ethics code covers major legal nuts and bolts. It also addresses discrimination, harassment, and violence in the workplace, as well as retaliation against whistleblowers.

See it at http://phx.corporate-ir.net/phoenix.zhtml?c=97664&p=irol-govConduct.

There we read that Amazon.com "will not tolerate any illegal discrimination or harassment of any kind" and "Violence and threatening behavior are not permitted."

Exercise

1. Should all Business Ethics codes address discrimination, harassment, and violence? State your opinion and make your case—aim to persuade someone who leans to the opposite side.

Works Cited

Alexander, David, "U.S. Military Sex Assault Reports Up 8 Percent: Officials," *Reuters*, December 3, 2014. http://www.reuters.com/article/2014/12/04/us-usa-defense-sexassault-idUSKCN0JI04J20141204 (accessed December 28, 2014).

Amazon.com, Code of Business Conduct and Ethics, http://phx.corporate-ir.net/phoenix.zhtml?c=97664&p=irol-govConduct (accessed December 28, 2014).

Belson, Ken, "Goodell Says Miami Case May Lead to New Workplace Rules," *New York Times*, December 11, 2013, http://www.nytimes.com/2013/12/12/sports/football/nfl-roundup.html?_r=0 (accessed December 28, 2014).

Bullying statistics.org, Workplace Bullying, http://www.bullyingstatistics.org/content/workplace-bullying.html (accessed December 28, 2014).

Branch, John, and Ken Belson, "In Bullying Case, Questions on N.F.L. Culture," *New York Times*, November 4, 2013, http://www.nytimes.com/2013/11/05/sports/football/for-the-nfl-a-question-of-hazing-or-abuse.html?_r=0 (accessed December 28, 2014).

Fidell, Eugene R., "Goodbye to George III," *Slate.org*, December 6, 2013, http://www.slate.com/articles/news_and_politics/jurisprudence/2013/12/sexual_assault_in_the_military_commanders_shouldn_t_be_the_prosecutors.html (accessed December 28, 2014).

Goldenberg, Suzanne, 'It Was Like They'd Never Seen A Woman Before,' *The Guardian*, February 3, 2006, http://www.theguardian.com/film/2006/feb/03/gender.world (accessed December 28, 2014).

Jenson v. Eveleth Taconite Co., 824 F. Supp. 847 – Dist. Court, Minnesota 1993; United States Court of Appeals, Eighth Circuit. 5 Dec 1997, http://caselaw. findlaw.com/us-8th-circuit/1136685.html (accessed December 28, 2014).

Lara, Alison Neumer, "A Case That Changed The Culture," *Chicago Tribune*, November 2, 2005, http://articles.chicagotribune.com/2005-11-02/ features/0511020328_1_sexual-harassment-lois-jenson-court-nominee-clarence-thomas (accessed December 28, 2014).

Miller, Zeke J., "Military Sexual Assaults: Obama Orders One-Year Review," *Time Magazine*, December 20, 2013, http://swampland.time.com/2013/12/20/ obama-orders-review-of-sexual-assaults-in-military/#ixzz2o3RF3fN7 (accessed December 28, 2014).

Nursing World, "Workplace Bullying: 8 Tips Before You Quit, *Navigate Nursing*, http://nursingworld.org/Content/NavigateNursing/AboutNN/Tip-Card-bullying.pdf (accessed December 28, 2014).

rt.com, "Reported Sexual Assaults In US Military Jumped By 50% In 2013," *RT*, December 28, 2013, http://rt.com/usa/sexual-assault-military-increase-899/ (accessed December 28, 2014).

Reuters. "U.S. Military Sex Assault Reports Up 8 Percent: Officials," http://www. reuters.com/article/2014/12/04/us-usa-defense-sexassault-idUSKCN 0JI04J20141204 (accessed December 28, 2014).

Shpigel, Ben, "A Classic Case of Bullying' on the Dolphins, Report Finds," *New York Times*, February 14, 2014, http://www.nytimes.com/2014/02/15/ sports/football/investigation-finds-pattern-of-harassment-in-dolphins-locker-room.html (accessed December 28, 2014).

Weissman, Jonathan and Jennifer Steinhauer, "Negotiators Reach Compromise on Defense Bill," *New York Times*, December 9, 2013, http://www.nytimes.com/ 2013/12/10/us/politics/house-and-senate-reach-compromise-on-pentagon-bill.html?_r=0 (accessed December 28, 2014).

Wicks, Andrew, "A Note on Sexual Harassment Policy" (1992), in Thomas Donaldson and Al Gini (eds.), *Case Studies in Business Ethics*, 4th edn, (Upper Saddle River, NJ: Prentice-Hall publishers, 1996).

Workplace Bullying Institute, "Results of the 2010 and 2007 WBI U.S. Workplace Bullying Survey," *WBI Research, Workplace Bullying*, http://www. workplacebullying.org/wbiresearch/2010-wbi-national-survey/ (accessed December 28, 2014).

Workplace Bullying Institute, "WBI 3-Step Action Plan," *Workplace Bullying*, http://www.workplacebullying.org/individuals/solutions/wbi-action-plan/ (accessed December 28, 2014).

3.5

Working for Change
Global Justice & Human Rights

Spotlight: *Sleep Dealer; Darwin's Nightmare; Fires of Kuwait*
Case Studies: Bangladesh's Sweatshop Collapse, Coca-Cola in
Colombia, Pfizer in Nigeria, Dunkin' Donuts Ad Campaign
Ethics Code: Dunkin' Donuts

> *Luz Martinez: Tijuana, Mexico, the biggest border town in the world.
> It pulls people in like a magnet even today, long after the border has
> been closed. Wandering souls keep coming, carrying nothing but their
> dreams. Today I met one. At first, I didn't think much of him. He
> looked like they all do, a little lost, holding on to whatever was left
> behind. Trying not to look scared coming to Tijuana, to work in the
> sleep dealers... He should be [scared].*
>
> —Sleep Dealer

For Memo Cruz of Oaxaca, Mexico, hacking is a lot more interesting
than farming. He looks at his father struggling to grow meager crops
and concludes that this is *not* the life for him. It's hard not to sympathize—if not identify—with someone who prefers hanging out in his
father's souped-up shack, eyes glued to his computer screen, to trying
to eke out a living as a farmer. And once they put in a dam, access to
water was limited to what you could purchase by the bagful. That his
hacking leads to a military response from the US sets in motion Memo's
journey north.

In the futuristic tale of *Sleep Dealer* (2008), we get a window into the
hardships—and injustices—facing those with neither money nor power.
We see that the gap between the rich and the poor and that we need do
more than infuse sums of money in trouble-spots around the world.
Rather, we are called to work together as a community that cares—and

Business Ethics Through Movies: A Case Study Approach, First Edition. Wanda Teays.
© 2015 John Wiley & Sons, Ltd. Published 2015 by John Wiley & Sons, Ltd.

cares to make systemic change so global justice and human rights can become a reality.

In this chapter we look at the thorny question of how to address global injustices—extremes of poverty, populations vulnerable to exploitation, human rights abuses, and so on. *Keep in mind:* Change usually comes a step at a time. The occasional avalanche brings transformation across a spectrum of social ills, but ordinarily moving from worse to bad to better and finally to good is a gradual process. To succeed we need strong analytical thinking skills, a reflective and resilient disposition, and a positive attitude. And don't forget the value of perseverance and the faith that we really can make a difference.

The human costs of wrongdoing on the part of corporations, institutions, and individuals can be demoralizing to examine and hard to address. However getting an overview of the global challenges and the tasks that lie ahead enables us to set goals. In this chapter we'll see how the movies *Sleep Dealer*, *Darwin's Nightmare*, and *Fires of Kuwait* provide a window on the sorts of global issues faced in Business Ethics. The first two show what happens when companies do *not* take the high road. Our last film, *Fires of Kuwait*, shows what can happen when we *do* work together across national and cultural boundaries. By setting aside differences and competitive instincts, we can more easily resolve problems and avert further catastrophes.

We'll look at four cases as well: First, the Bangladesh sweatshop collapse in 2013, and then two classic cases—one on Coca-Cola's bottling plant in Colombia and the other on pharmaceutical giant Pfizer's missteps in Nigeria. The last case is Dunkin' Donuts "racist" (or was it?) ad campaign in Thailand. Our ethics code here is that of Dunkin' Donuts.

SPOTLIGHT: *Sleep Dealer*

Memo leaves Oaxaca after he hacked into the US military's defense system and a drone destroyed his "office" (father's shed). His father was killed, leaving Memo overcome with guilt and grief. He figures the only solution is "El Norte"—head to Tijuana and hope for the best. Maybe in TJ he could get a job to send money back to his distraught and now impoverished mother. The movie traces his "progress" and the cyber world he enters. It's not a pretty picture.

Sleep Dealer portrays a dystopian future where workers are exploited and expendable. The picture is that of a militarized surveillance society (complete with drones blowing up "enemies" on a live reality TV shows), with laborers operating remote-control robots at construction sites around the world.

Memo and others who are desperate for work submit to a bizarre sort of bodily transformation. They are quite literally hooked to a machine—"wired" with nodes (data throughout their body) so they become human transmitters. The nodes are ports for wires that plug into the human recipient (= receiver) so they can control a robot "arm" to assist in construction projects. This allows workers to be located in Tijuana (or anywhere) and operate machinery around the world.

Workers live in fear of making mistakes or falling asleep on the job. Any slip-up and that's it! They could be fired—or worse. Such workers are easily replaced. Just think of all those undocumented workers lined up outside places like U Haul and Home Depot hoping for a day job. These workers could get the Marx "alienated laborer" stamp on their forehead, so thoroughly have they become tools of production with work lives devoid of meaning.

In an interview with the San Francisco Film Society, director Alex Rivera was asked, "Where did this idea of virtual labor come from for you?" He replied,

> The idea of the remote laborer came to me in the 1990s when the Internet was being pioneered and there was a lot of utopian dreaming about what the net would do for society. One of the things people were talking about was telecommuting, saying soon everybody could work from home… What if migrant farm workers who travel from Mexico to the US to work in the fields could work from home?

He adds: "I came up with this idea of workers who would physically stay in the South who would connect to a network and whose pure labor would cross the border to control machines in the North. Their pure labor traveled to the US but their bodies stayed out." He points out that:

> So it started as a kind of critique of the Internet utopianism but then slowly it started to reveal itself as a prediction when the call centers in India came online and all of a sudden America had this experience of dealing with people on an everyday basis who are, in effect, working in America but halfway around the world. …So, what started as political satire ended up being a way to think about globalization and a world that is summarily connected by technology but divided by borders.

CASE STUDY 1: Bangladesh Sweatshop Collapse

This could be subtitled "Trade-Offs From Hell." We already know that greed casts a long, dark shadow. The building collapse in Bangladesh makes that obvious. It illustrates how vulnerable workers are to the conditions within which they work.

The garment industry accounts for 80 percent of Bangladesh's exports. Yes, 80 percent. On April 24, 2013 an eight-story building in Bangladesh that housed five garment factories collapsed with more than 3,000 people inside. After days of rescue attempts, over 1,100 people were dead and scores injured or maimed. Eight months later, 200 people were still missing. The British newspaper *The Guardian* considers it "the worst industrial accident anywhere in the world for a generation" (Burke, 2013).

Jim Yardley of *The New York Times* (2013) calls it "the deadliest disaster in the history of the garment industry. " The international outcry is no surprise, especially when we learn that, "Workers earning as little as $38 a month were crushed under tons of falling concrete and steel."

The underwhelming response could be seen in the compensation: "Families were given a one-time payment of $257 when they collected the body of a relative in the days after the collapse, and the government has established annuities for survivors who lost limbs," Yardley (2013) reports. Is that fair? What would be reasonable reparations?

The building collapse was widely viewed as shameful, particularly since it was avoidable. As a result of the disaster, many international clothing companies pledged to help finance safety improvements in Bangladeshi factories. That said, there are conflicting views about whether such factories help the extreme poor (Yardley, 2013).

One respondent to the building collapse in Bangladesh points out all the benefits the country has gained by being a hub of manufacturing. Specifically, "Globalization, and with it the outsourcing of manufacturing labor from rich countries to poor ones, has lifted millions out of extreme poverty (defined as living on less than $1 a day). Shutting down sweatshops completely would only erase those gains" (Burke, 2013). What do *you* think? Is there a better option to deal with the inequities and bad safety conditions that wouldn't entail eliminating manufacturing jobs from the poor?

When asked if retailers cut and run from Bangladesh, Professor Kirk O'Hanson of the Markkula Center for Applied Ethics remarked that,

> There is plenty of blame to go around. The worldwide search for cheap production does contribute to unsafe conditions. If the U.S. companies want low-cost production, they have to resist doing business with the very

lowest-cost suppliers who are most likely to be cutting corners. They have to find suppliers who produce quality clothes in quality factories. Most are only screening for the first. I hope they stay in Bangladesh; they will have the same problem in another country in five years if they don't change their selection process (2013).

Repercussions

In March 2013 the Walt Disney Company, "considered the world's largest licenser, with sales of nearly $40 billion" ordered an end to the production of branded merchandise in Bangladesh and set out new rules for overseas production (Greenhouse, 2013).

> Journalist Steven Greenhouse also notes that Disney extended their ban to other countries, such as Pakistan, where a September 2013 fire killed 262 garment workers. He observes that, Disney's move reflects the difficult calculus that companies with operations in countries like Bangladesh are facing as they balance profit and reputation against the backdrop of a wrenching human disaster (2013).

One of the issues with outsourcing jobs, as with the Bangladesh sweatshop, is that workers may be exploited. It may take the form of low wages, long hours, use of children as laborers, and sometimes difficult or dangerous work conditions. Controversies have arisen with some of the biggest corporations in the world.

Just think of Apple and the controversy around work conditions in China and allegations of the use of child laborers by its supplier (Armitrage, 2013, Schundt and Zand, 2013).

Think also of Coca-Cola and accusations of brutal tactics to prevent unions, and the use of paramilitary operations to intimidate workers in their Colombia bottling plant (Borger, 2001). Two PBS *Frontline* fellows, Rob Harris and Tovin Lapan, went to Colombia in 2005 to investigate the story. You can watch their video report on the PBS website (see "The Coca-Cola Controversy" at http://www.pbs.org/frontlineworld/fellows/colombia0106/). Let's turn now to the issues that arose.

CASE STUDY 2: Coca-Cola in Colombia

As with the Bangladeshi building collapse, our second case also raises concerns about workers' safety. And it makes us aware of the power businesses can have over their employees' lives. One of the best-known corporations is the Coca-Cola Company—its reach is global and its catchy ads and slogans ("Coke is life," "The Real Thing," etc.) are etched into the popular culture. But its reputation came under fire when things went awry in its Colombia bottling plant. Julian Borger of *the Guardian* (UK) tells the story:

> Coca-Cola's bottling plants in Colombia used rightwing death squads to terrorise workers and prevent the organisation of unions, it was alleged in a Miami [Florida] court yesterday. The US union United Steelworkers is suing Coca-Cola on behalf of the Colombian union Sinaltrainal for what the lawsuit describes as "the systematic intimidation, kidnapping, detention and murder" of workers in Colombian plants. Sinaltrainal claims that five of its members working in Coca-Cola bottling plants have been killed since 1994 (2001).

Coca-Cola insists that they were not responsible for the "alleged atrocities," since they did not own the bottling plants. They place the blame on the contractor. Borger reports, "But union lawyers argued that the world's best-known soft drinks company closely controlled the operations of its contractors and was well aware of the brutal intimidation of workers in the bottling factories." Critics say this is passing the buck and corporations that outsource work to contractors should still ensure safeguards of their employees' basic rights (Borger, 2001).

As far as Coca-Cola sees it, they aren't responsible and that's that. "We deny any wrongdoing regarding human rights or any other unlawful activities in Colombia or anywhere else in the world." This elicited the following response:

> Daniel Kovalik, a US steelworkers' lawyer, said that Coca-Cola had stepped in to curb human rights abuses in Guatemala after three union leaders had been killed in the 1980s. That intervention showed that the company could stop the killings if it chose to, he argued (Borger, 2001).

So who's right? The Coca-Cola Company? Their critics? To answer this we need to assess corporate responsibility for its contractors and subcontractors. As we saw in the case of the tainted berries produced by Townsend Farms and sold by Costco (see Chapter 1.3), when problems arose the corporation—Costco—assumed responsibility and was held partially accountable.

Is the Colombia case analogous? Or are there significant differences between the two cases? If not, should the Coca-Cola Company take more control of the matter and use their considerable clout to see that changes are made? You tell me.

SPOTLIGHT: *Darwin's Nightmare*

Darwin's Nightmare lays bare the devastation wrought by the exploitation of the people and resources of Tanzania in exchange for guns from Russia. It portrays a real-life dystopia.

This unsettling movie was nominated for an Academy Award as Best Documentary in 2004. It gives us a sense of the dark underbelly of globalization. In this case, it's ex-Soviet cargo planes flying into Tanzania on a daily basis. They come to get fish. Lots of fish.

We watch the trade: Nile Perch from Lake Victoria for markets throughout Europe in exchange for guns and ammunition for the African fishermen. They are left with fish heads and bones to pick over, while the gunrunners reap the profits. It's a startling sight to see.

Neither Marx nor Rawls would have anything good to say about the conditions. For the one (Marx), the workers are on the losing end of the equation. For the other (Rawls), there is nothing we'd want to universalize here and the least advantaged members of the equation are not given any favors. Not a one.

Rawls' Difference Principle (Chapter 1.3) comes to mind. It prods us to strive for distributive justice, to help the most disadvantaged. We seek equality of opportunity and basic rights, but find them in short supply here in Tanzania. There's no question that this is a nightmare. We see the effect on the local people as the fruit of their labor (the fish) go to feed others around the world, while they are left with the rotten carcasses.

Director Hubert Sauper has an agenda—to show the world that what's happening in Tanzania is simply wrong. On his website (darwinsnightmare. com) Sauper speaks out. He says,

> The old question, which social and political structure is the best for the world, seems to have been answered. Capitalism has won. The ultimate forms for future societies are "consumer democracies," which are seen as "civilized" and "good." In a Darwinian sense the "good system" won. It won by either convincing its enemies or eliminating them.

He explains:

> In *Darwin's Nightmare* I tried to transform the bizarre success story of a fish and the ephemeral boom around this "fittest" animal into an ironic,

frightening allegory for what is called the New World Order. I could make the same kind of movie in Sierra Leone, only the fish would be diamonds, in Honduras, bananas, and in Libya, Nigeria or Angola, crude oil.

Sauper found it hard to film what he saw. He summed it up this way: "*Darwin's Nightmare* is a tale about humans between the North and the South, about globalization, and about fish." We see industrial nations taking advantage of Third World countries. We see the planes coming day after day, hauling off a staggering amount of fish. And we see the poor fishermen with the sad remains—the discarded leftovers—for their own families.

New York Times film critic A.O. Scott praises the film. He speaks of the huge cargo planes that fly into Tanzania to pick up the fish and notes:

> In any case, they leave behind a scene of misery and devastation that *Darwin's Nightmare* presents as the agonized human face of globalization. While the flesh of millions of Nile perch is stripped, cleaned and flash-frozen for export to wealthy countries, millions of people in the Tanzanian interior live on the brink of famine. Some of them will eat fried fish heads, which are processed in vast open-air pits infested with maggots and scavenging birds. Along the shores of the lake, homeless children fight over scraps of food and get high from the fumes of melting plastic-foam containers used to pack the fish (Scott, 2005).

As the movie indicates, when it comes to international business—and that means global Business Ethics—the power imbalance between the North and the South, the rich and the poor, needs to be recalibrated. All indications are the sooner the better.

CASE STUDY 3: Pfizer Meningitis Studies in Nigeria

Anyone who knows the Nuremberg Code or the Helsinki Declaration (see Chapter 2.2) knows that the first duty in undertaking human experiments is the voluntary and informed consent of the human subject. In the case of children or anyone deemed incompetent, a parent, guardian or surrogate decision-maker would have to give consent.

Basically it's a no-brainer: You want to run a clinical trial and your subjects are children, you'll need to get the parent-guardian to sign off. So what happened in 1996 when the pharmaceutical giant Pfizer tested its antibiotic Trovan in a meningitis epidemic in Kano, Nigeria? David Smith (2011) takes up the story:

> A hundred children were given an experimental oral antibiotic called Trovan, while a further hundred received ceftriaxone, the "gold-standard" treatment of modern medicine. Five children died on Trovan and six on ceftriaxone. But later it was claimed that Pfizer did not have proper consent from parents to use an experimental drug on their children and questions were raised over the documentation of the trial.

The 15-year battle that ensued "alleged that some received a dose lower than recommended, leaving many children with brain damage, paralysis or slurred speech" (Smith, 2011).

It's hard to think of ways to compensate for such harms. Here's what Pfizer did: It set up a compensation trust fund of $75 million and paid the families of four children who died $175,000 each. Pfizer also agreed to sponsor health projects in Kano and create a fund of $35 million to compensate those affected.

In 2006 *The Washington Post* obtained a copy of a confidential Nigerian report stating that, "A panel of Nigerian medical experts has concluded that Pfizer Inc. violated international law during a 1996 epidemic by testing an unapproved drug on children with brain infections at a field hospital."

The report concludes that "Pfizer never obtained authorization from the Nigerian government to give the unproven drug to nearly 100 children and infants" (Stevens, 2006). The publication of the report set off a firestorm, putting Pfizer on the hot seat. The company fought back. "Pfizer contended that its researchers traveled to Kano with a purely philanthropic motive, to help fight the epidemic, which ultimately killed more than 15,000 Africans. The committee rejected that explanation, pointing out that Pfizer physicians completed their trial and left while 'the epidemic was still raging'" (Stevens, 2006).

Pfizer is not alone in raising concerns around medical experimentation. Plenty of others—including the US government (e.g., in the Tuskegee syphilis studies of 400 poor black men in Alabama and the Guatemalan STD studies in the 1940s)—have cut corners that led to human rights abuses.

Pfizer called the lawsuit "frivolous" (see "Summary: Tovan—Kano State Civil Case—Statement of Defense," 2007). They contend that it is not certain that Trovan caused the deaths and bodily harm, because the disease itself can have the same or similar consequences. To many it looked like Pfizer was just trying to cover their butt (so to speak) and the fact they agreed to a settlement in the millions of dollars indicates some acknowledgement of at least potential culpability.

Take a moment to reflect on this. What if Pfizer is right about the cause of the deaths, brain damage, and other health problems? Assume they are right. Is there now a clean slate? Well, no, not really. That's because, as noted earlier, Pfizer did human experimentation without obtaining the proper consent. Had they not skipped this vital step they would have more credence in terms of ethical finger-pointing. But when one of the biggest pharmaceutical corporations in the world omits an obvious step, it doesn't look good. There's mud in their eye for sure! In its "Summary," Pfizer takes up the consent issue arguing,

> At Kano's Infectious Disease Hospital (IDH), parents or guardians of potential study participants were explained the details of the trial, including that participation was voluntary. Local Nigerian nurses explained *orally* to patients' parents and/or guardians in Hausa the details of the clinical trial. *Oral consent* was obtained before any patient was admitted into the study, and *at no point were the parents or guardians separated from the children* (2007, emphasis mine).

Of course we all know from the Helsinki Declaration that consent is preferably obtained *in writing*. So why wasn't it done here? Why assume an *oral* declaration is as good as one that is written? That seems a bit of a "he-said-she-said" defense. Secondly, why is Pfizer commenting on the parents/guardians not being separated from the children? Is that supposed to mean that parents bear some responsibility to watch what the researchers do to their children? Since when?

Pfizer further claims in its Defense Summary that it did not need to utilize an Independent Review Board. However, the Helsinki Declaration explicitly states that this is a moral obligation.

Pfizer contends that there was no regulation or law *in Nigeria* requiring that they seek ethical committee approval before conducting a clinical trial or investigative study. Therefore, *there was no need to obtain what the law did not require*. In addition, there was no formal ethics committee sitting at either Kano's IDH or at the nearby Bayero Teaching Hospital (Pfizer, 2007).

This argument has a weasel in it—namely, that Pfizer is not bound to abide by the Helsinki Declaration. Here's why: (1) There is no *law* in Nigeria that requires them to use an institutional review board (IRB) and (2) They are only required to obey the law of the country in question, not

American law or a code of ethics that is recognized around the world. Is this the honorable path for Pfizer to take? To look to the laws of the various countries that they turn to for clinical testing that they're doing in developing countries (not in the US or Europe)? And to overlook ethics codes that medical professionals and researchers have recognized as ethically binding?

Even if they had the most laudable goals when they headed to Nigeria to test Trovan on the 200 children, shouldn't Pfizer have maintained the highest of standards—ones in line with those of professional organizations?

That they *did* take steps to compensate the subjects/patients, families and the various parties affected by the Trovan experiments deserves to be acknowledged, even if the decision was years in the making. And we can all hope that Pfizer and all others doing clinical studies in developing countries—or right in our own backyard—would take care to prioritize the most vulnerable—the most disadvantaged in the equation as set out by Rawls' Difference Principle and any number of ethical codes.

CASE STUDY 4: Dunkin' Donuts Ad Campaign

So where can things go wrong? Sometimes when we least expect it. Consider a controversial Dunkin' Donuts advertisement for chocolate glazed donuts that stirred up trouble for the company in 2013. Let's see why there was a problem.

The ad: Picture a beautiful woman with a beehive hairdo, a dark chocolate-covered face and candy-pink lipstick who is holding a charcoal donut. She may look delectable, positively yummy, from one person's perspective or horrific, a chocolate ghoul, from another. It's all a matter of perspective.

Perceptions matter more than we may realize. If I look at a photo of you covered in dark chocolate, I may find you enticing, interesting, or even funny. I might also find you strange, weird, or over-the-top. But offensive? When does a chocolate-covered face cross an ethical line? Well, when it looks like blackface, for one. That's what happened to Dunkin' Donuts ad campaign.

Some thought it racist; some thought it bizarre; others thought it hilarious. None of these responses were what Dunkin' Donuts had hoped for when it launched its campaign in Thailand. Here's the nitty gritty:

> The advert shows a woman apparently wearing dark make-up and bright pink lipstick, with a 1950s beehive hairstyle. She is holding a "charcoal

donut," out of which a bite has been taken. The slogan next to the image reads: "Break every rule of deliciousness." The advert caused consternation on Friday morning, after Human Rights Watch said it would cause "howls of outrage" if it ran in the US (Gabbatt, 2013).

Dunkin' Donuts' head honcho in Thailand, Nadim Salhani, considered the racist charge preposterous. He called it "paranoid American thinking" (Gecker, 2013). In his opinion, "It's absolutely ridiculous." "We're not allowed to use black to promote our doughnuts?" he asked. "I don't get it. What's the big fuss? What if the product was white and I painted someone white, would that be racist?" (Gecker, 2013).

Exercise

1. One argument is that Thai citizens are used to the use of racial stereotypes. Specifically,

   The campaign hasn't ruffled many in Thailand, where it's common for advertisements to inexplicably use racial stereotypes. A Thai brand of household mops and dustpans called "Black Man" uses a logo with a smiling black man in a tuxedo and bow tie. One Thai skin whitening cream runs TV commercials that say white-skinned people have better job prospects than those with dark skin. An herbal Thai toothpaste says its dark-colored product "is black, but it's good" (Gecker, 2013).

   Does this information about the cultural context affect how you see the Dunkin' Donuts ad campaign? Share your thoughts.
2. Blackface is part of the American racist past. It is not something that is part of the past of other nations, including Thailand. Given that cultural reality, was it fair of Human Rights Watch to fault the Thai branch of Dunkin' Donuts?
3. How *do* we navigate these waters? What sorts of cross-cultural policies should be in place for businesses that have global operations?

ETHICS CODE: Dunkin' Donuts

Think about all the different ethics codes we've examined—from Amazon to Yahoo, from Exxon to Kellogg's, from Apple to Microsoft, from J&J to H&M, and on and on. Each code tells a story in setting out the ethical core of the corporation. As we have seen, they range over a set of values—not all the same, none of them completely different, but each one distinct. Each code speaks to the moral reasoning that holds the company in place as a "person"—an entity with legal status and, at least in some eyes, moral status as well. A great deal follows from this; all the more reason to examine the ethics code if you want to get a sense of the core values of the company and the business's ethics.

Our last ethics code is that of Dunkin' Donuts. We already saw the thorny problem they faced when their ad campaign went sideways.

Dunkin' Donuts: Living Our Values

- Honesty: Embrace the truth about oneself and the world
  Be honest no matter what … you can always recover from the truth
- Transparency: Demonstrate openness and vulnerability
  Share your thoughts without hesitation
- Humility: Acknowledge own mistakes and commit to learning
  It's about the team … never lose sight of those who helped along the way
- Integrity: Say what you think and do what you say
  Always act with integrity … character shows when no one is looking
- Respectfulness: Honor the dignity, inclusion, and diversity of others
  Give people their dignity, earn others' respect
- Fairness: Do what is right based on common principles
  Always do the right thing, especially when it is difficult
- Responsibility: Make yourself accountable to the community
  Own the outcome of your actions, good or bad

Looking over these values, we can see they all relate to the way that we interact with others and how we live in the world: Be transparent (open), humble (unpretentious, team-player), a person of integrity (honest, principled), respectful (treat others with dignity), fair (just); and, lastly, responsible (own up to your own actions).

You can see Dunkin' Donuts' Code of Business Ethics and Conduct at http://files.shareholder.com/downloads/abea-68scr9/0x0x486229/f034a2af-d186-4fee-9142-5cc5c3bba21c/May_2011_COC_Pages.pdf.

The CEO of Dunkin' Donuts, Nigel Travis, took an unusual step of acknowledging the complexity and occasional ambiguity regarding Business Ethics. Read his letter (which precedes the code) and share your thoughts.

Dear Colleagues:

Dunkin' Brands' success is dependent upon how we conduct ourselves and do business with our franchisees, vendors, suppliers, and other business partners. We strive to reach the highest standards of ethical behavior, and to live our core values—honesty, transparency, humility, integrity, respectful-ness, fairness and responsibility.

Although we have our values as a strong ethical foundation, today's business world is complicated—with gray areas, new regulations and government mandates to navigate and consider at all turns. Requirements such as the Sarbanes—Oxley Act [focusing on the accuracy of financial information and issues such as fraudulent activity] add an additional layer of complexity. Even when intentions are good, it's not always clear what is the right thing to do...

The Code cannot guarantee ethical conduct, nor can it cover every ethical issue that you may encounter. Ultimately, we are each personally account-able to act ethically, comply with the law, be watchful for questionable cir-cumstances, raise issues, and to ask questions—even when doing so may be difficult. ...

—CEO, Nigel Travis

Exercise

1. What can we learn from the four cases we've looked at in this chapter?
2. How might lessons learned help us understand how important are the ethics code of each business?
3. What stands out about Dunkin' Donuts' values (see above)?
4. Write a paragraph or two to Nigel Travis, responding to his letter.

Sometimes Things Go Wonderfully

There are times when we see how small we are compared to the forces of nature. An amazing documentary illustrates how people and corporations can work together and bridge differences in the face of an environmental disaster. This is *Fires of Kuwait* (1992). It's truly inspiring.

SPOTLIGHT: *Fires of Kuwait*

When Iraqi forces set fire to 600-plus oil wells as they were driven out of Kuwait in the first Gulf War, all hell broke loose. The skies were filled with smoke, smoke, and more black sooty smoke from the oil fires. They raged, seemingly without end. The skies got darker and darker, until day looked like night. The Sun? What Sun? The smoke was so thick it obscured the Sun. Putting the fires out seemed a task of such magnitude that it was unfathomable how it could be solved.

We watch as oil fire specialists from around the world try to extinguish all the fires—a feat that required extraordinary expertise. Among the teams was the famous crew led by Texan "Red" Adair. They put out the fires in 9 months, instead of the 5 years that was expected (Reed, 2004). The fact that cultural differences, competition and self-interest were set aside for the greater cause is downright heartwarming.

The film is a real life nail-biter and a testimony to human ingenuity. We see what was unleashed by the attacks on the wells and the nightmare the teams faced to make headway. The fact it was done at considerable risk underscores how fortunate we are to have individuals and businesses willing to attempt such daunting tasks.[1]

In addition to demonstrating collegiality, cooperation and collaboration, *Fires of Kuwait* raises important ethical issues about the tools of war. When the Iraqi military, presumably under orders from Iraqi dictator Saddam Hussein, set the wells on fire, they crossed a line. By torching the environment and causing damage on such a massive, destructive scale, the war took a radically different, and ominous, turn. With that gesture, the conflict was extended from a battle of warring "tribes" to a war against nature itself—the plants, the animals, the air we breathe, the creatures of the sea, and so on.

In the movie *Avatar*, the birds and mammals of the planet Pandora join its inhabitants in a battle-to-the-finish against the Marines seeking to colonize the planet and acquire its precious minerals. *Fires of Kuwait* is no *Avatar*, but it shares a concern about our relationship with the world around us. It calls us to our duties and obligations to care for the environment and preserve it for future generations.

The movie shows us how individuals and businesses can unite and put their knowledge and skills to work. We see them apply their expertise in fighting oil fires to the frightful task before them. *Fires of Kuwait* offers compelling proof of the way businesses can work in consort for the benefit of all. It's an uplifting moment in Business Ethics.

Works Cited

Armitage, Jim, "'Even Worse Than Foxconn': Apple Rocked by Child Labour Claims," *The Independent*, July 30, 2013, http://www.independent.co.uk/life-style/gadgets-and-tech/even-worse-than-foxconn-apple-rocked-by-child-labour-claims-8736504.html (accessed December 28, 2014).

Borger, Julian, "Coca-Cola Sued Over Bottling Plant 'Terror Campaign'," *The Guardian*, July 20, 2001, http://www.theguardian.com/world/2001/jul/21/julianborger (accessed December 28, 2014).

Burke, Jason, "Bangladeshi Workers Still Missing Eight Months After Rana Plaza Collapse," *The Guardian*, December 25, 2013, http://www.theguardian.com/world/2013/dec/25/bangladesh-workers-missing-rana-plaza (accessed December 28, 2014).

Dunkin' Donuts, "Code of Business Ethics and Conduct: Living our Values," http://files.shareholder.com/downloads/abea-68scr9/0x0x486229/f034a2af-d186-4fee-9142-5cc5c3bba21c/May_2011_COC_Pages.pdf (accessed December 28, 2014).

Gabbatt, Adam, "Dunkin' Donuts Apologises For 'Bizarre And Racist' Thai Advert," *The Guardian*, August 30, 2013, http://www.theguardian.com/world/2013/aug/30/dunkin-donuts-racist-thai-advert-blackface (accessed December 28, 2014).

Gecker, Jocelyn, "Dunkin' Donuts Criticized For 'Racist' Ad Campaign," *Associated Press*, August 30, 2013, http://news.yahoo.com/dunkin-donuts-criticized-racist-ad-124514391.html (accessed December 28, 2014).

Greenhouse, Steven, "Some Retailers Rethink Role in Bangladesh," *New York Times*, May 1, 2013, http://www.nytimes.com/2013/05/02/business/some-retailers-rethink-their-role-in-bangladesh.html?gwh=56E722B35EA01AF9D309515C08326620&gwt=pay (accessed December 28, 2014).

Guillen, Michael, "Q&A: Alex Rivera, *Sleep Dealer*," *San Francisco Film Society*, May 14, 2008, http://www.sf360.org/page/11194 (accessed December 28, 2014).

O'Hanson, Kirk, "Blog: Business Ethics in the News," Markkula Center for Applied Ethics, May 2, 2013, http://www.scu.edu/r/ethics-center/ethicsblog/business-ethics-news/16120/DISNEY:-Should-Retailers-Cut-and-Run-from-Bangladesh? (accessed December 28, 2014).

PBS, The Coca-Cola Controversy, http://www.pbs.org/frontlineworld/fellows/colombia0106/ (accessed December 28, 2014).

Pfizer, *Summary: Trovan, Kano State Civil Case - Statement Of Defense*, 2007, http://www.pfizer.com/files/news/trovan_statement_defense_summary.pdf (accessed December 28, 2014).

Reed, Christopher, "Red Adair," *The Guardian*, August 8, 2004, http://www.theguardian.com/news/2004/aug/09/guardianobituaries.usa (accessed December 27, 2014).

Sauper, Hubert, "The Film," *Darwin's Nightmare*, http://www.darwinsnightmare.com/darwin/html/startset.htm (accessed December 28, 2014).

Schundt, Hilmar and Bernhard Zand, "Undercover Report: Apple Faces Fresh Criticism of Factories," *Der Spiegel (Spiegel Online International)*, July 29, 2013, http://www.spiegel.de/international/business/labor-violations-rife-at-apple-manufacturing-partners-in-china-a-913652.html (accessed December 28, 2014).

Smith, David, "Pfizer pays out to Nigerian families of meningitis drug trial victims, *The Guardian*, August 11, 2011, http://www.theguardian.com/world/2011/aug/11/pfizer-nigeria-meningitis-drug-compensation (accessed December 28, 2014).

Stephens, Joe, "Panel Faults Pfizer in '96 Clinical Trial In Nigeria," *Washington Post*, May 7, 2006, http://www.washingtonpost.com/wp-dyn/content/article/2006/05/06/AR2006050601338.html (accessed December 28, 2014).

Yardley, Jim, "After Bangladesh Factory Collapse, Bleak Struggle for Survivors," *New York Times*, December 18, 2013, http://www.nytimes.com/2013/12/19/world/asia/after-collapse-bleak-struggle.html (accessed December 28, 2014).

Note

1 Another movie that shows the power of collaboration in the face of disaster is *Emergency Mine Rescue*, which centers on the rescue of 33 Chilean miners trapped half a mile below the surface. It is also well worth seeing.

3.6

Transformation
The Art of Personal Power

Spotlight: *Groundhog Day*, *Invictus*
Case Study: Kudumbashri's Work Skills Program
Ethics Code: The Coca-Cola Company

> *Phil: I'm a god.*
> *Rita: You're God?*
> *Phil: I'm a god. I'm not the God... I don't think.*
> —Groundhog Day

Phil Connors, a weatherman for WPBH TV in Pittsburgh, has covered the Groundhog Day festival in Punxsutawney, PA for four years in a row. This is nothing he is proud of. He'd like his job to be a stepping-stone to something better. From all appearances, Phil has a high opinion of himself and views others with disdain, calling them "Hairdo," "Pork Chop," or "Giant Leech." For him, "People are morons."

Unable to leave town because of a blizzard, Phil gets trapped in a time warp: He wakes up every day on Groundhog Day, over and over again. Nothing he does, even acts of suicide, make one bit of difference. His life has become a curse of relentless, and endless, repetition.

Groundhog Day (1993) is a classic of personal transformation. From a self-centered wretch declaring, "I'm a god," to the most sought-after bachelor in Punxsutawney, it's a dramatic trajectory and a story for the ages. We'll see that it also resonates with Business Ethics. Our vehicle is a framework of best practices set out by Buddhist monk, Thich Nhat Hanh in *The Art of Power*.

Business Ethics Through Movies: A Case Study Approach, First Edition. Wanda Teays.
© 2015 John Wiley & Sons, Ltd. Published 2015 by John Wiley & Sons, Ltd.

The Ethical Framework: Thich Nhat Hanh's Path of Power

A few years back we saw *The Art of War* craze. The catalyst was a got-to-have-it book by Sun Tzu. People scurried to get a copy and soak up its advice. It was no surprise that the very rich Gordon Gekko in *Wall Street* recommends it to Bud Fox, an eager beaver who craves wealth and power (see Chapter 1.3).

Gekko tells Bud, "I don't throw darts at a board. I bet on sure things. Read Sun Tzu, *The Art of War*. Every battle is won before it is ever fought." In his view, conducting business is pretty much like conducting a war. Winning battles before they are fought is to be preferred. More than a few people agreed, to gauge by the book's impact.

Gekko relishes having power over people. Not so Thich Nhat Hanh, who says, "Our society is founded on a very limited definition of power, namely wealth, professional success, fame, physical strength, military might, and political control" (2007, p. 1). For Hanh, "There is only one kind of success that really matters: the success of transforming ourselves, transforming our afflictions, fear and anger" (p. 2). You want power? Yes, power over others can bring short-term gains; but power over oneself is where long-term benefits can accrue.

So, how do we get there? Hanh proposes a set of *practices*. He parallels Aristotle's view that we develop our moral character by *doing something* and make a *habit* of a life of virtue. Hanh would agree that a life of moderation has much to commend it. In place of moral and intellectual virtues (as Aristotle set out), Hanh recommends the following:

Hanh's Five Aspects Of Personal Power

1 *Self-confidence*—trusting oneself
2 *Self-possession*—keeping a positive frame of mind
3 *Attentiveness*—being fully present to what's happening now
4 *Concentration*—staying focused on the task at hand
5 *Insight*—awareness of impact on self and others

Have the confidence to believe in yourself and the self-possession to think positive, holding out hope for a good result. Be present, not asleep at the switch. Both attentiveness (staying alert) and concentration (staying focused) should be our *modus operandi*. Otherwise, golden opportunities could slip like grains of sand through our fingers. And last but not least, foster insight to see the effect we have and what, if any, response is in order.

The Professional Dimension

These five practices help us build leadership qualities by developing inner strength. They also lay a foundation for collegiality and community building. "When we live without awareness, without the ability to truly see the world around us," Hanh observes, "our life is often like a runaway train" (p. 3). This is especially the case in our professional life, he says.

What we do on the personal level often reverberates on the professional level. And vice versa. When our professional lives suffer, so do our personal lives. In cultivating the right frame of mind and our "spiritual or true power," the quality of the work and our work lives will change (p. 3).

These remarks are in sync with Robert Solomon's key components of moral development (Chapter 3.1): Community, Excellence, Role Identity, Integrity, Judgment, and Holism. *Excellence* means we can't simply follow the maxims "do no wrong" and "avoid making mistakes," says Solomon (1992). Demonstrate benevolence in what we do. Strive to do our best, and not just follow along unthinkingly.

Turn the spotlight on ourselves Hanh would say. *Start here:* Be fully present to what is right here now, "in touch with what is going on inside and around us" (p. 3). The path to attentiveness, to being present, is with the five practices. We can see this in *Groundhog Day.*

SPOTLIGHT: *Groundhog Day*

First Power: Self-Confidence

Trust yourself. Have faith in what is inside of you and not directed toward anything external. This is the capacity of transformation and healing. What is crucial is *having a sense of direction*, a path, knowing where you want to go. Have confidence in your ideas and the concrete results of your practice. Believe in yourself, your vision, and what you think must be done to get there (pp. 15–16).

Phil Connors flunks this first step. On one hand he shows a bloated self-confidence when he calls himself "the talent" and makes fun of his co-workers. On the other hand, when confronted by his producer Rita his self-confidence withers. After she says, "I can never love a man like you because you only love yourself" Phil replies, "I don't even *like* myself."

In time he has a "dark night of the soul" where the gap between how he is living and what actually matters becomes apparent. This is the reality check that propels him to self-creation. Until then, he's like a horse with blinders, able to get only partial view of the world around him.

Second Power: Self-Possession

Keep a positive frame of mind. Be diligent. Don't get distracted from your goals. This is not a matter of *proving* yourself. You should already have the confidence in yourself (First Power) so there's no need to prove anything.

Hanh sees four aspects of self-possession:

- Don't let negative feelings manifest themselves: Do not nourish them and do not allow others awaken them.
- Don't allow negative feelings to take hold: Shrink them or replace them.
- Nurture the positive so understanding and compassion can develop.
- Keep a positive frame of mind to drive out the negative.

In Phil's case, negativity runs amok and wraps itself around him like a python about to devour its next meal. Until he takes hold of himself, Phil isn't going anywhere worth much. We see this most vividly when he tells the groundhog, "You want a prediction about the weather, you're asking the wrong Phil. I'll give you a prediction. It's gonna be cold. It's gonna be gray and it's gonna last you the rest of your life." His solution? Kill the messenger! He kidnaps the groundhog for a fiery murder-suicide at the quarry.

As you know, venting your anger or turning to violence rarely improves the situation. Phil is no exception. He can scream, act out all he wants, and grab poor groundhogs and drive off cliffs to end it all. That's not going to solve his problems or get him further down the road to self-transformation. Phil wakes up to Sonny and Cher singing, "I Got You Babe," just like every morning. Nothing has changed. Another Groundhog Day starts.

Unless he takes hold of himself in the right frame of mind, Phil is going nowhere. And no matter how destructively he behaves, he's no closer to his goal. He needs to cut the negativity and nurture the positive. Until he can do that, Phil is stuck in limbo. As local yokel Gus sizes up Phil, "I peg you as a 'glass is half-empty' kind of guy." Clearly, Phil needs an attitude adjustment.

Ethicist Michael Boylan has some pithy advice for the Phils of the world. He would tell Phil to reflect on his "Personal Worldview." Look at what he is doing and why he is doing it and take the four moral pillars to heart. These are wisdom, courage, justice, and self-control.

Without wisdom, we are morally blind and can't easily learn from the lessons of the past. Phil was happy to let go of moral rules and obligations, declaring: "We don't have to abide by their rules any more: 'Clean up your room', 'Stand up straight', 'Be nice to your sister', 'Don't mix beer and wine, ever' and 'Don't drive on the railroad tracks.'" Thinking he didn't have to deal with consequences (no tomorrow = no consequences), Phil could be as reckless as he wanted.

Without courage, we end up at extremes—one moment cowardly, the next moment rash. Phil tended toward the latter with his many suicide attempts. Without justice, our biases and desires take over. Being able to achieve fairness is then out of reach. Phil, for example, had no qualms about *his* staying in the fancy Bed & Breakfast, while his co-workers were stuck in the cheap hotel down the street.

Without self-control we are either at the mercy of others or unable to pull back when things veer off course. Phil abandoned self-control once he saw there was no price to pay for his excesses. This opened the door of gluttony, lust, and greed. Rita found him disgusting and, quoting Sir Walter Scott, judged him a "wretch, centered on self."

One lesson for our professional and personal lives is that a positive attitude goes a long way and can benefit others as well. It helps create an environment that promotes creativity and innovation. Think of the steps taken by companies to create a positive workplace and encourage workers (e.g., "Googlers") to be imaginative. That can't take place in an uptight, negative space, where supervisors or co-workers are quick to criticize. Companies can foster the interplay of ideas and the imagination, and create a space where colleagues can work together as equals.

Third Power: Awareness

Here we find "the energy of being aware of what is happening in the present moment." There are two aspects to this power: First, it helps clarify what to do and what not to do. These are the *parameters* shaping the boundaries of our objectives. Secondly, awareness helps us avoid difficulties and mistakes; "it protects you and shines light on all your daily activities" (p. 22). Think of it like the eye of a fly—able to see in all directions and gauge perils as well as benefits.

With a developed sense of awareness, we see what's going on here and now. Without it, we are in danger of becoming distracted, scattered, losing everything. It can be a challenge to stay present, as anyone who has ever done a monotonous or repetitive task can verify. Phil Connors fails here as well. Though he is repeating the same day, he shows little presence of mind, foresight, or hindsight. Until he is jolted out of his complacency, Phil is stuck in the dark. He hasn't the slightest inclination to put himself in the other's shoes and get a broader point of view.

Fourth Power: Concentration

Focused concentration is not as easy as you might think. It's like those meditation instructions that are so hard to follow: Don't let other thoughts shove their way into your mind, such as what route to take home, whether to skip lunch or grab takeout on the way home.

Concentration goes beyond being a problem-solving technique. It helps us look into ourselves and see what needs to be transformed, how to better ourselves. Look at Vaclal Smil, famous geographer and prolific writer. *Wired* magazine's Clive Thompson asked Smil how he managed to write 30 books—three alone in 2013.

Smil's answer was, "Hemingway knew the secret. I mean, he was a lush and a bad man in many ways, but he knew the secret. You get up and, first thing in the morning, you do your 500 words. Do it every day and you've got a book in eight or nine months" (Thompson, 2013). That is a testimony to both concentration and commitment.

We have examples from our films as well, such as Jeffrey Wigand of *The Insider* and Erin Brockovich. Both bring industry abuses to light and don't back down when the heat's on. We see this in the opening of *The Insider:* Wigand is gathering up his stuff. We don't yet know that the boxes he's carrying contain incriminating evidence and that he puts himself at risk to haul it away. Nor do we know that he's the whistleblower in one of the biggest product liability suits in US history. Doing what he did took courage and the ability to concentrate under the most trying of circumstances.

Erin Brockovich is also a powerhouse of concentration and commitment. She spent hundreds of hours single-handedly researching the Hinkley case of contaminated water and bringing the community together in a class action suit. At any point she could have thrown in the towel, given the obstacles she faced. But she didn't.

Phil Connors, however, isn't too swift when it comes to concentration. He's too focused on himself and trying to fill the void inside. Something needs to propel him out of self-indulgence. That's where the fifth power comes in.

Fifth Power: Insight

Insight is a companion to concentration. "If you are using your powers of concentration, insight allows you to fully see what you are concentrating on," says Hanh. Insight cuts through the layers of thoughts and feelings and brings clarity of mind. Insight is not a tool for *personal* power, because it is by way of insight that our world expands. This requires us to stay in the present and not get lost in past regrets or fantasies about future projects.

We may want things to stay the same, but they don't. In our lives and work, things are in transition. One day there are typewriters, the next day computers. One day there are telephone booths, the next day cell phones and tablets. One day we are young and frisky, the next day we need afternoon naps. And so on. "We have a tendency to think that we will live forever," Hanh observes (p. 25). And don't forget: "Without insight we think of power as something we gain for ourselves and ourselves alone" (Hanh, p. 26).

Phil Connors doesn't excel at this either. He sees that he is locked in a time warp and concludes that he has all the time in the world. He can do whatever he wants without any lasting cost. However, when indulgence runs its course and he can't escape the cycle of repetition, he hits bottom. He tries killing the groundhog. That doesn't work. He tries killing himself. That doesn't work either. Whatever he does lands him back in bed, waking up at 6:00 a.m. to "I Got You Babe" on the radio with nothing changed.

It's a game without end. Phil finally sees that he can play at his own death, but nothing he does, nothing at all, can stop others from dying. That reality hits like a thunderbolt. He then seizes hold of his life and starts to help those around him. One altruistic gesture after another transforms Phil from a cynical, sarcastic "wretch" to a man who is magnanimous and humble.

And so it is that Phil ends up beloved by those "morons" and "hicks" he so mocked at the beginning of his journey. His generosity of spirit that was so lacking when we meet him on February 1 is positively inspiring when he finally makes it to February 3.

Hanh says, "All of the first four powers lead to this fifth superpower. And with insight comes a tremendous source of happiness." For Phil yes, most certainly, and for us viewers too.

SPOTLIGHT: *Invictus*

Thich Nhat Hanh's practices also shed light on effective leadership. Our next movie, *Invictus* (2009), shows us how. It centers on Nelson Mandela after he became president of South Africa and sought to heal the country's scars from apartheid.

What he does is masterful. He affirmed what needed to be done and that it was the right thing—move beyond apartheid with a different model, one of respect and equality. Pay attention to detail and treat others with dignity. With his charisma as well as his "Don't take 'No' for an answer" managerial style, it's not surprising that Mandela was an agent of change. The instrument of transformation was South Africa's passion for rugby. Yes, rugby. Rugby is like a mixture of football and soccer, and a bit of basketball, with more players and at least as many demonstrative fans.

Just maybe rugby could unite the country as the national team, the Springboks, competes for the 1995 World Cup. It was a bit of a wild card on Mandela's part, but there's not much like sports to bridge personal and political differences. Mandela's instincts were that the Springboks could be such a bridge. Yes it was a beleaguered team—and the butt of a number of jokes by a TV sports commentator. And yes the players lacked dedication. But they *were* the rugby team and South Africans *do* like their rugby. Mandela brushed aside the criticism voiced by his aides and reached out to Francois Pienaar, the team captain. He did this with a self-confidence that Hanh would salute.

Let's face it: Against all odds, even a team down on its luck can unite people and bridge political, religious, economic, and cultural differences. As we see in *Invictus*, South Africa was no exception. Mandela saw the potential and set the wheels of change in motion. His was a three-pronged approach involving self, others, and the community. For Mandela that meant (1) educate himself about rugby; (2) reach out to the Springboks as collaborators, and (3) manifest enthusiasm and a call for national unity on the part of his fellow South Africans.

Mandela's approach is a model for those who supervise, plan, or engineer change in a complex or troubled work environment. His advice would be: Take control. With self-confidence and a positive attitude (self-possession), a leader can rally the troops. With attention to detail and concentration on the process, a leader can confront problems head on and oversee change.

This requires staying present to what's going on. Don't get stuck by what did or didn't work in the past. Don't get too far ahead of yourself or you may find yourself out of touch, detached, isolated. Teamwork requires *teams*, not just leaders. And, as Hanh indicates, leadership is fruitless without ideas—and insight—about how best to solve, or resolve, the issue.

We watch Mandela's hands-on method of leadership. He throws himself into learning as much as he can about rugby. That he became a fan didn't hurt. On the level of self-awareness, Mandela educated himself about the game and its importance to his country.

On the level of self and other, Mandela reached out to his fellow countrymen to celebrate the team as part of South Africa's history. This built national spirit. In the process Mandela taught rugby captain Francois a lesson or two about the human condition. This he did through conversation, encouragement, garnering wider support, sharing personal insights and words of inspiration.

He also made sure the Springboks got to tour the prison that housed Mandela for 27 years. This affected Francois quite dramatically when he entered the jail cell that held Mandela. We see how small it is, how dire the conditions. We see the window and the yard outside, where inmates did hard labor. We see Francois struggling to comprehend what 27 years of this must do to a man. But we also see that Mandela showed how the path of forgiveness could free people from the weight of the past and let go of long-held resentments and hatred.

We need to develop the sort of mindset that helps us achieve personal power. To be a transparent, humble, sincere, respectful, fair, and responsible person, I cannot be a moral wimp. I need the inner strength not to fold or give up under pressure. I need the personal power not to take the easy way out or to blindly follow the crowd and end up in a cul-de-sac of moral compromise. Carrying out our values requires us to have enough of a spine to stand up for those values when they are under siege.

In looking over Hanh's five practices, there can be no doubt that Nelson Mandela modeled each one of them. First, he showed self-confidence in the face of tensions from all quarters and was not deterred by the obstacles in his path. Hanh probably wouldn't care what order you listed his five aspects of personal power, but something is gained by putting self-confidence first. If we can't trust ourselves, it's hard to get anything off the ground. If we lack confidence, we'll be constantly second-guessing ourselves, waffling on decisions, and letting others steer our thinking. All the skills and talent in the world won't take you far if you don't trust yourself and show the confidence to be taken seriously.

Mandela had the confidence and trust that his instincts were square on. With his 27 years in prison, he'd seen the bottom of the pit and, so, what he now faced he took in stride. Whatever the challenges, he was prepared to meet them head on.

As far as self-possession goes, Mandela demonstrated a positive attitude and didn't waver in his optimism that things would work out. That it would take time came with the territory. While incarcerated, Mandela had nothing but time—and he saw the changes that *did* come over time.

As far as the practice of attention goes, Mandela modeled that by tending to details. This came out when one of Mandela's bodyguards said that he had always been invisible before (while with the previous president, F.W. de Klerk). With Mandela, the bodyguards were most definitely *not* invisible. Mandela took pains to learn their names and brought them back gifts from his travels.

We also see the concentration he showed the rugby team and encouraged them to do the same. Francois took this to heart. At one point the Springboks were bussed to a poverty-stricken area where children were playing—guess what?—rugby. The connection made with the children helped the team members see that they played a part in South Africa embracing a new beginning—one free of racism.

As for insight: Mandela showed a great deal of insight in deciding rugby could be a vehicle of transformation. We see this at the World Cup playoffs when the New Zealand team gave a pre-game spirited traditional performance called a "haka," to celebrate their heritage and draw power. The Springboks had no such chest-pounding exercise, but they found ways to channel some team spirit of their own. Mandela helped them see that what they were doing mattered. They also saw that it went beyond the game of rugby.

It's an inspiring movie on many levels. One is in the racial healing and the social transformation that came about, but also because of the power of perseverance, a positive attitude, and self-discipline. Another thing *Invictus* teaches us is how to *exercise* power. Clearly the president of a country has power, but Mandela doesn't misuse it. He meets people at their own level and treats them with respect and dignity.

He demonstrates restraint and a generosity of spirit. He shows us the high road by not giving in to the pressure to give the (white) Afrikaners a taste of their own medicine. He showed the world that the way to peace requires that we don't give in to vindictive urges; but, rather, see others as we would want to be seen and treat them accordingly.

CASE STUDY: India's Kudumbashree Program for Women—Building Skills

Hanh's practices are also helpful in offering words of guidance to businesses. Let's see how, by looking at one way to address poverty.

Journalist Mark Magnier (2013) reports on a state program in India called Kudumbashree (meaning "family prosperity"). It teaches skills such as farming to poor women. Created in 1998, the program is structured so that property owners with fallow land can lease it to cooperatives of four to 20 women. "After covering costs, the women split the proceeds," notes

Magnier. He adds, "Even more important than the money, many of the women say, is the respect." Furthermore,

> In a country where men often corner the best rural work opportunities, Kudumbashree offers a lifeline for 3.7 million women in Kerala, helping them till the soil, run shops and design garments and handicrafts, aided by their savings and government-subsidized loans. Farms run by women are a refreshing counter-narrative in a country that's been in the news more lately for sexual assaults, discrimination and low female social status.

Self-confidence on the part of the women and respect from those around them set a foundation for systemic growth and change. "The solidarity and management skills that participants learn have helped 5,000 women win election to local office in Kerala" (Magnier, 2013). One virtue of this success story is that it doesn't have to stop there.

Kudumbashree can serve as a model for other countries to follow, hopefully with the result of lifting up impoverished people. With such programs individuals and groups can be empowered so that further societal changes can come about, opening up new channels for doing and expanding businesses, and transforming the political and social structures in the bargain.

The practices set out by Thich Nhat Hanh and the underlying values that help build moral character are vital to self-transformation. These practices and the value frameworks that help sustain those practices—such as Virtue Ethics, Boylan's four moral pillars, and Solomon's five components of moral development—are enormously helpful for laying the ethical groundwork in Business Ethics as well. This is reflected in the thought and care that goes into the creation of a company's ethics code. Each code speaks to the moral reasoning treats the business as a "person"—an entity with legal status and, at least in some eyes, moral status as well. A great deal follows from this; all the more reason to examine the ethics code if you want to get a sense of the core values of the company—its ethical base.

Thich Nhat Hanh on Collegiality

Business Ethics is not just about big money or corporations working either in sync or in competition with other corporations. It is also about people working alongside other people, finding a way to a fulfilling job, to a vocation, to give purpose to our lives.

In *The Art of Power* Hanh says that whatever is our business we can learn to be "truly present, fully alive with a compassionate heart" (p. 77). As far as he's concerned, "Power is good for one thing only: to increase our happiness and the happiness of others." This means doing good—*beneficence* and trying to do no harm.

Throughout this book have been examples of those who turned their attention to right wrongs, to address inequities, and set things straight. From Johnson & Johnson's response to the Tylenol crisis to Costco's recall of the contaminated fruit mix, we have seen swift actions on the part of corporations and their CEOs to take affirmative steps to make things better for their customers or employees.

As for the concept of happiness, Hanh says,

> We must distinguish happiness from excitement, or even joy. Many people think of excitement as happiness. They are thinking of something, or expecting something that they can consider to be happiness, and for them, that is already happiness. But when you are excited you are not peaceful. True happiness is based on peace … You can buy conditions for happiness but you can't buy happiness … You have to cultivate happiness, you cannot buy it at the store. (p. 79).

Hanh warns us against being too attached or overly invested in *this* idea or *that* point of view. He puts it this way, "Attachment to views, attachment to ideas, attachment to perceptions are the biggest obstacle to the truth" (p. 88). That may be hard to grasp or to enact, given the turf wars we often see in the workplace. But if we can pull back from our attachments and focus on the problem at hand, we will be much more productive.

ETHICS CODE: The Coca-Cola Company

On its website, The Coca-Cola Company sets forth its Code of Business Conduct: "The REAL thing. The RIGHT way." In its preface/prologue, we find the following principle, "Act with integrity. Be honest. Follow the Law. Comply with the Code. Be accountable." We know by now that these are moral duties and obligations that give the Code a Deontological foundation. Reading on we find:

> *Integrity is fundamental to The Coca-Cola Company. Along with our other values of leadership, passion, accountability, collaboration, diversity and quality, it is a pillar of our 2020 Vision.*

Read the full Code of Conduct at http://assets.coca-colacompany.
com/45/59/f85d53a84ec597f74c754003450c/COBC_English.pdf
In a letter addressed to "Dear Colleague," we are told by Coca-Cola
that,

> We live in an era when public trust and confidence in business are among
> the lowest levels in history. We at The Coca-Cola Company are fortunate,
> however, to work for one of the most admired businesses in the world – a
> reputation that has been enhanced and safeguarded over the years by a rich
> culture of integrity and ethical conduct.

The Coca-Cola Code of conduct—like the others we have seen
throughout this text—underscores the importance of an ethics code and
the values that it sets out. As we saw in the previous chapter (3.5), events
can put a company's ethics to the test. And as we know from our own
lives, it is not always easy to act on the values we hold dear. But we have
seen in the movies and case studies that cast a spotlight on Business Ethics
that it is vital that to act with integrity. We need to do all we can to stay
true to what we believe in—for ourselves, and for others as well.

Works Cited

Boylan, Michael, *A Just Society*, (Lanham, MD: Rowman & Littlefield, 2004).
The Coca-Cola Company, *Code of Business Conduct*, http://assets.coca-colacompany.com/45/59/f85d53a84ec597f74c754003450c/COBC_English.pdf (accessed December 28, 2014).
Hanh, Thich Nhat, *The Art of Power*, (New York: Harper-Collins, 2007).
Magnier, Mark with Tanvi Sharma, "India Work-Skills Program Makes A Dent In Disrespect For Women," *Los Angeles Times*, September 8, 2013, http://www.latimes.com/world/la-fg-india-women-20130908,0,6847721.story (accessed December 28, 2014).
Solomon, Robert, "Corporate Roles, Personal Virtues: An Aristotelian Approach to Business Ethics" (1992), in Thomas Donaldson, Patricia H. Werhane, and Margaret Cording, (eds.), *Ethical Issues in Business: A Philosophical Approach*, 7th edn. (Upper Saddle River, NJ: Prentice Hall, 2002).
Thompson, Clive, "This Is the Man Bill Gates Thinks You Absolutely Should Be Reading," *Wired magazine*, November 25, 2013, http://www.wired.com/wiredscience/2013/11/vaclav-smil-wired/ (accessed December 28, 2014).
Tzu, Sun, *The Art of War*, MIT Classics Archive, Available at http://classics.mit.edu/Tzu/artwar.html (accessed December 28, 2014).

Appendix 1

Films Discussed in This Book

Film	Chapter
A Hijacking	1.1
Arbitrage	2.3
Big Men	1.3
Blue Jasmine	2.2
Civil Action	3.1
Contagion	2.2
Darwin's Nightmare	3.5
Disconnect	1.4 & 3.4
Erin Brockovich	2.4 & 2.5
Fires of Kuwait	3.6
Food, Inc	2.3 & 2.4
Groundhog Day	3.6
Her	1.4
Invictus	3.6
John Q	3.2
Local Hero	3.1
Made in Dagenham	3.3
Matewan	3.3
Michael Clayton	1.2
Murder by Proxy: America Goes Postal	3.2
North Country	3.4
Out of the Clear Blue Sky	2.5
Park Avenue: Money, Power, and the American Dream	2.2
Polytechnique	3.2
Quiz Show	2.3

Business Ethics Through Movies: A Case Study Approach, First Edition. Wanda Teays.
© 2015 John Wiley & Sons, Ltd. Published 2015 by John Wiley & Sons, Ltd.

Film	Chapter
Roger & Me	2.4
Salmon Fishing in the Yemen	2.4
Shattered Glass	2.3
Sleep Dealer	3.5
The Company Men	2.4, 2.5
The Insider	2.1
The Invisible War	3.4
The Net	1.4
Up in the Air	1.2
Wall Street	1.3

Appendix 2

Case Studies Discussed in This Book

Case Study	Chapter
Bangladesh Sweatshop Collapse	3.4
Beech-Nut's Apple Juice	2.3
Bullies in the NFL	3.4
Coca-Cola in Colombia	3.5
Costco's Tainted Berries	1.3
Dunkin' Donuts Ad Campaign	3.6
Edward Snowden and the NSA	1.4
European Horsemeat Scandal	2.4
Eveleth Mines	3.4
Exxon Valdez	3.1
Fast Food Workers' Strike	3.3
Film Recovery Systems, Inc.	2.5
Ford Pinto	2.2
Foster Farms' Chickens	2.3
Gunman at LAX	3.2
H&M and Child Labor	3.3
Kellogg's and Michael Phelps	2.4
Kudumbashri's Work Skills Program	3.6
Marriage Equality	3.3
Martha Stewart—Insider Trading	1.3
Minute-Maid Lemonade	2.3
Montreal Massacre	3.2
Pfizer in Nigeria	3.5
Target's Data Breach	1.4
Target's Online Tracking	1.4

Business Ethics Through Movies: A Case Study Approach, First Edition. Wanda Teays.
© 2015 John Wiley & Sons, Ltd. Published 2015 by John Wiley & Sons, Ltd.

Case Study	*Chapter*
Tylenol Case	1.2
UAW, H&M and Pay Equity	3.3
Virginia Tech Rampage	3.2
W.R. Grace Co.	3.1
West Virginia Chemical Spill	3.1

Appendix 3

Ethics Codes Discussed in This Book

Ethics Codes	Chapter
Amazon.com	3.4
Apple	1.1
Coca-Cola Company	3.5
Costco	1.3
Dole Foods, Inc	2.3
Dunkin' Donuts	3.6
Exxon Mobil Corporation	3.1
Ford Motor Co.	2.2
General Motors	2.4
Google	1.1
H & M	3.3
Johnson & Johnson	1.2
Kellogg's	2.4
Los Angeles World Airports (LAWA)	3.2
Microsoft	2.5
National Public Radio (NPR)	2.3
Yahoo!	1.4

Business Ethics Through Movies: A Case Study Approach, First Edition. Wanda Teays.
© 2015 John Wiley & Sons, Ltd. Published 2015 by John Wiley & Sons, Ltd.

Index

Business Ethics Through Movies: A Case Study Approach, First Edition. Wanda Teays.
© 2015 John Wiley & Sons, Ltd. Published 2015 by John Wiley & Sons, Ltd.

Made in United States
North Haven, CT
02 February 2022

15527210R00173